University of Toronto

THE CAMPUS GUIDE

University of Toronto

SECOND EDITION

AN ARCHITECTURAL TOUR BY
Larry Wayne Richards

PHOTOGRAPHY BY EUGEN SAKHNENKO

INTRODUCTION BY MARTIN L. FRIEDLAND
FOREWORD BY MERIC S. GERTLER

PRINCETON ARCHITECTURAL PRESS
NEW YORK

Published by Princeton Architectural Press
A MCEVOY GROUP COMPANY
202 Warren Street, Hudson, NY 12534
www.papress.com

Princeton Architectural Press is a leading publisher in architecture,
design, photography, landscape, and visual culture. We create fine books
and stationery of unsurpassed quality and production values. With
more than one thousand titles published, we find design everywhere
and in the most unlikely places.

Series Editor: Jan Cigliano Hartman
Editor: Linda Lee
Designer: Benjamin English
Mapmaker: John Wang

Special thanks to: Janet Behning, Abby Bussel, Susan Hershberg,
Kristen Hewitt, Lia Hunt, Valerie Kamen, Jennifer Lippert, Sara McKay,
Eliana Miller, Wes Seeley, Rob Shaeffer, Sara Stemen, Marisa Tesoro,
Paul Wagner, and Joseph Weston of Princeton Architectural Press
—Kevin C. Lippert, publisher

Library of Congress Cataloging-in-Publication Data:
NAMES: Richards, Larry, author.
TITLE: University of Toronto. The campus guide : an architectural tour
    / by Larry Wayne Richards ; photography by Eugen Sakhnenko ;
    introduction by Martin L. Friedland ; foreword by Meric S. Gertler.
OTHER TITLES: Campus guide (New York, N.Y.)
DESCRIPTION: Second Edition. | New York : Princeton Architectural Press,
    [2019] | Series: The campus guide | Includes bibliographical references
    and index.
IDENTIFIERS: LCCN 2018023206 | ISBN 9781616897253 (paperback : alk.
    paper)
SUBJECTS: LCSH: University of Toronto—Buildings. | University of
    Toronto—History.
CLASSIFICATION: LCC LE3.T53 R53 2019 | DDC 378.71354—dc23
LC record available at https://lccn.loc.gov/2018023206

Contents

How to Use This Guide

This guide is a resource for those interested in learning more about the three campuses of the University of Toronto. It is intended for visitors, alumni, and students who wish to have an insider's look at the university's buildings and places, from Cumberland & Storm's magnificent University College (1859) to John Andrews's megastructural Scarborough College (1966) and Patkau Architects / MacLennan Jaunkalns Miller Architects' striking Goldring Centre for High Performance Sport (2014). The guide reveals the university's extraordinary landscapes, architectural diversity, and spirited interior spaces.

The book opens with a foreword by the president of the university, Meric S. Gertler. An introduction by Martin L. Friedland discusses the history of the institution and its architecture, followed by eleven illustrated walks covering some 186 buildings, including many neighboring institutions. Each building is discussed within its architectural and social context and tied to the evolution of the university. An aerial perspective map orients the visitor-reader to nine of the walks and locates the buildings. A pocket, companion map is included at the back of the guide.

Visitors are welcome to tour the University of Toronto's three campuses: the downtown St. George campus, the University of Toronto Scarborough, and the University of Toronto Mississauga. The St. George campus's Nona Macdonald Visitors Centre is located at 25 King's College Circle, in the southeast corner of Knox College. For complete information on tours at the three campuses, visit www.utoronto.ca and search "campus tours."

The University of Toronto wishes to acknowledge the land on which the university operates. For thousands of years it has been the traditional land of the Huron-Wendat, the Seneca, and, most recently, the Mississaugas of the Credit River. Today, this meeting place is still the home to many indigenous people from across Turtle Island, and we are grateful to have the opportunity to work on this land.

Terrence Donnelly Centre for Cellular and
Biomolecular Research, sky garden

Foreword

A couple of weeks ago I took a taxi to my office at Simcoe Hall. The driver, who was new on the job, noted that this was his first time visiting the University of Toronto's downtown Toronto (St. George) campus. As I reached over to pay, I noticed him doing a double take across the Front Campus lawn in the direction of University College, Cumberland & Storm's Romanesque Revival masterpiece, completed in 1859. After a heartfelt "Wow!" he took some photos of the building with his phone and asked me about its history.

I am sure that University College's architecture will never lose its power to inspire such a response. I am also happy to report to readers of this indispensable guide that the wow factor is alive and well in the newest additions to U of T's architectural legacy across its three campuses.

Since 2012 the university has invested an astonishing C$1.2 billion in the construction of new buildings and the renovation of existing ones, and many of these projects have already won awards for their architectural merit or sustainability measures. This wave of capital construction has provided an abundance of proof points for me, as a geographer and planner whose academic focus includes the role of great universities in driving the economic and social prosperity of their host cities.

Top of mind as I write this is the newly opened Daniels Building at One Spadina Crescent, which houses the John H. Daniels Faculty of Architecture, Landscape, and Design. It incorporates an important nineteenth-century heritage structure, brilliantly restored and repurposed, and an awe-inspiring twenty-first-century addition in the midst of an imaginative new landscape. The transformation of this commanding site is a generational triumph for the university, the city, and indeed the country.

Readers will see in the following pages many other outstanding developments in the built form of U of T's downtown Toronto (St. George) campus, as well as its

Landscape panorama with Convocation Hall (left) and University College (right), circa 1908–14

Scarborough campus (UTSC) to the east and Mississauga campus (UTM) to the west—including some emphatic statements of the university's deep roots in and engagement with the communities around us. The Toronto Pan Am Sports Centre, the anchor of UTSC's emerging North Campus, is co-owned by the university and the City of Toronto. Built for the Toronto 2015 Pan Am & Parapan Am Games, the building seamlessly integrates community, intramural, national, and quadrennial uses, in fully accessible, state-of-the-art facilities. At UTM, the Innovation Complex, which includes the Institute for Management & Innovation, was made possible in part by a remarkable grant from the City of Mississauga. Whenever I attend an event in its sunlit rotunda, I am reminded of the exemplary town-gown partnership it represents.

Across all three campuses I am struck by the fact that the University of Toronto is a city-builder, figuratively as well as literally. In addition to their beauty and utility, U of T's newest buildings contribute to the city on another, even more important level—they enhance the university's role as a portal of opportunity for its students and their communities. Among U of T's undergraduate students, about a quarter come from families with household incomes of less than c$50,000 per year, and 20 percent are the first in their families to attend university. Combined with the fact that half of the Toronto region's population was born outside of Canada, we are one of the most culturally and socioeconomically diverse institutions anywhere on the planet. Like the city itself, Toronto's namesake university embraces this diversity as a crucial factor in its global standing as a teaching and research powerhouse. The growth of its physical infrastructure is ultimately driven by the university's commitment to support all members of the academic community, by providing them with the best possible environment for learning, discovery, and innovation.

Turning our gaze back to University College, in December 2017 we launched a major revitalization project to make the building more accessible and navigable and to ensure its renowned spaces can be used more fully. Moreover, the surrounding

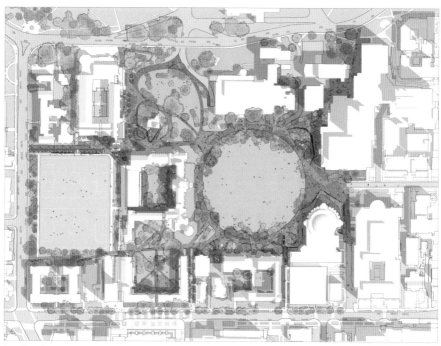

Landmark Project site plan

landscape is about to undergo its most significant renewal since U of T's founding almost two centuries ago. The Landmark Project will reunify the historic core of the university and repedestrianize King's College Circle, Hart House Circle, and Tower Road. Designed to foster interaction, the project will dramatically enhance the precinct as one of Toronto's great public spaces.

This second edition of *University of Toronto: The Campus Guide* provides ample reason for readers to explore and enjoy U of T's three campuses. Whether you are a student, a member of the faculty or staff, an alumnus, a neighbour, or a visitor, I commend this unique resource to you, and I encourage you to think of it as an invitation to experience the university's wonderful spaces, old and new, for yourself.

Meric S. Gertler
President, University of Toronto
March 2018

Introduction

Martin L. Friedland

The University of Toronto is a complex institution with a long history. Growing out of a federation of a number of colleges and an affiliation between many professional schools and bodies, it is today one of the largest universities in North America, with more than ninety thousand students on its three campuses. It has more than half a million alumni worldwide and consistently ranks as the leading university in Canada and in most surveys ranks among the top thirty universities in the world. Like all other major universities in Canada, it is a public university, primarily financed by the provincial government.

Since the founding of the university in 1850, a number of talented presidents have led the institution. Two presidents, in particular, stand out in their vision

William Nathaniel Wesbroom, detail from *Bird's-Eye View of Toronto*, with the University of Toronto grounds in the dark, forested area near the top; lithograph, circa 1886

concerning the physical growth and architecture of the university: Robert Falconer (president: 1907–32) and Claude Bissell (president: 1958–71). They helped transform the University of Toronto from its humble nineteenth-century beginnings as a successor of Toronto's first institute of higher learning, King's College, into today's hugely successful university with three campuses in and near the city of Toronto.

KING'S COLLEGE

On March 15, 1827, the Crown issued a charter to John Strachan, an Anglican minister, who had gone to England to establish a college in Upper Canada, now the Province of Ontario, "for the education of youth in the principles of the Christian Religion, and for their instruction in the various branches of Science and Literature."[1] The college, called King's College, was to be at or near the Town of York, later called the City of Toronto. Strachan, who would become the college's first president, wanted such an institution, he wrote, to avoid sending students for their education to the United States, where "the school books...are stuffed with praises of their own institutions, and breathe hatred to everything English."[2]

The council of the college purchased a site consisting of 150 acres of vacant forest land north of the Town of York—today downtown Toronto—from three owners at a price of £3,750, a sum about equal to the cost of Strachan's fine home on Front Street, overlooking Lake Ontario. In 1829 the eminent English architect Charles Fowler, who was then designing London's Covent Garden Market, completed drawings for the new college and sent a model to Upper Canada. His ambitious neoclassical design, employing Greek and Roman precedents, included four monumental courtyards. Fowler's proposal resembled Thomas Jefferson's Academical Village at

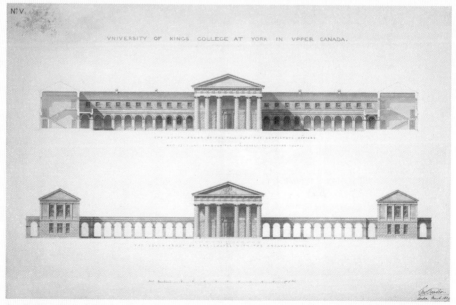

South elevations of Charles Fowler's 1829 neoclassical design for the university of King's College at York in Upper Canada

the University of Virginia (1817–25). Following the plan, some land was cleared and a title was purchased to create a grand avenue (now University Avenue), leading from Queen Street to the site where the legislative buildings of Ontario now stand. However, Fowler's design was never built.

Many people in Upper Canada strongly objected to the fact that the college would only accept members of the Church of England, and the Legislative Assembly of Upper Canada proceeded to condemn the charter—a position that the British House of Commons, which also opposed the charter, strongly endorsed. In response, the council of the college, with the approval of the colony's legislative assembly, made some changes: for example, professors no longer had to be members of the Church of England, although they still had to subscribe to the doctrine of the Holy Trinity.

Between 1837 and 1838, Toronto architect Thomas Young, who was in the process of designing St. James Cathedral on King Street, completed new plans for King's College. Young studied Fowler's grandiose proposal of 1829 and generated a compact version, 480 × 590 feet (146 × 180 meters), designed similarly in the neoclassical style. Young envisioned four buildings around a quadrangle, recorded in outline on an 1851 topographical map of the City of Toronto. The buildings were to contain a convocation hall, library, museum, chapel, lecture halls, classrooms, dining halls, and student residences. Only a student residence was built—completed in 1843 at the southeast corner of the imagined compound and representing only about one-twelfth of Young's vision. The student residence—a handsome structure employing the severe Doric order—was torn down in 1886 to make way for the present legislative buildings in Queen's Park. Classes were held in a vacant building on Front Street.

CREATION OF THE UNIVERSITY OF TORONTO

On January 1, 1850, the Parliament of Canada passed a law to secularize King's College, which was to be replaced by a new university that would no longer be connected with the Church of England. The University of Toronto, as the new institution was called, took over the charter, the land, and the buildings of its predecessor. Strachan denounced the "godless" institution and went on to create a new Anglican college, Trinity College, which was located on the site of the present Trinity Bellwoods Park, on Queen Street West. However, Trinity College would eventually join the University of Toronto in 1904.

Many members of the staff of King's College continued at the University of Toronto, including the president of King's, John McCaul. Only about fifty full-time students attended the new institution in the 1850s—roughly the same number that had been at King's College. In order to increase enrollment, President McCaul and others proposed a reorganization of the university that would give an incentive to other colleges, such as the various denominational colleges in Upper Canada, including the Presbyterian Queen's College in Kingston, the Methodist Victoria College in Cobourg, and the Roman Catholic Regiopolis College in Kingston, to affiliate with it.

Edwin Whitefield, view of the city of Toronto, lithograph, 1854

The University of Toronto Act was amended in 1853 to give these other colleges representation on the university senate. The new model was based on the University of London: University College became a nonreligious arts and science teaching college while the university itself, like the University of London, became an examining body.

University College was able to hire a credible group of professors. By the mid-nineteenth century, Toronto was a wealthy city of about forty thousand people and was growing rapidly. Daniel Wilson from Scotland, professor of British history and literature, and president of the university after McCaul, wrote to his wife shortly after he arrived in 1853 about his first impressions:

> It is a busy, bustling, active town…bearing such evident marks of rapid increase that I should not wonder if ten years hence it be found to number nearer a hundred thousand.…Everything indicates wealth and prosperity. As to the shops, many of them are equal to the best in Edinburgh, and if a person has only money, he need want for nothing here that he desires.[3]

The sense of bustle and prosperity described by Wilson is conveyed in a 1854 lithograph view of Toronto by Edwin Whitefield.

Not all the appointments were as good as that of Wilson. Sometimes politics played an undue role: the great Thomas Huxley was an applicant for a science chair and came recommended by the leading scientists in England, including Charles Darwin. The government, however, decided to appoint the undistinguished Reverend William Hincks, who just happened to be the brother of the premier.

The first college to become associated with the University of Toronto was Knox College, a Presbyterian divinity school that had broken away from the official

Church of Scotland; others would not join until several decades later. In 1875 Knox College opened a distinctive, church-like structure in the middle of Spadina Avenue, north of College Street, which still stands. It now houses the John H. Daniels Faculty of Architecture, Landscape, and Design. In a circa-1886 bird's-eye-view engraving of Toronto, Knox College appears prominently in a circle. (See page 11.)

One Spadina Crescent (Knox College), 1882

CONSTRUCTING UNIVERSITY COLLEGE

During the first few years of its existence, University College had to use temporary facilities to teach its students because the government wanted the site of the former King's College building at the top of University Avenue for a legislative building. Not only did University College need a proper home, the university also wanted to use some of its original endowment on a new building before the denominational colleges, which were now represented on the university senate, could get their hands on it. "Every stone that goes up in the building, every book that is bought," wrote, John Langton, the vice-chancellor at the time, "is so much more anchorage, and so much less plunder to fight for."[4]

The cornerstone for the magnificent University College building was laid in 1856, and the capstone for its 120-foot (36.6-meter) tower was set in place in 1858. Most people would agree that University College is the University of Toronto's finest historic building. It was designed by Frederic William Cumberland, one of Canada's greatest architects of the nineteenth century. Within a relatively brief period of time after arriving in Canada in 1847 at the age of twenty-seven, Cumberland had been involved in important building projects, including the Adelaide Street Court House (1852) and St. James Cathedral (1853). While working on University College, the architect was also busy with the equally fine expansion of Osgoode Hall (1857).

When the British author Anthony Trollope visited Toronto in 1862, he wrote that "the two sights of Toronto" were Osgoode Hall and University College, the latter of which he called "the glory of Toronto."[5] The two buildings are prominent in the aforementioned circa-1886 bird's-eye-view engraving, in which University College appears amid forested green and Osgoode Hall can be found at the south end of University Avenue.

Almost all of Cumberland's buildings survive today, including his residence, Cumberland House, completed in 1860 on the east side of St. George Street, just north of College Street and now home of the International Student Centre. (See Walk One, pages 88–89.) Even the government's Magnetic and Meteorological Observatory building (previously called the Royal Magnetical Observatory) by Cumberland, constructed in the early 1850s, still survives, although in a somewhat

William George Storm, Toronto University, watercolor, circa 1857

different form. Its stones were used to construct the observatory just east of University College, a building that in recent years housed the University of Toronto Students' Union organization.

At first, Cumberland and his partner, William George Storm, designed a Gothic structure for University College, but the governor general, Sir Edmund Walker Head, who wanted an Italian-looking building, was unhappy with the design. They then considered a Byzantine style. In the governor general's absence, however, they redesigned the building once again. The vice-chancellor of the university wrote, "We polished away almost all traces of Byzantine and got a hybrid with some features of Norman, of early English etc., with faint traces of Byzantium and the Italian palazzo, but altogether a not unsightly building."[6]

As Cumberland once explained, he chose the Norman Romanesque style because he "believed that its ruggedness was appropriate to Canada."[7] The architect had been influenced by John Ruskin, the nineteenth-century English art and social critic, who, using the example of English castles, urged young architects

"to conceive and deal with breadth and solidity" and stressed the importance of craftsmanship—all features that are found in University College.[8] An imposing structure, the main front of the south-facing building is nearly four hundred feet (122 meters) long and could then be seen, looking north, from the city and Lake Ontario.

East of University College was Taddle Creek, a stream that ran from Wychwood Park on the high ground north of what was then the city, along the present Philosopher's Walk and past University College, making its way to Lake Ontario. In 1859 a dam was built just east of University College to form a pond known over the years as McCaul's Pond. (See Walk One, page 51.) The creek appears and reappears in the history of the university. It was covered over in 1884 and made a city sewer, having become, as noted by a local newspaper at the time, "a holding tank for all the sewage discharged into Taddle Creek by residents of Yorkville upstream." Because of concerns with foundations and drainage, even after it was buried, the creek's existence played a role in the location and design of other buildings, including Hart House to the east of University College and Mount Sinai Hospital on University Avenue.

View from the southwest of Saint Basil's Church and College of Saint Michael, Toronto, as proposed by architect William Hay in 1855

The west wing of University College was a men's residence. President Daniel Wilson (president: 1880–92) advocated for a separate college for women, but the Ontario government preferred coeducational classes, and in 1884 the first female students officially attended lectures at University College. The college did not provide residences for women, however, and they were forced to find accommodations in boarding houses. The first University College residence for women, a home on Queen's Park Circle, since torn down, was not opened until 1905. A larger women's residence, Whitney Hall (now coeducational), was built in 1931.

OTHER COLLEGES

In the 1880s the university made another attempt to induce the denominational colleges to join. The Roman Catholic St. Michael's College, founded in 1852 and at the time primarily a theological college, affiliated with the university in 1881. A vision of what the college and its church, St. Basil's Church, might be—a tight cluster of Gothic-inspired structures—was presented by architect William Hay in 1855. A simpler version of the ensemble officially opened in 1856 on Clover Hill, the highest piece of land on the downtown campus. St. Basil's Church and the adjacent Odette Hall remain as the university's oldest surviving buildings. After World War One, St. Michael's developed more ambitious plans, with the establishment of the world-renowned Pontifical Institute of Mediaeval Studies on Queen's Park Crescent East.

The Presbyterian Knox College continued its affiliation with the university. Wycliffe College did as well—it was founded in 1877 by Low Church Anglicans, who wanted "to combat the Catholic heresies allegedly promoted by Trinity," and it joined the university in 1885. In 1891 Wycliffe moved to its present location on Hoskin Avenue. Both colleges offer only divinity degrees.

In 1890, after much debate following the passage of the Federation Act of 1887, Victoria University in Cobourg, Ontario, decided to federate with the University of Toronto, and the formal opening of the new Victoria College building took place two years later. William Storm, who had worked with Cumberland on the University College building, produced an impressive Romanesque Revival structure, borrowing heavily from the American architect Henry Hobson Richardson in the use of arches, colored bands, and cast-iron structural skeletons and stair-cases. The Old Vic building, as it is known, with its red sandstone and gray lime-stone, looks south to the Ontario Legislative Building, which was completed earlier that year.

Trinity College officially joined the University of Toronto in 1904, after its medical school had merged with the university's medical school the previous year. For Trinity, as for Victoria, the growing cost of science and research was a major factor in the decision to join the University of Toronto. Trinity received its present site in 1909 but did not physically move until after World War One. In 1923 the foundation stone of the current building was laid. (In fact, two foundation stones were laid, one on top of the other, because a month before this event, the original foundation stone from the college's old building on Queen Street was discovered. The two stones can be seen today to the left of the main entrance.) Architects Darling & Pearson, responsible for most of the major buildings on the university's campus during the previous twenty years, designed a Gothic building to resemble the old college. There were other changes. The present chapel, the last major work designed by the great English architect Sir Giles Gilbert Scott, was completed in 1955.

The denominational colleges were free to determine their own architectural styles and to choose their own architects. As a result, the University of Toronto, unlike many other universities, did not have a uniform style even in its early days. Gothic, Romanesque, classical, modernist, and other types of designs exist side by side, enlivening the campus and making it invitingly diverse.

SCIENCE BUILDINGS

From the university's beginnings, the teaching of science has played a major role. The institution's first science laboratory was in University College. The round building at the college's west end, now called the Croft Chapter House, served as Professor Henry Croft's chemistry laboratory. One can still see the ventilation openings at the top of the structure. In the 1890s a larger chemistry building—since demolished—was constructed at the south end of the campus. The chemistry department remained there until it moved to its present location on St. George Street in the 1960s. Known as the Lash Miller Chemical Laboratories, the new chemistry building was named after a long-serving chair of the department, who, surprisingly, refused to believe in atomic theory.

A physics laboratory took chemistry's place in University College's round house, but the space was clearly inadequate, and in 1907 Darling & Pearson designed a new physics building, later called the Sandford Fleming Building, just north of the old chemistry building. The space is now occupied by the engineering department, and a new physics building, named after the professor of physics John McLennan, is located just south of the Lash Miller Chemical Laboratories.

Victoria College, view from the southwest, circa 1900

The physics department had long lobbied for a proper astronomy facility—a story that has taken many twists and turns. In 1908 the federal government's Magnetic and Meteorological Observatory at the south end of the campus was taken down as a response to several problems: the smoke in the city obscured the view to the heavens, the new streetcar line on College Street interfered with magnetic readings, and the building's location made it difficult to create a straight entrance route into the university from the south.

Although parts of the old observatory were reconstructed east of University College and served astronomy study for a few decades, it was not until 1935 that a sophisticated facility—the new David Dunlap Observatory in Richmond Hill, north of Toronto—was finally built. At the time it contained the second largest telescope in the world. In 2008 the university sold the David Dunlap Observatory and the nearly two hundred surrounding acres to a developer on the condition that the 1935 building and the historic telescope be preserved. The proceeds from the sale were invested in a newly created Dunlap Institute for Astronomy and Astrophysics.

The biology department was originally housed in a structure on Queen's Park Crescent, which officially opened in 1889. It was demolished in 1966 to make way for the Medical Sciences Building. A new zoology building, named after Professor Ramsay Wright, who was responsible for the 1889 building, then moved to its current site on the southwest corner of St. George and Harbord Streets. The botany department had earlier split off from zoology and at first occupied one of the former private residences around Queen's Park Crescent and then moved into the building (now the C. David Naylor Building) on Queen's Park Crescent West, constructed in the 1930s. Today the department is housed in the Earth Sciences Centre on Willcocks Street. Its lovely greenhouses at the corner of College Street and Queen's Park were relocated in 2004 to a city park, Allan Gardens, to make room for the Leslie L. Dan Pharmacy Building.

PROFESSIONAL FACULTIES

Although King's College had included professional faculties, such as for law and medicine, the University of Toronto closed them down in 1853. The government believed that the professions should have the teaching responsibility for these students. The university continued, however, to examine candidates and offer degrees. The Federation Act of 1887 brought both law and medicine back as teaching faculties, although it was not until 1957 that the law school was fully recognized by the Law Society of Upper Canada (now the Law Society of Ontario).

After years in old houses on St. George Street, including Cumberland House and then at Glendon Hall, an estate in the north end of Toronto (now a part of York University), the law school moved to its present home, now consisting of Sir Joseph Flavelle's splendid mansion on Queen's Park, just south of the Royal Ontario Museum, Edward R. Wood's fine residence beside the museum, now named Falconer Hall after University of Toronto President Robert Falconer, and a new structure, the Jackman Law Building, behind and attached to Flavelle House.

The Faculty of Medicine was reestablished in 1887, its staff consisting of doctors from the private Toronto School of Medicine, situated a few miles away from the university, near the Don River. In 1903 a new medical school building opened on the site of the present Medical Sciences Building, built in the late 1960s.

Following the example of Johns Hopkins University, the University of Toronto made plans for a university-owned hospital on the campus. There were, however, strong and effective objections from residents near the proposed hospital on College Street at the top of McCaul Street. In 1913 the Toronto General Hospital, originally located in the present Regent Park near the Don River, moved to a site on the south side of College Street, east of University Avenue, and served as a teaching hospital. That original structure is now part of the dynamic MaRS Centre, affiliated with the university and designed to bring basic sciences and entrepreneurs together. The east and south towers were completed in 2005 and the three-quarters-of-a-million-square-foot (seventy-thousand-square-meter) west tower was completed in 2016. (See Walk Seven, pages 244–46.)

A large number of other professional schools became associated with the University of Toronto in the 1880s and later decades. The Royal College of Dental Surgeons of Ontario, which had been running its own school since 1875, affiliated with the university in 1888. In the late 1890s, the dentistry division opened a school on the south side of College Street, east of University Avenue. The site was, however, needed for the new Toronto General Hospital, and in 1909 a five-story building on the northeast corner of College and Huron Streets—designed by Edmund Burke, who would later design the Bloor Viaduct—opened for students. Dentistry stayed there until 1959, when it moved to a new International Style building on Elm Street, north of Dundas Street.

The architecture division, which had grown out of the Faculty of Applied Science and Engineering, then took over the former Royal College of Dental Surgeons of Ontario building in 1961 and moved to the old Knox College site in 2017. The university had established the department as Canada's first architectural program in 1890, and it later gained its independence from engineering.

Pharmacy followed much the same pattern as dentistry. The Ontario College of Pharmacy affiliated with the university in the early 1890s, but it did not physically move from its site on Gerrard Street East to the campus until 1963. Its new home, the Leslie L. Dan Pharmacy Building, designed by Foster + Partners, opened in 2006 at the northwest corner of College Street and University Avenue.

The Faculty of Applied Science and Engineering was established in 1873 as the School of Practical Science. A three-story red-brick building, which was torn down in the 1960s to permit the construction of the Medical Sciences Building, opened in 1878 on King's College Circle, and the school formally affiliated with the University of Toronto in 1889. In 1904 another engineering building, the Mining Building, was constructed on the north side of College Street, and over the next century the faculty's expansion, with its many divisions, rivaled that of the Faculty of Medicine.

Later, other professional schools were established, including a Faculty of Education (1906), School of Forestry (1907), and School of Nursing (1933), all of which originally had purpose-built, stand-alone facilities. They are now, for the most part, absorbed into the general architectural fabric of the campus.

KING'S COLLEGE CIRCLE

By the early years of the twentieth century, King's College Circle was increasingly ringed with buildings: University College to the north, the School of Practical Science to the southeast, the library and the medical school to the east, and Knox College, which had moved from Spadina Crescent in 1915, to the west. An important addition to the east side of the circle had been the new university library, which was fully in operation in 1893.

A new library had become necessary in 1890 because of a devastating fire in University College caused by a careless worker carrying kerosene lamps up a wooden staircase, which destroyed the entire collection of about thirty thousand books. The new library building, designed by David B. Dick and generally shaped like a medieval church, was isolated from other structures to prevent fires from spreading and was constructed with noncombustible material. The stacks were made of cast iron and the floors of massive sections of glass, which allowed light to penetrate from floor to floor. The architect copied the front doorway from a twelfth-century Scottish abbey that President Daniel Wilson had described in one of his early books. By 1910 a five-story glass-floored expansion into the ravine to the east was completed. The building, which was the second largest library in Canada after the Parliamentary Library in Ottawa, served the university until after World War Two, when a large addition was made to the building.

When University College was rebuilt after the 1890 fire, it did not include a convocation hall, and convocations were temporarily held in such venues as the gymnasium and the examination hall of the School of Practical Science. Eventually, with the support of the alumni and the government, the university built the present Convocation Hall at the southwest portion of King's College Circle. Designed by Darling & Pearson, who had just completed the residence for the businessman Flavelle in Queen's Park, it was intended to seat two thousand people. It was modeled on the Sorbonne's main lecture theater in Paris, completed in 1901. Convocation Hall opened in 1906, in time for President Falconer's 1907 inauguration ceremony. An alluring panorama, circa 1908–14, shows the building soon after it was completed. (See Foreword, pages 8–9.) In 1923 Simcoe Hall, a striking new administration building, was attached to Convocation Hall, further enclosing and giving definition to King's College Circle.

STUDENT FACILITIES

Compared to most other universities, the University of Toronto provided relatively few student residences in its early days. The majority of its students were from the Toronto area and lived with their families or in boardinghouses. Moreover,

Library (left) and Medical Building (right), on King's College Circle, with the city skyline beyond, 1912

the University College residence was closed at the end of the nineteenth century because the space was needed for teaching purposes. The university encouraged fraternities in those early years, some of which still survive around the campus. In 1907 the university planned a residence quadrangle at the corner of Devonshire Place and Hoskin Avenue. Due to funding problems, only three wings of the residence were completed. They now house an international studies center as well as the Trinity College library.

The various affiliated colleges added residences over the years. Victoria College opened Annesley Hall, a residence for women, on Queen's Park near Bloor Street in 1903. Trinity College opened St. Hilda's College, a residence on Devonshire Place, in 1939. St. Joseph's College, which occupied the grand home formerly owned by the Christie family (famous for biscuit manufacturing) at the corner of Wellesley Street and Queen's Park Crescent, affiliated with St. Michael's College in 1912. A number of men's residences were built, including Victoria's Burwash Hall and St. Michael's Teefy Hall, both designed in the collegiate Gothic style.

One of the university's greatest benefactors has been the Massey family, who made their fortune in farm equipment. The Masseys were intensely interested in architecture and helped bring about Annesley Hall, Burwash Hall, and the Household Science Building (at the southeast corner of Bloor Street and Avenue Road), and in the early 1960s contributed Massey College for graduate students. Their greatest gift, however, was Hart House, a student center for men, which was not fully opened to women until 1972. It is unique in combining athletic facilities with spaces for music,

A. Scott Carter, *Map of the University of Toronto*, commissioned for Hart House by the Honorable Vincent Massey, oil on panel, 1937

art, debate, and many other activities. The construction of Hart House started before World War One, and it was used for training soldiers during the war. Designed by Toronto architects Sproatt & Rolph, who had been responsible for Victoria's Burwash Hall, the collegiate Gothic building officially opened in 1919. The Map Room on the first floor of Hart House contains on one of its walls an imaginative, colorful map of the university, painted in 1937 and commissioned by the Massey family. Sproatt & Rolph was awarded the American Institute of Architects prestigious Gold Medal in 1925 in recognition of their expertise in collegiate Gothic architecture.

Female students would not get suitable athletic facilities until the Clara Benson Building, designed by Fleury, Arthur & Barclay, was constructed on the west campus in 1959. Additional athletic facilities for men and women went up to the west of the Benson Building in the 1970s. In the 1980s many student services, such as the housing service and the bookstore, were incorporated into the Koffler Student Services Centre, the former Beaux Arts–inspired reference library at the northwest corner of College and St. George Streets. A twenty-four-hour student commons opened in 2018 in the former architecture building on College Street.

The university's first stadium, Varsity Stadium, was created in 1911, evolving from a cinder track and a five-hundred-seat grandstand constructed south of Bloor Street in 1901. It continued to expand during the next four decades. By 1950 an average of over twenty-five thousand people would attend each intercollegiate football game. In 2002 the university demolished the stadium and replaced it with a state-of-the-art facility that seats only about five thousand spectators. An ice arena, built in 1926 just east of the stadium, seats four thousand, perhaps reflecting the relative popularity of ice hockey over field sports at the University of Toronto. The

Hart House, view looking northwest from Queen's Park, circa 1920

Women's Hockey Team (from left: unknown official, Evelyn McDonald, Minnie Barry, Annie Hunter, Olive Bonnar, and Anne Sutherland), 1910

Goldring Centre for High Performance Sport was recently completed on Devonshire Street, just west of Varsity Stadium—described by Larry Richards in "Walk Four: The North Campus" as "one of the most innovative and elegant buildings completed by the university in the past decade."[9]

THE 1920S AND 1930S

After the devastation of World War One—in which so many students, staff, and alumni lost their lives—the 1920s were good years for the University of Toronto. On the first anniversary of the armistice, the cornerstone for a memorial tower was laid between Hart House and University College. The magnificent bell tower, designed by the architects of Hart House, Sproatt & Rolph, was completed in 1924.

Under President Falconer's strong leadership, the university constructed a number of buildings, including the splendid 1920 Darling & Pearson-designed Electrical Building (now the Rosebrugh Building) fronting on Taddle Creek Road. But two events at the institution in 1922 had a particularly profound effect and indirectly led to new structures. The first was Frederick Banting and Charles Best's discovery of insulin in 1922, with the subsequent awarding of the Nobel Prize in Physiology or Medicine jointly to Banting and to the head of the department of physiology, J. J. McLeod. Research money poured into the university, resulting, for example, in a new research institute for Banting on College Street opposite Toronto General Hospital. Insulin aided in putting the University of Toronto on the medical map.

The other event was the creation in 1922 of the School of Graduate Studies, which helped increase enrollment of graduate students. Up until then, the number of doctoral students at the university had been very low, even though the doctorate degree had been available since 1897. The School of Graduate Studies has occupied various homes on the campus and presently inhabits two historic houses at 63 and 65 St. George Street—the former the nineteenth-century home of Canada's first prime minister, Sir John A. Macdonald. The new Pontifical Institute of Mediaeval Studies at St. Michael's College also attracted graduate students, resulting in a building for the institute on the east side of Queen's Park Crescent. Additionally, the red-brick-and-stone, Rockefeller-funded School of Hygiene, which was constructed in 1927 on College Street, drew many foreign graduate students.

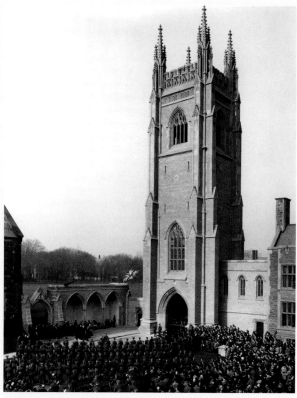

Dedication of the Soldiers' Tower, 1924

President Falconer's successful twenty-five-year term of office ended in 1932, and the chair of the Governing Council, Canon Henry Cody, became president. It was difficult for the president to be creative or to encourage construction during the Great Depression, when the government was cutting its expenditures. Some construction took place, however.

The principal addition to the university in the 1930s was the expansion of the Royal Ontario Museum, which was an integral part of the University of Toronto until it formally separated for financial reasons in the 1960s. In 1914 the west wing of the museum—a three-story Byzantine-style building designed by Darling & Pearson—opened beside Philosopher's Walk. Using construction as an opportunity to create jobs during the Depression, the building was expanded in 1933 to three times its capacity with a handsome new wing and an entrance on Queen's Park.

WORLD WAR TWO AND ITS AFTERMATH

During World War Two, enrollment decreased from about eight thousand students to roughly seven thousand, although the number of engineering students actually increased. There was very little change in the physical structure of the university, although there was considerable war-related work within the institution. One result

East facade of the Electrical (now Rosebrugh) Building, facing Taddle Creek Road, 1920s

Students in the Hart House Library during World War Two, circa 1942

of the war was that Canada drew closer to the United States. This would promote the flow of graduate students to the United States and result in the shaping of the University of Toronto's own graduate programs along the lines of the United States'.

After the war, enrollment soared as the University of Toronto absorbed about a quarter of all the Canadian veterans who went on to university. In the academic year between 1946 and 1947, there were more than seventeen thousand enrolled students, about half of them veterans. At the same time, the number of female students at the university declined from almost 50 percent of the student body to a little over 25 percent, as many women were expected to stay home, get married, and have children. This largely accounted for the arrival of the baby boomers at universities twenty years later.

Due to the increased number of students, the engineering department, which then included architecture, needed more space. Temporarily it moved into the federal government's large former munitions plant in the town of Ajax, about twenty-five miles (forty kilometers) east of Toronto. The federal government offered to give the land permanently to the university. "It seems to me," wrote Minister of Reconstruction C. D. Howe, "that you will be driven out of the city eventually, and I doubt if there is any more suitable location than the one you have [at Ajax]."[10]

Fortunately, the university declined the government's offer and eventually built new engineering facilities on the downtown Toronto (St. George) campus, including the Mechanical Engineering Building on King's College Road and the Wallberg Memorial Building for chemical engineering on College Street, as well as new facilities for the Institute of Aerophysics in the north end of the city. Architecture also returned from Ajax to the main campus and was temporarily housed in the old skating arena on Huron Street.

BABY BOOMERS

By 1950 almost all the veterans had graduated, and overcrowding was no longer a serious problem. The economy was strong and there was relatively little unemployment, yet the university constructed only a few buildings during that decade—a short-lived lull in construction that would end in the 1960s.

By 1955, under President Sidney Smith (president: 1945–57), it had become clear that the baby boomers would hit the universities in the 1960s. Experts predicted that enrollment in Canada would at least double and that the numbers of students seeking to attend the University of Toronto would be disproportionately higher. A 1956 internal university report, created by the university senate's Plateau Committee—created to deal with the increase in enrollment—set the stage for future planning: the university should be prepared to double its enrollment; residences should be expanded; and new colleges, both downtown and on the outskirts of the metropolitan area, should be established.

It was evident that the Toronto campus would have to expand, but in what direction? An earlier 1949 report by a committee headed by Professor Eric Arthur of the School of Architecture and Landscape Architecture had agreed with a still earlier 1947 report by architect and planner James Murray that the downtown campus should expand to the west. Murray had concluded that it should not extend north because of the "serious barrier of heavily traveled Bloor Street," coupled with the expense of purchasing properties in the area to the north. Murray's guiding principle was that it should take no longer than ten minutes—the time allowed between lectures—to walk from one part of the campus to another. (It takes about ten minutes to walk between Bloor and College Streets.) "A circle with its centre just south of Hart House and a diameter stretching from College Street to Bloor Street," Murray noted, "extends...west as far as Spadina."[11]

The campus, the Plateau Committee concluded, should therefore extend west to Spadina Avenue. Up until then, the university, with a few exceptions, such as the dentistry, nursing, and education divisions, did not extend west of St. George Street. In the late 1950s, the University of Toronto started quietly buying properties in that area and eventually expropriated numerous properties west of St. George Street between Bloor and College Streets.

PLANNING FOR EXPANSION

The board of governors set up an advisory planning committee, which produced a comprehensive plan for the new thirty-three-acre campus south of Harbord Street and extending to Spadina Avenue: The campus would be reserved for pedestrian use only. Deliveries would take place via underground routes from the main city streets, and parking would be confined to lots on Spadina Avenue, which would provide a buffer from the then-contemplated Spadina Expressway. (As it turned out, the expressway was never built, primarily because of the opposition inspired by Jane Jacobs, who had recently moved to Toronto from New York City, only to find her own home in the path of the proposed expressway.) Two large playing fields would be created in the middle of the west campus, between the residences and athletic buildings to the west and the academic buildings on or close to St. George Street. The Faculty of Arts and Science and some other divisions were to move to the new west campus.

The planning committee also made detailed proposals for the university as a whole, most of which were later implemented under Bissell's presidency, between 1958 and 1971. It was a veritable building boom: University College received a new north wing in 1964, which completed the quadrangle; a centrally located arts building named after former president Smith opened on the west side of St. George Street in 1961; the Ramsay Wright Zoological Laboratories, the Lash Miller Chemical Laboratories, and the McLennan Physical Laboratories with its Burton Tower appeared on the west campus; and the Galbraith Building for engineering, named after the first dean of engineering, was constructed in the 1960s on the east side of St. George Street. A University of Toronto fund-raising campaign had brought in c$15 million, higher than its original target. Unfortunately, the government would not provide the necessary additional funding to meet the cost of the west campus expansion and the new construction, which had risen from an estimated c$12 million

Officials examining a model of the west campus expansion in the late 1950s (from left: Vince Kelly, president of the Students' Administrative Council [SAC]; Neil McKinnon, member of the board of governors; and Adrienne Poy, vice president of SAC)

to over c$50 million, not including the cost of the land and projects already in progress.

The government was faced with additional demands from other Ontario universities, such as McMaster University, which was now eligible for provincial funding, and newly created institutions, such as Carleton University and University of Waterloo. In the summer of 1957, the chair of the university's board of governors, Eric Phillips, wrote to President Smith that although he was "much in sympathy" with the closing of the roads and the construction of two playing fields, his feeling was that "no such luxury will be accepted by the Government."[12] These, of course, were the two crucial aspects of the west campus expansion plan. "It is my feeling," Phillips wrote, "that the layout as a whole should be based on the complete absence of playing fields from this area, and that such open space as is involved in the overall plan should be limited to what I call 'quadrangles.'" The plan was thereafter effectively emasculated. New buildings were constructed using the existing street pattern, cars were not excluded, and there were no playing fields. This would have long-term consequences for the university.

A FLURRY OF BUILDINGS

At no period in the university's history did so much construction take place in so short a time as in the 1960s. In addition to the buildings mentioned above, there were new buildings at the denominational colleges, such as the new John M. Kelly Library and Loretto College women's residence at St. Michael's, the new Margaret Addison Hall for Victoria College, and the Gerald Larkin Academic Building for Trinity College.

The university also constructed new professional buildings, such as the massive concrete Medical Sciences Building on the site of the old engineering building on King's College Circle and the previously mentioned Galbraith Building. The law school moved from Glendon Hall to occupy Flavelle House, with a library and moot courtroom built behind it. The Faculty of Music opened a building overlooking

Philosopher's Walk, with two large concert halls, and the Royal Conservatory of Music (at the time closely associated with the university) took over the building that had once housed McMaster University.

As had been recommended by the Plateau Committee, the university also established two new colleges on the west campus. In 1964 the cornerstone of the first phase of a new undergraduate college—appropriately called New College—was laid at the corner of Willcocks and Huron Streets. It was, as President Bissell said at the ceremony, "a new chapter in the history of the University of Toronto." It would be the first college directly under the control of the university constructed since University College was built in the 1850s. Innis College, named after political economist Harold Innis, admitted its first students in 1964, but the sod was not turned for the building at the corner of St. George and Sussex Streets until 1973. Unlike New College, it did not initially have a residence, until one was built across the road on the east side of St. George Street in the 1990s.

The university's flurry of construction in the 1960s was accompanied by a marked shift to modernist styles. This shift reflected the changing mindset of the city at large, which had held an international design competition for a new city hall in 1958, which is widely recognized as a defining moment for modern architecture in Toronto. Coordinated by Professor Arthur from the University of Toronto, the jury chose a design by Finnish architect Viljo Revell. The university had played a role in forcing the establishment of a design competition for the task, the result of which

Toronto City Hall during construction, view from the southeast, August 17, 1964

was announced in 1958. The competition brought a number of talented architects to Toronto, such as John Andrews, who later designed Scarborough College, and Macy Dubois, who would design New College. Others came to Toronto because of the newly recognized potential for exciting architectural work in the city, such as Jack Diamond, who would design Innis College and other buildings on the campus, Eberhard Zeidler, who would design the first Rotman School of Management buildings, and Ron Thom, who would design Massey College. So the decision to hold a competition for the new city hall helped change the face of Toronto and the university.

FOUNDING OF SCARBOROUGH AND MISSISSAUGA

Even the creation of New and Innis Colleges, as well as the establishment of York University (which first admitted students in 1960 and was affiliated with the University of Toronto until 1965), would not be able to satisfy the expected demand for university education in the Toronto region. The University of Toronto, therefore, founded two new colleges on the outskirts of Toronto. With the encouragement of the Ontario government, it purchased two large blocks of land—a two-hundred-acre site in Scarborough about twenty miles (thirty kilometers) east of the main campus, and a hundred-fifty-acre site on the Credit River in Mississauga, the same distance west of the campus. The two new colleges, now known as University of Toronto Scarborough (UTSC) and University of Toronto Mississauga (UTM), were to be like other colleges in the University of Toronto system, though it was envisioned that they would gradually achieve greater autonomy.

Three members of the School of Architecture and Landscape Architecture, Andrews, Michael Hough, and Michael Hugo-Brunt, worked together on the site plan and the bold design for Scarborough College—a facility that incorporated televised instruction in the classrooms. Andrews, an Australian architect (and a University of Toronto professor at the time), created an imposing concrete megastructure in 1964

Aerial view of Scarborough College, September 1966; Science Wing (left) and Humanities Wing (right)

Erindale College, South Building, 1971

that sits dramatically on a ridge overlooking the heavily wooded valley of Highland Creek below. The *Architectural Forum* magazine gave it a rave review, stating that "the visitor succumbs most willingly to the sheer power of the whole, to Andrews' ingenious blending of light, form, and space into a single experience."[13] Not everyone was thrilled, however. Some members of the board regarded it as "conspicuous waste," and the use of television for teaching was not entirely successful.

The Mississauga campus started life with a preliminary building, the North Building, to greet the first class that started in 1967. Meanwhile, Andrews developed the initial site plan and architectural vision for the campus, then known as Erindale College. Somewhat similar with Scarborough, he proposed a megastructure, which was developed further by the engineering firm of A. D. Margison and Associates in 1968, but it lacked the design finesse characteristic of Andrews. (See Walk Ten, page 300.) Certain aspects of the megastructure concept were given form in the pleasant South Building (1971), designed by Raymond Moriyama in association with A. D. Margison and Associates.

By the end of the 1980s, the two colleges were each approaching some four thousand full-time students and were poised to increase their size and range of activities.

GRADUATE STUDIES

The growth in the number of students attending postsecondary institutions meant that universities required more teachers and more graduate programs to produce those teachers. The University of Toronto played a major role in this endeavor. To handle the increase of graduate enrollment in engineering, for example, the university doubled the number of engineering faculty members during the 1960s. The engineering department took over the Sandford Fleming Building on King's College Road, which became physically linked to the new Galbraith Building on St. George Street.

Medicine also greatly increased its number of postgraduate students. The Medical Sciences Building was ready for use by the end of the 1960s and the Faculty of Medicine also acquired the former veterans' hospital, Sunnybrook Hospital, in the northeast part of the city from the federal government. Other affiliated teaching hospitals expanded. On University Avenue alone, there were major additions to the Hospital for Sick Children and the Toronto General Hospital. Mount Sinai Hospital

Vincent Massey and Claude Bissell, president, with a model of Massey College, September 1963

built a wholly new structure, because the presence of Taddle Creek did not permit additional stories atop its existing building. Princess Margaret Hospital and the Ontario Cancer Institute expanded at their old site on Sherbourne Street, both later taking over one of the Hydro Buildings on University Avenue in the 1990s. (A list of hospitals and centers affiliated with the health sciences at University of Toronto is included on page 232.)

At the same time, research grew in importance at the university. The new Ontario Institute for Studies in Education (OISE) was established in 1965 by the Ontario government. It later became part of the University of Toronto and had the largest number of graduate students in the university. In 1969 it moved into its present twelve-story building on the north side of Bloor Street, constructed specifically for OISE. Other centers and institutes followed, like the Centre for Mediaeval Studies and the Marshall McLuhan Centre for Culture and Technology.

In the early 1960s, a final great gift by the Massey Foundation enabled the establishment of a graduate college. Massey College opened in 1963 at the corner of Devonshire Place and Hoskin Avenue. Vincent Massey's son, the architect Hart Massey, wanted a modern treatment; the elder Massey, however, according to Bissell, was "determinedly traditionalist." [14] The Frank Lloyd Wright–inspired Vancouver architect Ron Thom managed to satisfy both father and son while creating a universally acclaimed building. Massey College has the feel of a traditional English college, with its inner courtyard and grand dining hall, but it is also strikingly modern in design.

With the increased number of graduate students, the university needed more graduate residences and acquired two apartment buildings on Charles Street West for family housing and a low-rise apartment building at the southeast corner of Bloor and St. George Streets. It was not until Graduate House opened in 2000 with its over 420 student places—and with its huge steel O dramatically hovering over the street at the corner of Spadina Avenue and Harbord Street—that the university added significantly to its accommodations for graduate students.

The university library system also had to expand in order to provide facilities for the expected increase in the number of graduate students. A separate research library devoted to the humanities and social sciences was a high priority for President Bissell. The university had not originally planned a major expansion north of Harbord Street, but it became clear that this was the only reasonable possibility for a major library complex. The New York firm Warner, Burns, Toan & Lunde proposed a bold cluster of linked structures, assembled around an enormous triangle-shaped building, each side of which would be 330 feet (101 meters) long—the length of a Canadian football field. The John P. Robarts Research Library, the complex's central triangular area, was named after the Ontario premier who authorized the project. It officially opened in 1973. The monumental sixteen-story building (including underground floors) is said to be the largest academic library building in the world. The north wing of the library complex houses the Faculty of Information, and the south wing has one of the most spectacular sights in the university—a rare book library with an awe-inspiring six-story open interior and soaring wood shelving. (See Walk Six, page 214.) A third wing, imagined to the west in the original master plan, will be completed in 2019.

The colleges and departments also expanded their collections. New libraries were built at University College and at Victoria, Trinity, and St. Michael's Colleges. At the end of World War Two, the Toronto library system had only five hundred thousand books and was ranked thirty-sixth among university libraries in North America. By 1965 it was ranked eleventh, and by the end of the century, it had eight million volumes and ranked second only to Harvard Library in acquisitions.

THE 1970S AND 1980S

The 1970s and 1980s were difficult years for the University of Toronto, as for other Canadian universities. The Ontario government wanted to control its expenditures on universities, which had grown between 1965 and 1969 from 1 percent to about 10 percent of its budget. Within the first six months of University of Toronto President John Evans's tenure, the government imposed a freeze on all new provincially funded capital expenditures, including the renovation of old buildings. A fund-raising campaign in the latter half of the 1970s was used primarily for renovations, including a comprehensive restoration of University College, for which the principal consultant was Arthur, the highly respected professor of architecture who did much to enhance and preserve Canada's architectural heritage while simultaneously promoting modernism. The campaign also funded a new athletic center on Harbord Street, the Koffler Student Services Centre (incorporating the former Toronto Reference Library on College Street), and a new Earth Sciences Centre on the west campus. Financial constraint continued—even intensified—after Evans left office in 1978. The new president, James Ham, spent much of his five years in office cutting budgets.

Despite the financial difficulties, the university established Woodsworth College in 1974 for part-time students. Until then, part-time students had been under the umbrella of the extension division, which had operated successfully since its establishment in 1929 in President Falconer's day. The extension division, today called the School of Continuing Studies, with quarters on the west side of St. George Street, near Bloor Street, continues its successful outreach program. At first operating out of several historic houses located across the road from the School of Continuing Studies, Woodsworth College continued to grow. A new award-winning building designed by KPMB Architects in association with Barton Myers Associates was completed in 1992, imaginatively combining the historic houses with an old drill hall. Now that the college includes full-time students, an ambitious Woodsworth College Residence was built at the southeast corner of Bloor and St. George Streets in 2004.

The Earth Sciences Centre, located between Huron Street and Spadina Avenue, accommodates botany, forestry, geology, and related disciplines. It was officially opened in 1989, during President George Connell's incumbency.

Robarts Library, nearing completion in 1972

A. J. (Jack) Diamond's thoughtful design incorporated Bancroft Avenue as a pleasant pedestrian street.

President Connell, who took office in 1984, inherited a demoralized university, mainly due to financial constraints. He was, however, able to lay the foundations for his successor Robert Prichard's successful ten-year presidency in the 1990s. President Connell supported increased research at the hospitals, introduced long-range budgeting, and restructured the university's governing process to give the faculty a greater role and therefore a greater stake in the university. A turning point in the history of the university was the Nobel Prize in Chemistry awarded to John Polanyi in 1986. In part because of Polanyi, both the federal and provincial governments started to fund "centres of excellence" instead of limiting their funding to a formula based on student enrollment. Funding based on quality gave the University of Toronto a natural advantage.

RECENT YEARS

Prichard became president in 1990 and made a great contribution to the physical shape of the university. He had taken an elective course in modern architecture while an undergraduate at Swarthmore College, which sparked a lifelong interest in building design and construction. He and his four talented vice presidents were able to raise large sums in a fund-raising campaign, which was primarily devoted to supporting academic chairs. At the end of Prichard's tenure in 2000, the university had raised c$700 million, and during his successor Robert Birgeneau's presidency, the campaign reached c$1 billion. Impressive fund-raising activity continued under President David Naylor, who took office in 2005, and his successor, Meric S. Gertler, who became president in 2013, both of whom are recognized as strong presidents.

A new campaign, entitled "Boundless," was launched in 2013 and raised its original goal of over c$2 billion six months ahead of schedule. The campaign continues with a higher goal.

Over the past thirty years, the university has been both acquiring existing buildings and actively constructing new ones on the downtown Toronto (St. George) campus and at the Scarborough and Mississauga campuses. The sight of numerous cranes continues to be a feature of life on all three campuses. One can see the extraordinary growth by observing recent changes at various vantage points on the downtown campus.

From the corner of University Avenue and College Street, for example, one can see a number of existing buildings purchased by the university, such as 500 University Avenue for rehabilitation science and the former Board of Education buildings on College Street for the faculties of nursing and medicine. On the north side of College Street is the Leslie L. Dan Pharmacy Building designed by Norman Foster (2006) and the Terrence Donnelly Centre for Cellular and Biomolecular Research (2005) designed by Behnisch Architekten of Stuttgart, Germany. Further west is the Bahen Centre for Information Technology (2002), designed by Diamond Schmitt Architects. The immense MaRS complex on the south side of College Street, stretching from University Avenue to Elizabeth Street—incorporating the original 1913 Toronto General Hospital building—has recently been completed and brings entrepreneurs and scientists together in one setting.

Farther north, at the corner of Bloor Street and Queen's Park, one can see Daniel Libeskind's striking addition to the Royal Ontario Museum, once an integral part of the university and still closely associated with it; Victoria College's Isabel Bader Theatre designed by Lett/Smith Architects; and additions to the Royal Conservatory of Music by KPMB Architects. A new addition to the law school, designed by Hariri Pontarini Architects, can also be seen behind Flavelle House. This multistory curved structure around Queen's Park Crescent is named after major

donor Hal Jackman, a law graduate and former lieutenant governor of Ontario and chancellor of the university. Plans are now being completed for a large building on the site of the planetarium between the museum and the law school.

Along St. George Street are new buildings constructed over the past thirty years, such as the Joseph L. Rotman School

President Robert Prichard (rear) and his four vice presidents in the fall of 1999 (from left: Michael Finlayson, Jon Dellandrea, Heather Munroe-Blum, and Adel Sedra)

of Management, and two new residences—Woodsworth and University Colleges—
as well as additions to the chemistry building and the previously mentioned Bahen
Centre for Information Technology, both by Diamond Schmitt Architects. Another
major engineering building—to house the Centre for Engineering Innovation and
Entrepreneurship—is presently under construction on what had been a parking
lot behind Convocation Hall. The university also acquired the existing Medical Arts
Building at the northwest corner of St. George and Bloor Streets, which now
accommodates humanities disciplines. From the corner of St. George and Harbord
Streets, one can see Graduate House, designed by the Pritzker Prize–winning
Thom Mayne of the US firm Morphosis.

There have also been significant changes in the physical landscape of the
university. In 1994 Judy Matthews, a philanthropic alumna, donated funds to
transform St. George Street with a new urban design infrastructure supporting
pedestrian flow that would also include flowerbeds and trees. It was the start of
a comprehensive program to improve the quality of public open spaces and to
enhance the physical beauty of the university. In 1999 the university launched its
Open Space Master Plan initiative, "Investing in the Landscape," which aims to
knit together the campus, create more green space with more trees and less concrete, eliminate cars on the Front Campus, and recognize the importance of
pedestrians. The new entrance gates at College Street and the redesign of King's
College Road to the Front Campus were part of the first phase of this plan. The
university's 2017–22 Landmark Project, which includes construction of a grass-
roofed underground parking garage below King's College Circle, will eliminate
parking on the Front Campus.

Greater awareness of the importance of art in the university has become
evident in recent decades with the 1996 creation of a new art venue in University
College to compliment the art collection and gallery at Hart House. The university
has also encouraged architects and planners to include outdoor public art. See,
for example, the sitting statue of Northrop Frye on a bench at Victoria College.
Richards's "Walk Eight: The Museum and Gallery Walk" describes the many important galleries and museums within and near the university.

The planning and urban design process at the university changed dramatically
under President Robert Prichard's tenure. The university and the city of Toronto
concluded an agreement in 1997—with the support of local residents' groups that
sometimes oppose development—to permit the use of twenty-eight specific sites on
the downtown campus for future expansion. In determining the development sites,
the university agreed that future buildings would conform to certain urban design
guidelines rather than density provisions. These criteria became the evaluative tool
for development permissions in the City of Toronto Official Plan and remain in force
today. At the same time, the university established a physical planning and design
advisory committee, the Design Review Committee, to review design policy, partici-
pate in architect selection, and consider the design of future university buildings
as well as revisions to the university's master plans.

Planning for future growth has been a priority in the past several decades. In 2000 the university prepared plans to expand enrollment on all three campuses to meet the future growth of demand for university places for children of the postwar baby boomers. The principal growth has been at Scarborough and Mississauga, where enrollment has almost tripled on each campus since the turn of the millennium.

The Scarborough and Mississauga campuses had been established in a rural setting with significant conservation lands in their midst, and on these campuses expansion is limited to certain areas that will not impact the flood plains or the protected areas. The increased enrollment and recent expansion on both campuses have led to institutions that are now each as large as many other North American liberal arts colleges or universities. As on the downtown Toronto (St. George) campus, many of the new structures at Mississauga and Scarborough, such as the Communication, Culture & Technology Building at Mississauga and the Academic Resource Centre at Scarborough, are by award-winning architects with strong national, even international, reputations.

In recent years there have been many new buildings on the suburban campuses. In "Walk Nine: University of Toronto Scarborough (UTSC)," Richards describes a number of other new buildings at Scarborough. The university was able to take advantage of the federal government's Knowledge Infrastructure Program, announced in 2009 following the economic downturn of 2008, to obtain c$35 million to build an instructional laboratory center at Scarborough, as well as a similar amount for a comparable center on the Mississauga campus. That same year the City of Toronto was awarded the Pan American Games to be held in 2015. As a result, a major complex for aquatics, to a great extent paid for by the three levels of government, was built at the far north end of the Scarborough campus. That enabled about a hundred acres of land that had been used as a dump to be remediated and available for future development by Scarborough. That is ample land, considering the original downtown Toronto (St. George) campus was only 150 acres. Many new developments will appear on the north campus, such as student housing and a new science building.

There has been comparable activity on the Mississauga campus. Of particular note is the new Terrance Donnelly Health Sciences Complex. Having a medical academy has raised the campus's status and increased the range of research projects it can undertake. Again, Richards's text describes the many award-winning buildings that have been constructed. These include the Health Sciences Complex, the Instructional Centre, the Hazel McCallion Academic Learning Centre, the Recreation, Athletics, and Wellness Centre, and the Communication, Culture & Technology building. In 2013 the City of Mississauga committed to help build the new Innovation Complex, a c$35 million building that houses the Institute for Management & Innovation, as well as a business incubator.

Growth will also continue on the downtown Toronto (St. George) campus over the next decades, both in numbers of students and buildings. Much of the growth of students will be in the graduate programs. It is reasonable to predict, as stated in the second edition of *The University of Toronto: A History* (Martin L. Friedland, 2013), that by the two hundredth anniversary of the university in 2027 there could be 80,000 students on the St. George campus, with a total of 120,000 on all three campuses. New projects are under discussion. Expect a major development on the north side of College Street, across from the MaRS complex, to replace the Banting and Best Institutes. The engineering department has a number of sites that can and probably will be developed, such as underused space behind the Wallberg Memorial Building. Another potential replacement site is Cody Hall on the corner of St. George and Russell Streets. The north section of the Goldring Centre for High Performance Sport has the structural capacity for a tall building. There is discussion about a large development on the planetarium site, and on and on. In the summer of 2017 the university announced that it had acquired a c$123 million four-acre site on the southwest section of the campus, from College to Russell Streets and between Huron Street and Spadina Avenue, where the Centre for Addiction and Mental Health is located.

An application to establish a new plan for the downtown Toronto campus to replace the 1997 plan was submitted to the City of Toronto in 2016.

FROM PASTURES TO TWENTY-FIRST-CENTURY URBANITY

The University of Toronto started out in the early nineteenth century in a pastoral setting far outside the city limits, growing its own vegetables for the students in residence. It is now an intensely urban institution embedded in and integral to Toronto's dense downtown and to the economy of the city and the province. The Greater Toronto Area today possesses one of the largest populations in North America, and recently Toronto became the third largest North American city outside of Mexico, after New York and Los Angeles. Almost half of immigrants to Canada end up in the Toronto area.

The University of Toronto flows into the city and the city flows through the campus. It is often difficult to tell where the university ends, with its many buildings south of College Street and north of Bloor Street. As an urban entity, the University of Toronto is more like New York University than Columbia University. The growth of the many affiliated teaching hospitals throughout the city likewise contributes to this effect. The two suburban campuses, Scarborough and Mississauga, also started life in rural settings, but like the St. George campus, they are becoming part of the urban landscape.

While there is no prevailing architectural style at the university—in part because each denominational college was and still is responsible for the design of its buildings—it contains some of the finest architecture in Canada, starting with Cumberland's masterpiece, University College, and it includes more than ninety-five heritage sites on the three campuses. In the coming years, there will continue to be growth, particularly at the suburban campuses, and the panorama of designs and styles will also continue. Campus planning has become of increasing importance

View of the St. George campus from the west with the Back Campus in the foreground and the city skyline beyond

in recent years and incremental landscape projects, as Richards rightly argues in this guide, have the potential to be the "glue" that binds the architecturally diverse campuses together.

I trust that readers will enjoy their tour of the University of Toronto through Richards's descriptions and through their own walks through the campuses. The university's diverse treasury of buildings and their landscapes provide the opportunity to learn much about the history of architecture in Canada and beyond. Moreover, readers will learn about more than just architecture, because the history of the University of Toronto mirrors the history of Toronto, the history of Ontario, and the history of Canada.

NOTES

Much of the material for the introduction is drawn from Martin L. Friedland, *The University of Toronto: A History* (Toronto: University of Toronto Press, first edition, 2002: second edition, 2013).

1 *Charter of the University of King's College*, University of Toronto Archives.
2 J. George Hodgins, *Documentary History of Education in Upper Canada*, vol. 1 (Toronto: Warwick and Rutter, 1984), 222.

3 *Sir Daniel Wilson's Journal*, September 21, 1853, University of Toronto Archives.

4 W. S. Wallace, *A History of the University of Toronto* (University of Toronto Press, 1927), 72.

5 Geoffrey Simmins, *Fred Cumberland: Building the Victorian Dream* (University of Toronto Press, 1997), 92.

6 John Langton, "The University of Toronto in 1856," *Canadian Historical Review* 5 (1924): 142.

7 Simmins, *Fred Cumberland*, 103.

8 Douglas Richardson, *A Not Unsightly Building: University College and its History* (Toronto: Mosaic Press, 1990), 61.

9 Larry Richards, "Walk Four: The North Campus," *infra*.

10 University of Toronto Archives, C. D. Howe to Eric Phillips, February 7, 1947.

11 James Murray, "A Report on Problems of Building Expansion in the University of Toronto," 1947, 6-7, University of Toronto Archives.

12 Eric Phillips, letter to Sidney Smith, July 30, 1957, University of Toronto Archives.

13 Oscar Newman, "The New Campus," *Architectural Forum*, May 1966.

14 Claude Bissell, letter to Eric Phillips, January 15, 1960, University of Toronto Archives.

The Historic Core

HOSKIN AVENUE

QUEEN'S PARK CRESCENT WEST

Back Campus

Front Campus

HART HOUSE CIRCLE

KING'S COLLEGE CIRCLE

ST. GEORGE STREET

KING'S COLLEGE ROAD

COLLEGE STREET

TORONTO

The Historic Core

The city of Toronto is densely built and, in its collective mindset, overtly modernist. It has also become a city of towers with more than 150 tall buildings under construction in 2018, second only to New York among North American cities. Toronto's vertical surge is accelerating with some 450 tower proposals moving through the city's planning process. Within this changing urban context lies the University of

Back Campus, looking southeast

Toronto's downtown (St. George) campus and its historic core, a milieu of substantial masonry buildings, courtyards, lawns, playing fields, and mature trees. The historic core is not only distinctive but also increasingly of great value as a network of public open spaces. Here we find an oasis of calm amid metropolitan fervor.

As well, the historic core has a significant collection of heritage structures. Given the quality and range of designs—from the moody, mysterious University College to the noble, imposing Convocation Hall to the comforting, embracing Hart House—the core of the St. George campus presents a living exhibition of architectural excellence, mirroring the university's history. In his introduction to this book, Martin Friedland recounts the establishment of the university in 1850 and its

gradual settling of the forest lands to the north of the Town of York, now the city of Toronto. Completely urbanized today, the campus nevertheless retains gentle traces from more than a century and a half ago. One of my favorite escapes is to sit on the porch of Cumberland House at 33 St. George Street, the house that Frederic Cumberland, architect of University College, designed for his family at the end of the 1850s. Looking across the fenced-in lawn, it's inviting to imagine a scene from a century and a half ago, with a game of croquet underway and horse-drawn carriages clicking along nearby College Avenue (now College Street). From the second floor of the house, Cumberland could have gazed through the trees northward and seen his magnificent new creation, University College.

While the world of the 1850s seems far off, the buildings and landscapes that survive from that era (and the 160 years since) help us imagine and fantasize about the past and in turn better understand our complicated present. Encased by modern, vertical Toronto, the university's historic precinct is an instructive jewel.

1   Alumni Gates, Entrance Plaza, and King's College Road

Andropogon Associates, Ltd., in association with Elias + Associates Landscape Architects, 2003

Alumni Gates, the University of Toronto's "front door" on College Street, is marked by limestone-clad gateposts enveloped in wisteria. The lower parts of the gateposts are heavily rusticated, similar to the base of the neighboring Lassonde Mining Building. Constructed fifteen years ago, they commemorate the one hundredth anniversary of the University of Toronto Alumni Association. The gates and the entrance plaza have taken on an aura of formality and tradition, reinforced by the stone paving of King's College Road as well as by the handsome walkways and seating, elegant lampposts, and tree plantings. Together, these elements strengthen the axial view north to King's College Circle and University College that has existed ever since the obstructive Magnetic and Meteorological Observatory was dismantled in 1908.

Alumni Gates

Lucius O'Brien, McCaul's Pond with University College in the background, watercolor, 1876

2   King's College Circle (Front Campus)
Landmark Project

KPMB Architects with Michael Van Valkenburgh Associates, Inc., Urban Strategies, Inc., and ERA Architects Inc., expected completion 2020

King's College Circle, comprising twenty-two acres, is the university's most important open space. Also known as Front Campus, it is the institution's historic heart—a place of ceremony and everyday collegial activity. After a century and a half of casual evolution, the circle and the surrounding precinct are being comprehensively transformed to clarify, reimagine, unify, and connect. The Landmark Project is an ambitious undertaking for the university, and, when completed, it is expected to add immeasurably to daily life on campus and in the surrounding city.

University College originally had a picturesque, meandering approach from the southeast, across Taddle Creek, near McCaul's Pond. In the 1860s or 1870s, the university built a road from College Avenue (now College Street), on an axis with University College, but it only extended about halfway as far north as today's King's College Road. Early photographs of the area show unpaved dirt and gravel roadways in front of University College forming a squarish circle. For many years this area contained a cricket pitch. In landscape architect Bryant Fleming's 1917 "Preliminary Plan for the Landscape Improvement and General Expansion for the University of Toronto," this large open space is labeled "The Green," while contemporary maps refer to it simply as the "Front Campus."

Although Fleming asserted that the primary entrance to the campus should be from the east and fully integrated with Queen's Park, he somewhat begrudgingly accepted that the King's College Road entrance "is probably conceded to be the most important." For King's College Road, Fleming proposed "properly located walks paralleling the roadway" and suggested that double rows of trees should be "considerably spaced...as to form an avenue of vision to and from Main Building [University College]." He envisioned a new plaza at the north end of this avenue, next to Convocation Hall. Interestingly, he also focused on the south vista from University College, calling for a visual termination to that axis on the south side of College Street. He imagined "the approach from the north being axial with the tower of Main Building, and to the south upon some strong architectural monument or motif, located across College Street upon land condemned for such purposes." Fleming's 1917 vision was rekindled at the start of the twenty-first century by Philadelphia-based Andropogon Associates, the landscape architects for Alumni Gates and King's College Road. Their work was part of a much larger initiative for the area that included the redesign of King's College Circle as part of the university's Open Space Master Plan, an ambitious vision launched in 2000. Their concept proposed that the Front Campus lawn within King's College Circle would be retained as a playing

ABOVE: View looking southwest toward the Medical Science Building and Convocation Hall
TOP: The Landmark Project, architectural rendering of an aerial view

field but also become more formal—a pure circle—and that automobile parking around it would be eliminated. Andropogon Associates also designed a new plaza at the north end of King's College Road, between Convocation Hall and the Medical Sciences Building, in the exact location that Fleming had foreseen; however, the landscape architects did not engage the notion of a southern plaza across College Street, accepting that the distant silhouette of the CN Tower (1976) would suffice for the foreseeable future as a termination of the south axis from University College. As with Fleming's 1917 vision for King's College Circle, Andropogon Associates' 2000 plan was unrealized.

In 2015 the University of Toronto hosted an "Innovative Ideas and Design" competition for the King's College Circle precinct. The winning team, led by KPMB Architects and landscape architects Michael Van Valkenburgh Associates, created a new vision that will further pedestrianize the open spaces within the historic core of the campus, including Front Campus, Back Campus, Hart House Circle, Tower Road, Sir Daniel Wilson Quad, and the Medical Sciences Building plaza. The design work commenced in January 2016. The project will consist of a grass-roofed, underground parking garage for three hundred cars; elegant, glass-enclosed loggias providing access to the garage; granite-paved roads and walkways for pedestrians and cyclists; and a tapestry of integral gardens and social spaces. The project's tentacles extend far and wide, reaching Queen's Park to the east and Hoskins Avenue to the north.

Although the comprehensive Landmark Project, focusing on King's College Circle, emphasizes a forward-looking "healthy urbanism," from tree preservation and planting, to the promotion of walking and cycling, it can also be understood as an organic reconnection with the historic core's nineteenth- and twentieth-century spirit. The colors of the granite paving—purples, greens, russets—are derived from the colors of University College's historic, slate-roof tiles; the circle will be soft-edged and gently flowing, recalling the meandering gravel roads that once led to University College. Architectural renderings (see pages 53–54) suggest that the transformed character of the university's most important open space will be a comfortable synthesis of formality and informality—an inventive "modern picturesque."

3   Back Campus Playing Fields for the Toronto 2015 Pan Am & Parapan Am Games

Bregman & Hamann Architects, 2015

Tower Road Modifications

KPMB Architects, Inc. and Michael Van Valkenberg, Inc., expected completion 2020

The counterpoint to the Front Campus is the smaller Back Campus, located north of University College and south of Hoskin Avenue. Looking at the pale green artificial turf that carpets most of the area now, there are few hints of the original landscape or its historical associations. This was where the university's first military unit, the K Company, drilled and paraded at University College in 1861. During World War

One, the Back Campus was the place where city regiments, cadet corps, and the University of Toronto Contingent of the Canadian Officers Training Corps completed military exercises. In 1939, with World War Two looming, King George VI and Queen Elizabeth appeared here before thousands of spectators for the queen's presentation of colors to the Toronto Scottish Regiment.

For more than a century, the grassy rectangle has been a student playing field and casual open space available for a host of activities by the university and its surrounding community. Although cherished as a flexible space for sports, picnics, and hanging out on the grass, the Back Campus had poor drainage and frequently became a muddy pit. With the Pan Am & Parapan Am Games coming to Toronto in 2015, the university received an opportunity for federal and provincial funding to reconstruct the Back Campus, including the insertion of two field hockey pitches for the games. Following two years of controversy and debate, the historic landscape of green—if sometimes muddy—grass was replaced with artificial turf, surrounded by tall sports-field lighting elements. The field is now used year-round and has provided much-needed space for teams, clubs, and casual sports players.

The university's Landmark Project includes improvements to the north edge of the Back Campus—the verge along Hoskin Avenue—and redesign of Tower Road along the east.

4   University College
Cumberland & Storm, 1859
Restoration and renovation
David B. Dick, 1892
Restoration and renovation
Wilson Newton, Roberts Duncan, and Eric Arthur, 1979
Laidlaw Wing
Mathers & Haldenby, 1964
Revitalization project
Kohn Shnier Architects in association with ERA Architects Inc., 2018

Towered, turreted, majestic University College is arguably the most important structure on the St. George campus, both historically and architecturally. The university approved funding for the building in February 1856. Frederic Cumberland, a member of the University of Toronto senate, and the highly artistic William George Storm were appointed as the project architects the same month. Construction started on October 4, 1856, and the building, designed in the rugged Romanesque Revival style rooted in medieval architecture of the eleventh and twelfth centuries, opened three years later on October 4, 1859.

Major changes to the natural landscape have occurred over the years, causing "UC," as it is affectionately known, to forfeit the full power of its original picturesque setting. However, the building continues to have great significance as the university's iconic set piece. In 1968 University College was designated by the

OVERLEAF: University College

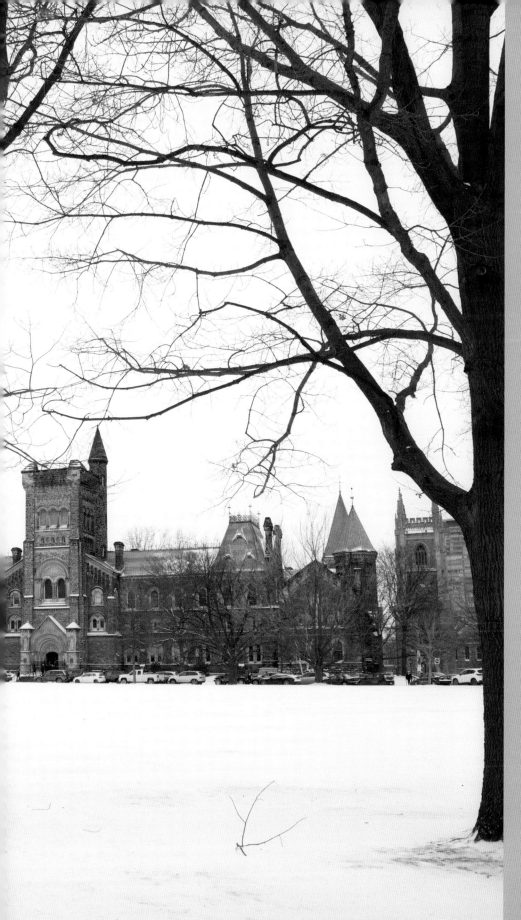

Historic Sites and Monuments Board of Canada, sealing its status as a national treasure.

In his authoritative book *A Not Unsightly Building: University College and Its History* (1990), Douglas Richardson reminds us that in the early 1850s Toronto was hardly a city but rather "a small town" of about thirty thousand people with "only fields and scattered houses north of Dundas," and the university grounds were "set apart in the semi-rural outskirts of the city." (The city was also rebuilding following the devastating fire that destroyed four entire blocks of its core in 1849.) The completion of University College brought substantial construction activity and, finally, fame and architectural glory to sleepy Victorian Toronto.

University College, main entrance

The building became a key stop for prominent visitors, including Edward, Prince of Wales, who included it in his 1860 Canadian itinerary. By 1883 horse-drawn streetcars rattled along College Avenue (now College Street) just south of University College, and Toronto was in the midst of major urban expansion to the north and west. University College and its pastoral setting had become an island in the midst of a bustling city with a population of more than eighty thousand. (See Introduction, *Bird's-Eye View of Toronto*, page 11.)

Cumberland & Storm's "First Study" for University College shows a layout inspired by Oxford and Cambridge Universities, forming a large rectangular quadrangle. As the design developed, Cumberland & Storm were considerably influenced by John Ruskin and the Dublin architects Deane & Woodward—in particular their work between 1855 and 1859 on the Oxford University Museum of Natural History. It seems that the University of Toronto and the architects wanted to avoid the Gothic style, which was strongly associated with churches and denominational colleges; they thought the rugged Romanesque Revival approach was more suitable for Toronto's northern climate than the more intricate Gothic.

The resulting building was U-shaped with a quadrangle opening to the north at what would become known as the "Back Campus." In addition to its massive main tower and arched entrance on the south, University College was distinguished by the circular chemistry lab at the southwest corner, now the lovely Croft Chapter House. About a third of the structure is made of stone, incorporating substantial amounts of sandstone from Georgetown, west of Toronto, along with stone imported from the United States and France. Due to budget constraints the remainder was

Southeast tower, University College

constructed mostly of brick, although the building displays an astonishing array of sculptural, carved ornament in stone and wood, along with spectacular polychrome tile floors and beautiful stained glass. Indeed, one must explore the interior to fully appreciate this masterful work of architecture.

On February 14, 1890, a fire broke out in the southeast corner of University College and spread rapidly, following an accident involving kerosene lamps. The following Sunday, more than fifty thousand Torontonians showed up to survey the disaster. Although many interior spaces were destroyed in the eastern portions, the stone structure survived, and the university, provincial government, and broader community immediately rallied to restore the magnificent building. David B. Dick, a talented architect who was born in Scotland and trained in Edinburgh before moving to Toronto in 1873 (where he became university architect and designed the new university library), was placed in charge of the restoration in September 1890, and University College was fully reoccupied by January 1892. With minor exceptions, the overall configuration of the restored structure changed very little. UC's burned-out Convocation Hall was replaced with needed lecture rooms and offices, and a new boiler house and men's lavatory were added in the quadrangle at the north end of the east wing. Dick also deviated somewhat from the original High Victorian style of Cumberland & Storm, particularly for the east wing, adding a then-more-fashionable late-Victorian layer.

In 1964 the yellow brick and buff stone, neo-Norman-style Laidlaw Wing, housing the College Library, was built across the north end of the U-shaped building. It was designed by Mathers & Haldenby, a two-generation-old Toronto-based firm that exemplified "Ontario establishment" in the fullest sense, with its low-key, conservative architecture. The new wing finally enclosed the quadrangle in a manner somewhat similar in plan to Cumberland & Storm's "First Study," but it lacks sophistication and finesse in terms of proportion and detailing. Along the Laidlaw Wing's south-facing arcade is the University of Toronto Art Centre, housing part of the university's extensive art collection. (See Walk Eight, page 249.)

In 2017 University College launched the rejuvenation of several of its key spaces, the most prominent being the reinstatement of the library, with a new mezzanine in the grand east hall on the second floor. Other components of the renewal project include a new reading room in the west hall, converting the Croft Chapter House into a conference center, creating a third-floor student café beneath an existing clerestory, updating HVAC and IT systems, and providing complete accessibility. A new elevator will be added in the cloister—a contemporary, sculptural play on the Norman-Gothic architecture of University College. The renovation project will respect and complement the historic building. In the words of architect John Shnier, "We intend to integrate the new design elements as though they had always belonged." Revitalization of the quadrangle will be implemented as part of the Landmark Project.

Other buildings constituting the college include Whitney Hall, the University College Union, Sir Daniel Wilson Residence, and Morrison Hall.

Whitney Hall

University College Union

5 Whitney Hall
Mathers & Haldenby (with John M. Lyle as consulting architect), 1931
Ferguson Wing
Mathers & Haldenby, 1960

University College's Whitney Hall is named for the wealthy lumber baron Edward C. Whitney, brother of James P. Whitney, who was premier of Ontario from 1905 to 1914. The residence was originally for women only but is now coeducational and accommodates 250 students in four houses composed around a well-defined quadrangle that opens on the east to the Back Campus.

In 1930 St. George Street formed the western boundary of the campus. To establish a consistent style and character to the public face of the institution, the administration had mandated since 1920 that all new buildings along College and St. George Streets be "Georgian in character," and Mathers & Haldenby—in consultation with John M. Lyle, one of Canada's outstanding architects of the first half of the twentieth century—responded accordingly with this red-brick structure that has finely articulated doorways, railings, and lanterns.

In 1960 a wing designed by Mathers & Haldenby was added at the southeast corner, seamlessly continuing the same Georgian Revival vocabulary used thirty years earlier.

6 University College Union
Architect unknown, 1885
Addition
Darling & Pearson, 1923
Renovations
Stinson Montgomery & Sisam Architects, 1987

Originally a fine late-Victorian residence, this building was first occupied by George H. Watson, partner in the successful law firm of Watson, Smoke & Masten, Barristors & Solicitors, and later by Lieutenant Colonel Frederic Nicholls, president

Sir Daniel Wilson Residence

of Canadian General Electric. The facade facing St. George Street displays what is sometimes referred to as "Toronto bay and gable" style and presents a projecting third-floor gable clad in fluted shingles. An intricate wrought-iron fence is found in front of the house.

In 1916 the university acquired the building for University College's Women's Union, and between 1922 and 1923 architects Darling & Pearson completed a major addition to the east. The union supports a broad range of University College activities and includes the Helen Gardiner Playhouse. With the construction of Morrison Hall tower to the south, in 2005 pathways around the UC Union were landscaped, giving the building a more gracious setting.

7 Sir Daniel Wilson Residence

Mathers & Haldenby, 1954

Now coed, the Sir Daniel Wilson Residence was first opened by University College sixty-five years ago for men. It is announced to the viewer on St. George Street with a large clock tower that rises above a portico marking the main entrance. The building honors Sir Daniel Wilson, president of University College from 1880 to 1892—he was later the first president of the newly federated University of Toronto.

The Sir Daniel Wilson Residence was completed twenty-five years after neighboring Whitney Hall. Mathers & Haldenby again employed the conservative Georgian Revival style, but the two buildings are quite different: Whitney Hall is made of red brick, while Sir Daniel Wilson is built of yellow buff brick; whereas Whitney Hall forms a pleasing, square quadrangle, Sir Daniel Wilson's quadrangle is ill-defined and drifts ambiguously toward the main University College building. In 2005, when Morrison Hall was added directly to the north, Sir Daniel Wilson's Howard Ferguson Dining Hall (the north wing of the quasi-quadrangle) was renovated and expanded to serve both residences.

8   Morrison Hall

Zeidler Partnership Architects, 2005

The realization of coeducational Morrison Hall in 2005 ended a lengthy discussion about where and how University College might add another student residence. Each site the college considered generated a heated debate about preserving green space and existing views, retaining mature trees, and considering the always contentious matter of architectural style. Eventually, a very tight infill site fronting on St. George Street was selected for the 270-bed residence, to the north of and adjacent to Sir Daniel Wilson Residence.

Morrison Hall's thirteen-story, zinc-clad tower, rising from a two-story yellow brick podium that integrates seamlessly with Sir Daniel Wilson Residence, evokes the gray-blue of neighboring slate roofs. The tower steps back three times near the top to refer to nearby collegiate Gothic structures, such as the Soldiers' Tower, its volumetric twin to the east. A large decorative gate thoughtfully screens the delivery area from St. George Street. Zeidler Partnership Architects' design is thoughtful if unassuming, possibly the result of many years of university wrangling about site, context, and style. The building seems to be waiting for a flourish at the top—perhaps a crown relating to the iron finials pointing skyward from its mother ship, the original University College next door.

Morrison Hall

9   Louis B. Stewart Observatory

Cumberland & Storm, 1855; moved and rebuilt, 1908

The Louis B. Stewart Observatory was originally located south of King's College Circle as part of the Toronto Magnetic and Meteorological Observatory, completed in 1855 in a mild Venetian style by the same architects selected one year later to build University College. A landscaped area commemorating the original facility, which consisted of a main structure with a domed corner tower and smaller surrounding buildings within a walled compound, is located at the northeast corner of the Sanford Fleming Building.

In 1908 the observatory was dismantled to make way for the northward extension of King's College Road. The materials were reused to build the Stewart Observatory in its present location, including a tower similar to the original one. The structure served meteorological and astronomical studies until 1953. In recent years it housed the University of Toronto Students' Union (UTSU) offices and became a rallying point for student concerns, frequently sporting creative graffiti. On the building's east face, a wall-mounted relief designed by Johnny Koo and Bruce Parsons incorporates a smashed bicycle. It commemoratively reads: "Those Who Gave Their Lives for Democracy on June 4, 1989 in Tiananmen Square, Beijing."

With the UTSU moving their offices to the Student Commons building on College Street in 2018, the Stewart Observatory will once again be rethought, this time as part of the encompassing Landmark Project.

Louis B. Stewart Observatory

Hart House

10 Hart House

Sproatt & Rolph, 1919

Hart House Circle Modifications

KPMB Architects, Inc. and Michael Van Valkenberg, Inc., expected completion, 2020

Hart House impresses through the beauty of its materials, detailing, and crafts-manship. The construction of this fine student facility at the beginning of the twen-tieth century was made possible by its generous patron, Vincent Massey, the first Canadian-born governor general of Canada. The Massey family had acquired con-siderable wealth via the Massey Manufacturing Company, later merged as Massey-Harris. Hart Massey, Vincent Massey's grandfather, who had serious interests in efficiency through design, died in 1896, and the philanthropic funding that he left behind enabled the creation of the Massey Foundation. However, it was Vincent Massey who was particularly interested in the cultural role of progressive architec-ture. A graduate of the University of Toronto's University College and Balliol College, Oxford, Vincent Massey became convinced that the University of Toronto needed a central student facility and in 1910 confirmed funding from the family's estate for an ambitious new kind of campus center. The YMCA supported the project as well.

From 1910 to 1919 Massey closely monitored and participated in design and construction decisions for Hart House, named in honor of his grandfather. He was also influential in shaping matters of use, social interaction, and governance at the new campus center. (For him "common fellowship" meant "men." Women were not admitted to Hart House on equal terms until 1972.) A lengthy dedicatory inscription at the east end of the first-floor corridor records the aspirations of the facility. A passage from it reads:

> The prayer of the founders is that Hart House…may serve in the generations to come the highest interests of this university by drawing into a common fellowship the members of the several colleges and faculties, and by gathering into a true society the teacher and the student, the graduate and the undergraduate; further that the members of Hart House may discover within its walls the true education that is to be found in good fellowship, in friendly disputation and debate, in the conversation of wise and earnest men, in music, pictures and the play, in the casual book, in sports and games and the mastery of the body.

As architectural historians William Dendy and William Kilbourn have claimed, Hart House is perhaps Canada's finest example of Beaux-Arts Gothic Revival. A plaque in the main lobby honors the memory of the architect, Henry Sproatt: "His skill as a master of the Gothic form is woven into the fabric of this house." The building's planning is superb, with common rooms in the south and west wings, athletic functions in the north wing, the Great Hall to the east, and a theater placed underground below the narrow, central quadrangle. Hart House embodies the picturesque qualities of Oxford and Cambridge, balancing small-scale comfort with moments of real grandeur.

The Great Hall, designed for serving meals for up to three hundred people, is covered by a hammer-beam roof of steel and oak. A monumental traceried south window features armorial glass honoring ten of the university's benefactors and college founders. Below the window are panels bearing the arms of the British Royal Family, along with arms of fifty-one universities in the British Empire of the early twentieth century. Rising from the south-end dais is a mysterious "corkscrew" Gothic stair tower that originally led to the second-floor Faculty Union Senior Common Room (now the receiving room and bar of the Gallery Grill, a gourmet dining destination on campus). Running along the top of the oak paneling is an inscription chosen by Massey from John Milton's *Areopagitica*—an attack on censorship of the press.

Visitors should not miss the civilized lecture room, library, map room, reading room, and east common room. (See map in Introduction, pages 24–25.) Hart House also includes a music room featuring an exquisite ceiling structure of British Columbia cedar. The tiny chapel on the first floor features work by artist Will Ogilvie, including windows completed in 1969, celebrating Canadian nature and containing fragments of stained glass from ruined churches in France, Belgium, and Italy. The architectural feast continues with an intimate, five-hundred-seat theater tucked

PREVIOUS: Hart House, the Great Hall, circa 1920

into the basement level, under the central courtyard. Interestingly, it was the location of a lecture by the famous American architect Frank Lloyd Wright, on November 30, 1949.

Hart House, University College, and the Soldiers' Tower (1924), with its arched colonnade, contribute two sides of Hart House Circle, a space loosely defined on the south by the Gerstein Science Information Centre. The Queen's Park Crescent West overpass, constructed in 1949, forms the rather rude eastern boundary of this historic zone, which was originally contiguous with Queen's Park. (See Introduction, page 26.) The University's Landmark Project calls for the future dismantling of the high-speed overpass, allowing Hart House Circle and Queen's Park to once again flow gently together.

Making cider at Hart House Farm, November 28, 1969

Today Hart House embraces superb theatrical performances, literary activities, and an outstanding collection of Canadian art. As well, the Hart House community enjoys a 150-acre farm in the Caledon Hills, 34 miles (55 kilometers) northwest of Toronto. Acquired by the university in 1949, Hart House Farm includes the rustic Ignatieff House and a sugar shack where maple syrup is produced.

Hart House remains a vibrant, collegial place and continues to fulfill the vision of its forward-thinking patron. Indeed, the claim in the University Board of Governors' 1921 book *Hart House, University of Toronto* that "the passage of time will leave the building more and more beautiful" resonates as fact.

11 Soldiers' Tower

Sproatt & Rolph, 1924

Modifications

Mathers & Haldenby, 1949

Located at the northwest corner of Hart House Circle, the Gothic-style Soldiers' Tower and its carillon were sponsored by the university's Alumni Federation, now known as the University of Toronto Alumni Association. The cornerstone was laid on November 11, 1919, the same day that Hart House was officially opened, and the tower was dedicated in 1924 to honor students and alumni who lost their lives in World War One. (See Introduction, page 28.)

The composition of Soldiers' Tower is more complex than it first appears. Standing at the south end of Tower Road, it links University College and Hart House. To the east it is tied to the latter by a volume containing the stair that leads to the Muniment Room, a vaulted space halfway up the tower that contains archival material and memorabilia related to both world wars. Joined to the tower's base is a colonnade with large stone tablets bearing the inscribed names of members of the university who perished in World War One. The base of the tower incorporates a fan-vaulted passageway, whose side walls were redesigned in 1949 by Mathers & Haldenby and inscribed with the names of members of the university killed in

ABOVE: Workers unload a 2.5-ton bell for the Soldiers' Tower carillon, September 14, 1927
OPPOSITE: Soldiers' Tower

World War Two. The sophistication of the Soldiers' Tower was duly recognized in 1990, when it was awarded a City of Toronto Urban Design Award.

The tower's carillon was not dedicated until 1927. The first carillon had twenty-three bells, with nineteen added in 1952. The tower was renovated, and major improvements were made to the carillon in the mid-1970s, increasing the total number of bells to fifty-one.

12   Wycliffe College
David B. Dick, 1891
Convocation Hall (Sheraton Hall)
George M. Miller, 1902
Refectory, library, and residence hall addition
Gordon & Helliwell, 1907
Principal's residence and new chapel
Gordon & Helliwell, 1911
New library (Leonard Hall)
Chapman & Oxley, 1930

Named for the Oxford theologian, priest, and professor John Wycliffe, this college is an Evangelical Anglican graduate school of theology that prepares students for the ministry. The seminary was founded in 1877 as the Protestant Episcopal Divinity School by the Church Association of the Diocese of Toronto, a lay Evangelical group at St. James Cathedral that championed the doctrinal points of the English Reformation.

Wycliffe College, Soward Reading Room

Wycliffe College

The school's first building, designed by William George Storm and opened in 1882 (demolished circa 1925), was located north of College Street and east of King's College Road. Becoming a federated college in 1889 and growing rapidly, the school constructed a new building on campus in 1891, fronting on Hoskin Avenue. The red-brick Victorian ensemble that one sees today resulted from numerous additions, including a seventeen-room principal's residence added in 1911. The whole speaks of austerity and sobriety; however, a closer look reveals unpretentious architectural delights such as the highly detailed brickwork surrounding the large windows to the left of the main entrance.

The elegant 1930 library addition at the southwest corner, Leonard Hall, seems curious at first because its collegiate Gothic style and stone cladding are more akin to nearby Hart House than to Wycliffe College itself. The intention was to eventually replace Wycliffe's older, modest brick buildings with new stone buildings in the collegiate Gothic style, but this vision was never realized.

Besides Leonard Hall, Wycliffe College has numerous interior spaces worth visiting, including the Soward Reading Room, Founder's Chapel, Sheraton Hall, old Cody Library, and the Refectory. This last space captures the sense of simplicity and common moral life that are deeply valued by the Wycliffe community. These charming spaces, connected rather higgledy-piggledy, exude humanity and warmth. Moreover, the intriguing architectural "jigsaw puzzle" that has evolved over 127 years at Wycliffe College flies in the face of the mechanistic, "same thing everywhere" monotonous buildings spawned by globalization. In this sense, Wycliffe College is a distinctive, comfortable, welcoming place.

Gerstein Science Information Centre

13 Gerstein Science Information Centre

Original library (Sigmund Samuel Building)

David B. Dick, 1892

Bookstack wing

Darling & Pearson, 1909

North wing

Mathers & Haldenby, 1954

Morrison Pavilion

Diamond + Schmitt Architects, 2003

Heritage Wing restoration and renewal

Diamond + Schmitt Architects, Inc., 2008

This sprawling complex houses Canada's largest academic science and medicine library. The development of the center spans nearly 130 years, from the construction of the highly eclectic 1892 structure facing on King's College Circle, to the suave Morrison Pavilion of 2003 nestled into the ravine and facing the provincial legislative buildings, to the thoughtful restoration of the magnificent reading room in 2008.

The pivotal piece of the composition is the original New University Library designed by David B. Dick, now the Sigmund Samuel Building. (See Introduction, page 23.) By the 1880s the university urgently needed a new library, having outgrown the one housed in University College; the devastating fire that destroyed University College in 1890 made this even more imperative. Dick's cruciform plan for the new structure included a tower (influenced by Kelso Abbey in Scotland, Dick's place of birth) that marked an exuberantly sculpted entrance porch. These elements can still be enjoyed today, although the original gorgeous entrance has been demoted to an emergency exit. The magnificent five-story bookstack wing by Darling & Pearson was completed in 1909. Its structural glass floors allow natural light to flow down through the building. A major wing by Mathers & Haldenby, clad in Queenston limestone, was added at the north in 1954. Together with the earlier buildings, it functioned as the university's library until 1973, when Robarts Library was completed.

The Morrison Pavilion, providing 650 additional study spaces, was imaginatively grafted onto the east side of the center's north wing in 2003. An octagonal tower, topped by four abstract copper-clad planes, authoritatively completes the 1954 entry axis and serves as a strong orientation point. A copper-clad vault runs the length of the slender pavilion, whose walls are faced in rough-cut stone, giving the library an appropriately weighty aspect. Contrasting with this, alternating thin planes of gray glass seem to defy gravity and float across the stone face. The elongated pavilion feels entirely sympathetic with the early parts of the complex without being historicist.

In 2008, as part of the Heritage Wing renewal project, the historic reading room was restored. A dropped ceiling was removed, revealing the original hand-carved wood trusses, rafters, and dramatic glass skylight from 1892.

14   Volunteers' Monument

McDougall & Skae (site planning); Mavor & Co. (Robert Reid, sculptor), 1870
Restoration
Spencer R. Higgins, 2008

This major monument—Toronto's first public sculpture—commemorates Canadians lost in the June 1866 skirmish with the Fenians—Irish Americans who sought to revenge accumulated wrongs to their native Ireland—at the Battle of Ridgeway in Canada West (present-day Ontario). The story leading to the monument starts during the American Civil War, when, during a crisis in British-American relations, the threat of an American attack on Canada emerged. This led to the formation of volunteer rifle companies, including one at University College in 1862. In 1866 after the Civil War, a new threat appeared from the Fenians, who selected nearby English Canada as a target. The Fenians, some eight hundred strong, crossed the Niagara River in force, and the Queen's Own Rifles K Company, which included the University College group of volunteer faculty members and students, joined troop trains going to the border. A battle unfolded at Ridgeway, and although the Fenians finally withdrew and retreated across the border, three University College men were killed in the confusion.

The monument was financed through public subscription of one dollar per contributor and erected in 1870 in a sylvan setting that overlooked the now-buried Taddle Creek. What was built was much less ambitious than the vision put forward in 1869 by William Storm, who had proposed a brick caretaker's lodge, trees, and elaborate walkways leading to and surrounding the monument. Montreal

Volunteers' Monument

sculptor Robert Reid eventually executed the Volunteers' Monument in the Italian Renaissance style, composed of a tiered, rectangular gray-brown sandstone pedestal with diagonal buttresses, on which white marble figures are displayed. The east figure symbolizes "Grief"; the west, "Faith"; and the north and south figures represent Canadian volunteer riflemen. A statue of Britannia rises at the top.

15 Canadiana Building
Mathers & Haldenby, 1951
Addition
Mathers & Haldenby, 1957

Donated by Dr. Sigmund Samuel, a noted philanthropist, this building was originally known as the Archives and Canadiana Building and housed Samuel's extensive collection of Canadian decorative arts. (This superb collection is now displayed at the Sigmund Samuel Gallery of Canada at the Royal Ontario Museum, three blocks to the north. (See Walk Eight, pages 253–55.) In 2008 the university's Centre for Criminology and the School of Public Policy and Governance moved into the building.

    The Canadiana Building is curious architecturally. Presenting a stone-clad single volume capped by a sloping slate roof, it embodies Canadian architect John M. Lyle's plea from the 1920s onward for "solidity and simplicity" and a certain Canadian leitmotif. The four sculptures commanding the building's facade—figures of Samuel de Champlain, General James Wolfe, Sir John Graves Simcoe, and Sir Isaac Brock—were designed by Jacobine Jones and carved by Louis Temporale. They underscore

Lyle's nationalizing agenda. Throughout, the detailing and materials represent an engaging mixture of classical and modern impulses, from the handsome front doors with circular motifs, to the precisely detailed staircase, to the chevron-pattern, inlaid cork floor in the main room to the right of the foyer.

This small but monumental building commands our attention because it is so fascinatingly transitional in terms of style. It marks a mid-twentieth-century period in Canada when modernism was, for the most part, in the crevices and still far from full-blown.

16   McMurrich Building

Darling & Pearson, 1922

Opened in 1923 as the Anatomy Building, the McMurrich Building today hosts various university divisions, such as the Office of Campus and Facilities Planning, Office of Space Management, Office of Research Ethics, and Research Services. Its original setting was surely spectacular, along the ravine of Taddle Creek, traces of which are still evident, particularly where the landscape rolls downward at the building's north end. The west face has been altered by an unsympathetic stair

McMurrich Building

tower and the abutting plaza of the Medical Sciences Building; renovations in 1977 erased the original interiors.

Approaching the building from Queen's Park, one can appreciate what remains of this splendid structure. The grand east facade features massive anchoring end towers, with five soaring stone pilasters in between, an elegant rhythm of fenestration, and a subtle row of arches and stonework marching across the top edge of the building. The beautifully carved stone doorway has a pair of sumptuous oak doors.

It is inviting to imagine that the university will soon bring the grounds surrounding the building up to a high standard, incorporating it within the University's Landmark Project for the precinct.

17   J. Robert S. Prichard Alumni House

Mathers & Haldenby, 1958

This foursquare stone building served as the home of the University of Toronto Press from 1958 to 1989, when the press moved to a commercial office building on Yonge Street. The university bookstore was also located here until 1985, when it moved to the Koffler Student Services Centre on College Street. In 2000 the building was named the J. Robert S. Prichard Alumni House to honor the university's thirteenth president. It currently houses advancement and alumni-related divisions.

Executed in a mildly Canadian chateau style featuring a steep slate roof and numerous dormer windows, it is similar to the university's Canadiana Building, completed seven years earlier by the same architects.

J. Robert S. Prichard Alumni House

John Bryce Kay House

SCHOOL OF GRADUATE STUDIES

Although master's degrees were first awarded in 1843 at King's College and the doctorate degree was offered starting in 1897, the School of Graduate Studies (SGS) was not formally established until 1922. Today there are more than eighteen thousand graduate students registered in nearly three hundred graduate degree programs, making it the largest graduate school in Canada. SGS has student services and administrative offices in two historic houses at 63 and 65 St. George Street.

18   John Bryce Kay House, 65 St. George Street
David B. Dick, 1891

It is not entirely surprising to discover that the talented David B. Dick, designer of the university's first library, was the architect of this superb house at 65 St. George Street, a rambling brick and stone Tudor-inspired building that stretches deep into the block. It was built for John Bryce Kay Jr., one of the founders of the John Kay and Son household furniture stores, and purchased by the university in 1954. The SGS administrative offices are located here, including workspaces for the dean and the vice-provost for graduate research and education.

19   Macdonald-Mowat House, 63 St. George Street

Nathaniel Dickey (builder), 1872
Renovations
The Ventin Group, Ltd, 2016

To really appreciate this house— designed in the Second Empire style with a mansard roof and later transformed in the Italianate Style—one must stand at the south-facing front door and imagine the pastoral setting that spread before it in 1872. The fancy suburban villa surely impressed Sir John A. Macdonald, Canada's first prime minister (1867–73), who purchased the house from Nathaniel Dickey in 1876 and lived there for two years before serving again as prime minister (1878–91). It is interesting to think of Macdonald as a suburban neighbor of architect Frederic Cumberland, whose villa had been realized a few years before, just 820 feet (250 meters) to the south. In 1888 Oliver Mowat, premier of Ontario from 1872 to 1896, bought the house and kept it until 1902. Knox College has owned the house since 1910.

TOP: Macdonald-Mowat House, 1926
BOTTOM: Sir John A. Macdonald Room

In 2016 the house was extensively renovated by the Ventin Group to provide better accommodation for School of Graduate Studies Student Services. New HVAC systems and heritage replacement windows were added. Original wood paneling was preserved in some rooms, as well as the handsome English encaustic tile floor in the vestibule and main entry hall. (The tile pattern can be found in Maw & Co catalogs of the 1860s.) The renovation achieved an admirable marriage of twenty-first-century innovation with historical preservation.

20   Knox College

Chapman & McGiffin, 1915

Institutionally, Knox College is not part of the University of Toronto, but the dignified, architecturally commanding structure has great presence on the campus, both along St. George Street and on King's College Circle.

Presbyterian Knox College's first home was on Spadina Crescent and opened in 1875. (See Introduction, page 15.) The college moved to its present location in 1915, where it plays a crucial role in defining the western edge of the vast Front Campus. The best views of Knox College are from the east, looking across King's College Circle at the handsome chapel and library volumes.

The building's U-shaped configuration creates a memorable exterior space that is divided in half by a covered walkway, making two cloisters. Wrapping around these pleasing cloisters are student dormitory rooms, classrooms and offices, a magnificent library, and a glorious chapel. Knox College's collegiate Gothic style is perhaps somewhat low-key on the outside, but inside, the college's full architectural glory abounds.

The main entrance hall off King's College Circle is supported by a forest of elegant columns rising to exquisitely crafted fan vaults. Stone balustrades with tracery ring the mezzanine level. From the entrance hall one can go up to the chapel on the south side or the Caven Library on the north side, both featuring enormous windows of amber stained glass.

Knox College

Knox College

Knox College's distinctive architecture has made it popular with the film industry. The movie *Cocktail* (1988), starring Tom Cruise, included segments filmed there. In *Harold and Kumar Go to White Castle* (2004), Knox College represents Princeton, and in the epic film *The Incredible Hulk* (2008), the college served as the fictional Culver University. The landscaped Nona Macdonald Walkway runs along the south side of Knox College, leading to the university's Nona Macdonald Visitors Centre, which is tucked into the ground level of the college.

21   Convocation Hall

Darling & Pearson, 1906
Renovation and restoration
ERA Architects Inc., 2007–10

The view of the connected Convocation and Simcoe Halls from the northeast, diagonally across the sweeping Front Campus lawn, has long been a familiar and inspiring

Convocation Hall

one. Now, with the completion of the nine-story Myhal Centre for Engineering
Innovation & Entrepreneurship to the west of these buildings, the reading of that
long, low, horizontal composition of Convocation and Simcoe Halls has changed
significantly. This layered arrangement was not always so: when completed in 1906,
Convocation Hall stood alone without Simcoe Hall, and what became King's College
Circle was then a horseshoe-shaped gravel road leading to University College.
(See panorama, pages 8–9.) The approach to Convocation Hall was originally from
the east (centered on the building's eastern apse) along Taddle Creek Road (where
the Medical Sciences Building is now), and Convocation Hall was set back considerably from the evolving King's College Road as part of a V-shaped view corridor
from College Street to University College.

   The University of Toronto Alumni Association first promoted the idea of a
large hall in memory of those fallen in the Fenian raids and the Boer War; the proposition subsequently expanded, and by the time the cornerstone was laid in the summer
of 1904, the university required government support beyond the generous funding

provided by alumni. At the time, the hall's two thousand seats probably seemed extravagant. Today, however, with several thousand graduates passing through Convocation Hall annually with family and friends, multiple packed-to-the-rafters convocation ceremonies are held each year.

The designers of Convocation Hall, Darling & Pearson, had become Toronto's preeminent architecture firm, with Frank Darling recognized as the guiding light. He studied and trained in England between 1870 and 1873 before moving to Toronto. His name or his firm's name appears in conjunction with more projects at the University of Toronto than any other architect or firm. Darling received the Royal Institute of British Architects' Gold Medal in 1915 and died in 1923. His successor firm completed numerous buildings at the university, the Banting Institute (1930) being the last. Darling was fluent in many architectural styles. For Convocation Hall he chose the Beaux-Arts approach and followed through with rigorous execution. To some extent the building is modeled on the Sorbonne theater in Paris. The cylindrical, central auditorium space features a splendid dome. Considering its size, the hall has a remarkably intimate feel.

In 2007 the university launched an ambitious restoration and refurbishing project that both brought back much of Convocation Hall's original dignity and propelled it into the twenty-first century. The university's current Landmark Project includes plans for a new plaza adjacent to Convocation Hall, which will further the usefulness of this great building. Convocation Hall is typically one of the first and last grand architectural experiences of a student's University of Toronto years.

Soldiers in front of Convocation Hall, circa 1914

Simcoe Hall, with construction of the Myhal Centre for Engineering Innovation & Entrepreneurship in the background, fall 2017

22   Simcoe Hall

Darling & Pearson, 1924

Simcoe Hall, a long bar-shaped building running north–south behind and adjacent to Convocation Hall, houses the university's provost, president, and senior administration. Its primary facade, facing the southwest corner of King's College Circle, was astutely set at an angle to negotiate between the "bar" and the infill wing joining Convocation Hall. Darling & Pearson placed an elegantly scaled, templelike front at the bend, complete with a pediment and two pairs of engaged pilasters topped by Ionic capitals. A Palladian window graces the center of this lovely composition.

From the entrance hall to the council chamber, interior spaces are handsomely proportioned, elegantly detailed, and quietly inviting. Although somewhat dwarfed now by the new Myhal Centre for Engineering Innovation & Entrepreneurship directly behind it, Simcoe Hall continues to have a dignified presence.

23   Physical Geography Building

Darling & Pearson, 1925

Originally called the Forestry Building, this stately three-story brick structure first stood next door to Cumberland House, two hundred feet (sixty-one meters) south

Forestry Building (now the Physical Geography Building) in its original location on St. George Street, April 1927

of where it is now. In order to make room for the Galbraith Building in 1960, the Forestry Building was moved northward on steel rollers and placed on foundation walls that were about three feet (.9 meter) higher than the original ones and faced in brick instead of limestone, resulting in an unfortunate change in the proportional sense and appearance of the building. It now serves as the home for Arts & Science programs, primarily the Department of Mathematics. Stylistically a hybrid of Georgian and other classical influences, the Physical Geography Building offers several architectural pleasures, from the pediment-adorned entrance, to the stone quoining at the corners, to the balustraded parapet.

24 Cumberland House, 33 St. George Street

Frederic Cumberland, 1860

Renovations

William Storm, 1883

This historically and architecturally important house provides office and meeting space for the International Student Centre. Sadly, Cumberland House has largely been stripped of its bucolic setting and is now surrounded on three sides by asphalt. Its main entrance was originally on the east, and a long lawn stretched southward to College Street. (The house turned its back to St. George Street on the west until it was remodeled in 1883. What appears today as the front yard was originally the backyard.) Today, a small fenced lawn momentarily recalls nineteenth-century Toronto.

Inside, it is still possible to enjoy the fine proportions, superb moldings, and elegant fireplaces in the principal rooms on the ground floor. The circular stained-glass light above the main stair is spectacular. Amid these few preserved spaces, one can imagine how splendid the entire mansion must have been nearly 160 years ago, when Frederic Cumberland and his family lived there.

Cumberland, who was one of Canada's most distinguished architects and an accomplished civil engineer, railway manager, and politician, was thirty-seven in 1860 when he finished his house, which he called "Pendarves." He had just completed his masterpiece, University College, the year before. How interesting to think that he could rise in the morning and gaze from the second floor, across the pasture fields filled with grazing cows and sheep, and see his other creation, University College, a thousand feet (three hundred meters) to the north.

Cumberland lived at Pendarves for twenty-one years. After his death, his business partner, architect William Storm, remodeled the house for A. Morgan Cosby. Storm moved the main entrance from the east side, running the entrance hall through to a new vestibule and front door on the west. The University of Toronto purchased the house in 1921, and it served the law and business schools before becoming a gathering place for international students in 1966. This most recent use seems quite appropriate, given that Pendarves means "meeting place" in Cornish.

Cumberland House, view from the south, circa 1886

Faculty of Applied Science and Engineering

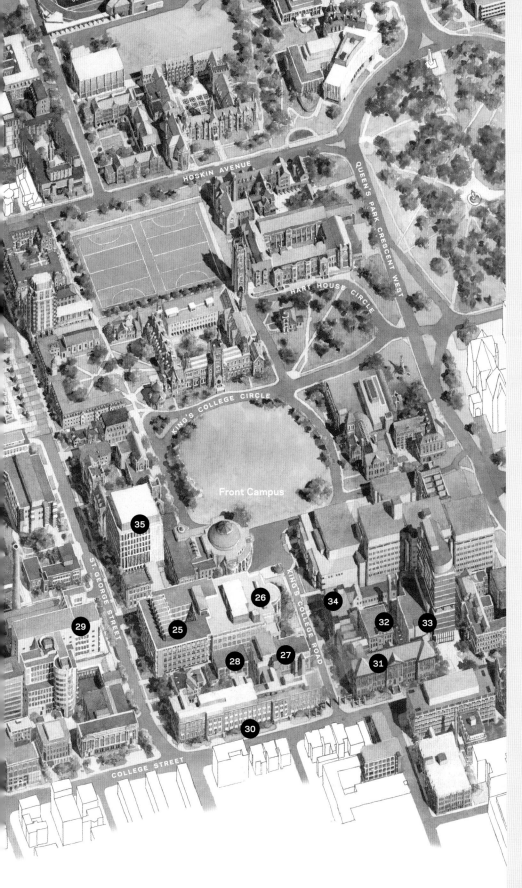

HOSKIN AVENUE

QUEEN'S PARK CRESCENT WEST

HART HOUSE CIRCLE

KING'S COLLEGE CIRCLE

Front Campus

ST. GEORGE STREET

KING'S COLLEGE ROAD

COLLEGE STREET

35

29

25

26

34

32

33

31

27

28

30

Faculty of Applied Science and Engineering

The Faculty of Applied Science and Engineering is the premier engineering school in Canada, embracing a creative community of 5,298 undergraduate students, 2,415 graduate students, 261 faculty members, and over 50,000 alumni. Founded in 1873 as the Ontario School of Practical Science, the school has a complicated institutional genesis, recorded in *The Skule Story: The University of Toronto Faculty of Applied Science and Engineering, 1873–2000* and brought to the present in *A Contemporary History of the Faculty of Applied Science & Engineering, University of Toronto, to 2018.*

Engineering's story begins in 1871 when the Ontario provincial government decided to create a college of technology supporting advanced study for the scientific professions. Models included the practically oriented Sheffield Scientific School at Yale and the Lawrence Scientific School at Harvard, both kept operationally independent from their respective universities. The Province of Ontario allocated c$50,000 in funding, purchased the Mechanics Institute building at Church and Adelaide Streets, and commenced renovations in September. Strangely, the College of Technology opened in May 1872 as a kind of fledgling evening school for artisans, tradesmen, and clerks, rather than focusing on advanced studies for the scientific professions. Among the offerings were courses in architectural and mechanical

Ontario School of Practical Science, circa 1904

drawing, antecedents of Canada's first architecture program, introduced at the University of Toronto in 1890.

In January 1873 the Legislative Assembly of Ontario brought forward a bill to establish and fund a new provincial institution, the Ontario School of Practical Science (OSPS). The assembly's act of March 29, 1873 provided arrangements whereby OSPS students could attend University College lectures at the University of Toronto and vice versa. The College of Technology at Church and Adelaide began to call itself the School of Practical Science. University College's role in the new school increased when Professor James Loudon was appointed chair of Mathematics at UC in 1875, the first Canadian-born person to occupy a permanent professorial position at the university. He promoted the use of more UC teaching staff within the OSPS, which became a kind of de facto applied science department within University College. Loudon also brought forth the idea of the school being in a new structure on the university campus, a vision realized in 1878.

The new red-brick facility for OSPS, costing c\$30,000 and paid for by the government, was located at the southeast corner of King's College Circle and faced north. Designed by architect Kivas Tully, it became known affectionately, as "The Little Red Schoolhouse." Between 1889 and 1890 the building was tripled in size, following the original style and including a landmark tower and new main entrance facing east. The structure remained on King's College Circle until 1966, when it was demolished to make way for the new Medical Sciences building.

In addition to the realization of the new school on campus, 1878 was also significant because the school finally had a professor of engineering—the newly appointed John Galbraith, who went on to have an illustrious, legendary career in Engineering. The new OSPS offered three, three-year diploma courses: Engineering (Civil, Mechanical, and Mining), Assaying and Mining Geology, and Analytical and Applied Chemistry. Student fees of c\$80 per year were considered substantial at the time but enrolment nevertheless rose steadily.

Among the required courses in the 1880s, the centerpiece was engineering drawing, consisting of technical drawing, mapping and topography, projections and perspectives, and descriptive geometry, with students spending fourteen of their forty weekly class hours on this core of visualization studies. This emphasis applied uniformly to the three areas of engineering education: civil, mining, and mechanical. The prominence given to engineering drawing and visualization remains at the heart of the undergraduate programs in today's Faculty of Applied Science and Engineering, bolstered now by digital technologies.

Following the Federation Act of 1887, which among many changes brought denominational colleges under the auspices of the university, the School of Practical Science affiliated directly with the University of Toronto, forfeiting its role as a branch of University College. Finally, as had been proposed in 1871, the school became an independent professional school for engineering and applied sciences. In 1906 the School of Practical Science officially became part of U of T, and the name was changed to the Faculty of Applied Science and Engineering (known simply by some as "Engineering"). With the growing success of the faculty, it expanded rapidly, including completion of the grand Sandford Fleming Building in 1907.

Now, with the completion of the Myhal Centre for Engineering Innovation & Entrepreneurship in 2018, Engineering occupies all or part of seventeen buildings: sixteen on the St. George campus and the Institute for Aerospace Studies at the north edge of the city. (See Walk Eleven, pages 326–27.) This represents more than 775,000 net assignable square feet (72,000 square meters). Collectively, the Engineering buildings present 114 years of architectural history, from Edwardian and Bauhaus styles to twenty-first-century, yet-to-be-named styles that emphasize energy efficiency and long-term sustainability.

25   Galbraith Building

Page & Steele Architects, 1960

The Galbraith Building is Engineering's main administrative center. It is named for John Galbraith, the university's first professor of engineering (appointed 1878), principal of the Ontario School of Practical Science, and first dean of the faculty.

Designed in the spare International Style, the building was composed as a kind of square donut around a courtyard. Its architecture is for the most part unremarkable, although there is provocation in the rational marking of the structural bays, particularly on the north side, where a rigorous rhythm of limestone-clad columns and dark-brown and light-brown brick infill occurs. The courtyard itself, which was originally open to the main lobby but later modified at the west, still has a late-1950s feel, including a lively cantilever stair at the north side.

A bold 1972 minimalist steel sculpture called *Becca's H* by Robert Murray stands in front of the Galbraith Building, and a terra-cotta frieze from the former "Little Red Schoolhouse" Engineering Building (which stood where the Medical Sciences Building is now) is displayed near the front entrance.

26   Sanford Fleming Building

Darling & Pearson, 1907
Addition (Burton Wing)
Horwood & White, 1948

From 1905 to 1908, the King's College Road area was a beehive of building activity. Convocation Hall was completed in 1906; the old observatory was dismantled in 1908, allowing the northern extension of King's College Road; and a new physics building, the McLennan Physical Laboratories (now the Sanford Fleming Building) was finished in 1907. Sir Sanford Fleming was chief engineer of the Intercolonial Railway of Canada from 1864 to 1876, and in 1871, he was appointed chief engineer on Canadian Pacific Railways surveys. He was instrumental in establishing the standardized, twenty-four-hour system of international time zones.

Confidently executed in the Beaux-Arts style, the Sanford Fleming Building originally had a U-shaped composition; following a fire that gutted the building in 1977, the inside of the U was filled in to make a student commons area. The most distinguished aspect of the building is the monumental east facade with its convex,

ABOVE: Physics Building (now the Sanford Fleming Building), view looking northwest, circa 1909
OPPOSITE: Galbraith Building

semicircular volume rendered in yellow brick and limestone. This volume, which now houses the Engineering and Computer Science Library, originally contained a large lecture hall. Three pairs of grand doors that led to the hall were retained. At the piano nobile level, six pairs of Ionic columns rise to support a classical cornice.

27   D. L. Pratt Building
Page & Steele Architects, 1964
Additions and Alterations
Dunlop Farrow Inc. Architects, 1988

A single-story wing for metallurgy was constructed at the northeast corner of the Wallberg Memorial Building along King's College Road in 1964. In 1988 three floors were added to the wing, realized through the generosity of D. Lorne and Lucille Pratt.

28   Engineering Annex
Darling & Pearson, 1920
Addition
Darling & Pearson, 1926

This small brick structure was originally the home of the University of Toronto Press and simply known as the Press Building. Founded as a printing program in 1901, the press's first home was on the top floor of the original, 1882 Wycliffe College building. The 1920 Press Building, designed by the prestigious firm Darling & Pearson had a large library and reading room. In 1976 the Press Building was taken over by Engineering, renovated, and renamed the Engineering Annex. It currently houses facilities for Electrical & Computer Engineering.

Press Building (now the Engineering Annex), November 1920

Bahen Centre for Information Technology

29 Bahen Centre for Information Technology

Diamond + Schmitt Architects, 2002

The Bahen Centre for Information Technology's multidisciplinary program, which includes the Faculty of Arts and Science as an integral partner, supports facilities for teaching and research in computer science, electrical engineering, engineering science, mechanical engineering, and industrial engineering.

Although its front door is on St. George Street, the L-shaped, cream-color brick structure extends deep into the block and can be entered from the north, east, south, and west. Sitting on top of an underground parking garage, the building is attached to the Koffler Student Services Centre, abuts the Central Steam Plant, and incorporates and reuses a historic Victorian house. It also embraces the Fields Institute for Research in Mathematical Sciences to the west.

The Bahen Centre's sprawling composition—pulling activities and people together to reinforce its multidisciplinary agenda—is held together by a monumental

Bahen Centre for Information Technology, atrium

atrium that runs east-west through the building. Soaring, polished concrete columns articulate this beautiful space, which is flooded with natural light from above. At the atrium's west end, a cylindrical volume incorporating stairs and lounges rises dramatically through eight levels and marks the minor cross-axis running north–south.

A sculpturally ambitious convex volume pushes out at the building's south side and terminates into a narrow visual corridor and gently rising pedestrian route from College Street. At the base of this volume is a granite-paved courtyard enclosed by the Bahen Centre, the Koffler Centre, the Fields Institute, and the Student Commons building. A series of cylindrical towers (which store rainwater for irrigation) give further definition to the western edge of the courtyard. Cascading pools flow from the courtyard down to College Street.

The Bahen Centre was one of the university's early examples of implementing a green agenda, which extends from the building's systems to its underlying urban infill and densification strategies. Moreover, the center's laudable infill and "urban octopus" strategies can be traced back to architect Jack Diamond's small but seminal York Square project, completed in Toronto's Yorkville area with Barton Myers in 1968.

30 Wallberg Memorial Building

Page & Steele Architects, 1949
Penthouse addition
Atria Architects, 2012

The Wallberg Memorial Building, which primarily serves the chemical engineering department, resulted from a bequest by Ida Marie Wallberg in 1933 to commemorate her brother, Emil Andrew Wallberg, the former president of Canada Wire and Cable who died in 1929. The start of construction was delayed until after World War Two, and the building's design reflected a fascinating fusion between essentially classical and modern directions.

Wallberg Memorial Building, circa 1948

Stretching a full block along College Street, the symmetrical facade featured a pair of identical, moderne entrances, Roman-like urn balustrades, and handsome steel-casement windows associated with the 1920s and 1930s. In 2012 an architecturally prosaic penthouse was added that houses the BioZone, a laboratory space for applied bioengineering research. In 2017 the Wallberg's original, finely scaled steel-casement windows were replaced with pragmatic, energy-efficient units. The new units lack the design finesse and delicacy of the original 1949 windows.

31   Lassonde Mining Building
Francis Riley Heakes with Frank Darling, 1905
Goldcorp Mining Innovation Suite
Baird Sampson Neuert Architects, 2010

Francis Riley Heakes was chief architect of the Ontario Public Works Department, designer of the province's nearby Whitney Block, and creator of the minor Mill Building (now called the Haultain Building) for the university. He and and colleague Frank Darling were awarded the large, important commission for the Lassonde Mining Building (originally called Chemistry and Mining Building) on College Street.

At the beginning of the twentieth century, this section of College Street was still on the outskirts of Toronto, but the street was becoming an important east–west artery, and the city was expected to rapidly expand westward. The location and grandeur of the Mining Building signaled and encouraged this westward expansion. Executed in a turn-of-the-century Beaux-Arts style with a bilaterally symmetrical front facade and monumental brick columns, it followed architectural ambitions at Cornell University, the University of Pennsylvania, and Columbia University,

Lassonde Mining Building, attic

Lassonde Mining Building

where imposing schools of metallurgy and mineralogy had been constructed. Heakes and Darling's original plans included two wings at the east and west, which extended north to form a quadrangle. Due to budget constraints, however, the wings were not realized.

The Lassonde Mining Building is now home to the Mineral Engineering Program, the Lassonde Institute for Engineering Geoscience, the Institute of Biomaterials and Biomedical Engineering, the Lassonde Institute of Mining, the Goldcorp Mining Innovation Suite, and the Canadian Mining Hall of Fame. The hall of fame recognizes and honors legendary mine finders and builders who contributed to the vast Canadian mining industry.

During 2009 and 2010 the huge attic was imaginatively renovated to accommodate the Goldcorp Mining Innovation Suite, with a "blue sky" conference room topping the new rooftop composition. A dramatic glass-enclosed elevator, mimicking a mine-shaft elevator, whisks people to the new suite of handsomely designed laboratories, studios, and offices. Over the years, students had secretly accessed the attic and, decade after decade, scribbled graffiti on the brick walls and wood beams. Extensive areas of graffiti were retained during the attic-renovation project, preserving this unique tradition at the Mining Building.

32 Haultain Building

Francis Riley Heakes with Frank Darling, 1904

Expansion and rebuilding

Craig & Madill, 1931

One of the university's hidden surprises is the seventy-foot-square (twenty-one-meter-square) Edwardian style Haultain Building, which was originally called the Mill Building. Constructed of red brick, it was a milling building for the School of Practical Science, housing machinery for experiments on the mechanical processing of ores. In the early 1930s, several floors were added. In its present state, it feels like a piece of late-nineteenth-century Liverpool transported to Toronto, waiting for film crews to discover it.

33 Rosebrugh Building

Darling & Pearson, 1920

Originally known as the Electrical Building, the Rosebrugh Building is attached to and architecturally similar to the Thermodynamics Building (1909). An early photograph shows the splendor of the Rosebrugh Building when it stood proudly on Taddle

ABOVE: Rosebrugh Building (right) and the atrium of the Centre for Cellular and Biomolecular Research
OVERLEAF: Rosebrugh Building, exterior

Creek Road, which was removed in 2003 to make way for the new Terrence Donnelly Centre for Cellular and Biomolecular Research (Donnelly CCBR). (See Introduction, page 29.) Rosebrugh's west facade is still fully exposed, but its east facade is now incorporated into the Donnelly CCBR's atrium. Both facades display grandly arched windows and sophisticated brickwork.

Although the structure is largely embedded in the dense built fabric of the southeast campus precinct, it is still possible to grasp the extraordinary talent of Frank Darling, the primary designer of the building.

34 Mechanical Engineering Building
Thermodynamics Building
Darling & Pearson, 1909
New (west) building
Allward & Gouinlock Architects, 1948

Darling & Pearson's original design for the Thermodynamics Building was ambitious, consisting of a laboratory wing running east–west and a taller, more imposing office and classroom wing facing west, fronting on King's College Road; due to budgetary problems in 1908, only the laboratory wing, which is now part of the Mechanical Engineering complex, was completed. The north face of this wing features a handsome doorway composition with fine stonework rising to an elegant pediment. The wing's seven rhythmic brick arches are brought into magnificent relief when late afternoon sun strikes them from the northwest. Embedded in the old Thermodynamics Building was a boiler plant, vented by a pair of tall brick chimneys that are joined at the top. Although largely hidden today by new buildings, it is worth the effort to find these sculpturally captivating elements.

After World War Two, funding was available to complete the missing wing along King's College Road. The new, functionalist Mechanical Engineering Building opened in 1948. Designed by Allward & Gouinlock Architects, it is one of Toronto's most significant mid-twentieth-century modern buildings, showing influences from both the Bauhaus and the Dutch de Stijl movements.

The limestone-clad building's classrooms, shops, laboratories, offices, and lecture theaters are efficiently distributed within a simple rectangular plan. An austere stairway, rising near the entry and incorporating vertical corner glazing and an elegant stainless steel clock, divides the west-facing facade into two parts. The larger left

Steam, Gas and Hydraulic Laboratory Building of the University of Toronto   Darling & Pearson, Architect
This shows the building as it will appear when completed. At present the whole laboratory part is completed which comprises all of the building to the left of, and including, the first window to the right of those protected by awnings.
Faculty of Applied Science and Engineering

Thermodynamics Building (Steam, Gas, and Hydraulic Laboratory Building) as designed in 1908

Mechanical Engineering Building (west building)

part features three bands of horizontal windows, while the right part has one band at the top of an otherwise blank wall. This upper band continues at the south elevation and wraps around the east face. A wonderful two-story steel casement window with a slightly projecting balcony graces the south elevation.

Behind the mechanical engineering wing is a tight web of alley-like service spaces between the Haultain, Rosebrugh, and Mining Buildings. Here, in a compact secretive zone, one can quietly feast on architectural history.

35   Myhal Centre for Engineering Innovation & Entrepreneurship
Montgomery Sisam Architects, Inc. with Feilden Clegg Bradley Studios, 2018

Surrounded by significant heritage buildings—Knox College, the Physical Geography Building, and Simcoe Hall—the Myhal Centre for Engineering Innovation & Entrepreneurship filled in the last unbuilt site on St. George Street, the main artery of the campus. Shoehorning the facility's complex program and requiring 77,500 net assignable square feet (7,200 square meters) onto the restrictive urban site proved formidable.

The MCEIE celebrates multidisciplinary collaboration and houses a five-hundred-seat auditorium; sixteen Technology Enhanced Active Learning (TEAL) rooms; design, fabrication, and prototype laboratories; and a myriad of research facilities incorporating robotics and mechatronics. An entrepreneurship hatchery supports collaboration with industry, from concept to prototype, underscoring Toronto's reputation as one of the top ten cities in the world for startups.

Volumetrically, the MCEIE is rationally configured: a 148-foot (45-meter) cube comprising eight floors and a glass-enclosed mechanical penthouse. Floors five through eight surround a skylit atrium. The exposed structural frame, made of fly

Myhal Centre for Engineering Innovation and Entrepreneurship (right), view from the west (architectural rendering)

ash concrete, recalls the grided structure of the Yale Center for British Art (1974) by Louis Kahn, while the manipulation of natural light and warm, Baltic birch interior finishes are reminiscent of the Finnish architect Alvar Aalto's humanizing work.

On the exterior, prefabricated panels of creamy-yellow brick tiles relate the MCEIE to the brick colors of nearby Convocation Hall, Simcoe Hall, the Bahen Centre, and the Sanford Fleming Building. In this sense the MCEIE is admirably contextual. Landscaped, pedestrian walkways surround the structure, successfully connecting it to the university's open space network.

The dignified, carefully detailed building aggressively embraces flexibility, a low carbon footprint, sustainability, low maintenance, and longevity. Ultimately, the MCEIE can be understood as a skillfully contrived spatial framework for twenty-first-century engineering innovation.

In addition to the eleven buildings presented here, Engineering has a large facility at the north edge of the city, the University of Toronto Institute for Aerospace Studies (UTIAS). (See Walk Eleven, pages 326–27.) Engineering also shares space in three other buildings: 256 McCaul Street, the Fields Institute, and the Donnelly Centre for Cellular and Biomolecular Research. (For more on the Fields Institute, see Walk Five, pages 181–83; for more on the Donnelly Centre for Cellular and Biomolecular Research, see Walk Seven, pages 235–36.)

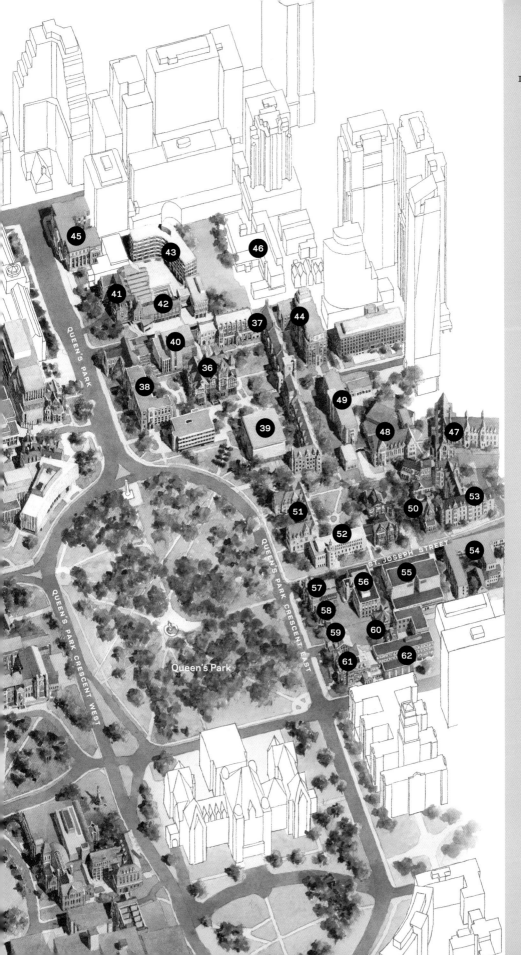

The East Campus

A mere five-minute walk across Queen's Park, the east campus presents a different world from the historic core: the topography is more varied, the architecture more conservative, and the pace slower. Moreover, two of the university's oldest colleges dominate this verdant part of the campus: the University of St. Michael's College (which affiliated with the University of Toronto in 1881) and Victoria University (which joined in 1890).

This rich history is underscored by the fact that the oldest building of the university is found here, St. Basil's Church (1856), which is part of St. Michael's College. Commanding a hilltop, the stoic St. Basil's overlooks Bay Street and bears silent witness to the intense real estate development that has burst forth along this street during the past five decades. Modern high-rise apartment towers, hotels, and office blocks line the north–south thoroughfare cheek by jowl. A pair of glassy

Courtyard, St. Michael's College

towers, designed by the noted Toronto architect Peter Clewes, was added at the northeast corner of the St. Michael's campus in 2014. (See page 126.) These were realized when, in order to generate needed revenue, St. Michael's College sold a major land parcel to a developer that constructed these two residential high-rises and a group of town houses next door to St. Basil's Church. The peaceful inner sanctum of St. Basil's is still there, but the church's gentle yet commanding presence in the cityscape has been forever changed.

The story of the changing east campus goes beyond St. Michael's: Victoria University similarly sold land for a twenty-three-story condominium on Charles Street West at the northeast corner of "Vic," as the university is known. The ringing and infiltration of the University of Toronto campus with condominium towers has called forth varying opinions: some find this dynamic flowing together of town and gown a positive change, while others regard it as the development of an ambiguous "cultural soup." But even with these changes, the east campus continues to be a distinctive part of the university and the city.

VICTORIA UNIVERSITY

Victoria University evolved from the Wesleyan Methodist Church's Upper Canada Academy, located in Cobourg, Ontario, sixty-eight miles (110 kilometers) east of Toronto. The academy changed its name to Victoria College in 1841 and became Victoria University in 1884. During the late 1880s, it went through a complex process of affiliation with the University of Toronto, left Cobourg, and commenced construction of a grand new building at the northeast corner of Queen's Park. Today Victoria University consists of Victoria College, a nondenominational arts and science college, and Emmanuel College, a United Church theological college. Together they support more than 3,600 students.

Vic's campus is roughly divided into two halves by Charles Street West, with the main quadrangle, centered by Victoria College, located in the southern half. Following allocation of land for the new building in 1886, the university held a limited architectural competition between four firms. Langley & Burke's proposal was deemed "most attractive," but the selection committee found some of the internal planning unsuitable, and the firm was eventually replaced by architect William Storm, a former Vic student.

Storm put forward various designs, including a "Proposed Grouped Design" consisting of three buildings—the main building, the residence hall, and the gymnasium—forming a quadrangle. This idea might have stemmed from Nathaniel Burwash, who was president of Victoria College when it moved from Cobourg to Toronto; Burwash was also inspired by a trip he had taken in the summer of 1888 to the United States to study campuses and new college buildings there. Only the Main Building (Victoria College) was eventually realized. The Vic quadrangle as it exists today is a mature composition of buildings and spaces anchored by Storm's sculptural essay of 1892. Traditional and modern buildings coexist, balancing formality and informality.

Victoria College

36 Victoria College

William Storm, 1892

Work on Victoria College began in January 1891, and, although the building was not completely finished, it opened in October 1892, providing accommodation for administrative offices, classrooms, a chapel, a library, and students' and professors' rooms. The entire cost of Victoria College, including furnishings, landscaping, and fencing, amounted to C$212,000.

Victoria College is a powerful edifice, commanding a gentle hill at the north end of Queen's Park. Designed by William Storm in the Romanesque style developed by Henry Hobson Richardson in the United States (defined by his Trinity Church [1877] in Boston), it is a strong object-building while simultaneously playing an important role in urban space making. Its monumental presence centers the main Victoria University quadrangle but also breaks that urban space into two smaller, comfortably scaled zones.

The building itself displays all of the characteristics of the highly integrated Richardsonian Romanesque style: massive stonework, large semi-circular arches, expressive towers and turrets, and colorful decorative patterning. Storm's asymmetrical composition of the grand south portal and main tower are particularly striking, achieving both balance and tension. This was the last work of the artistic Storm, who died on August 8, 1892, two months before the new Victoria College opened.

Victoria College, main stair

37 Burwash Hall
Sproatt & Rolph, 1912
Upper Burwash House
Sproatt & Rolph, 1913
Lower Burwash House
Sproatt & Rolph, 1931

When the new Victoria College was conceived, both Nathaniel Burwash and the architect William Storm called for a group of buildings, but only one was realized. In 1903 Annesley Hall was completed on a separate plot of land to the north, but two decades passed before the additional structures imagined by Burwash and Storm for the central Victoria College campus appeared: the Birge-Carnegie Library in 1910 and Burwash Hall and Residences (now Burwash Hall and Upper Burwash House) between 1912 and 1913. With the addition of Emmanuel College and the Emmanuel College Residence (now Lower Burwash House) in 1931, there was the semblance of a quadrangle as imagined in Sproatt & Rolph's 1928–29 master plan. The quadrangle was finally completed with the construction of the E. J. Pratt Library (1960), Northrop Frye Hall (1967), and the Isabel Bader Theatre (2001).

Burwash Hall (and what is now Upper Burwash House) was made possible through a gift from the Massey Estate, and Chester Massey took great interest in the design, having in mind no ordinary building for the one hundred male students that it would accommodate. Sproatt & Rolph, who would conceive the magnificent Hart House student union for the University of Toronto a few years later, designed the linked Burwash Hall and Residences in the collegiate Gothic style, forming an L and giving meaningful definition to the main Vic quadrangle. The residence hall consists of four houses in the style of English colleges, each with an entrance onto the quad. The dining hall, which features six huge Gothic windows on both the north and south facades, seats 260 students at sixteen large tables. Hanging on the western wall is Queen Victoria's burial flag, given to Vic soon after the queen's death.

Burwash Hall (**ABOVE**) and its dining hall (**OPPOSITE**)

In 1931 an L-shaped residential wing was added to the south for Emmanuel College, the theological division of Victoria University. Also designed by Sproatt & Rolph, it continued the collegiate Gothic vocabulary of gray Credit Valley rubble stone with Indiana limestone trim and high-pitched roofs finished in green slate. Similar to the organization of the 1913 residence to the north, Lower Burwash House has five houses.

A walkway along the west side of the building, which is built into a slope, steps down to the south and passes alongside the Lester B. Pearson Garden for Peace and Understanding adjacent to the E. J. Pratt Library. Walking from Charles Street along Upper and Lower Burwash Houses down to Queen's Park is one of the most rewarding spatial experiences offered on the east campus.

38 Birge-Carnegie
Sproatt & Rolph, 1910
Emmanuel College
Sproatt & Rolph, 1931

Although today they appear to be one continuous structure, the Birge-Carnegie building (formerly the Birge-Carnegie Library) at the north and Emmanuel College to the south were constructed separately, the former finished in 1910, the latter in 1931. Together they face the northern extension of Queen's Park Crescent (Avenue Road) and form the western side of the Victoria University quadrangle.

In 1906, following Vic's request for funding, Pittsburgh industrialist Andrew Carnegie agreed to allocate US$50,000 for a new library if the institution could match these funds with an endowment for permanent maintenance. A wealthy Vic alumnus, Cyrus Birge, agreed to do so in 1907, and the university launched a design competition in 1908 that invited three of Toronto's leading firms to compete: George M. Miller (who had completed Annesley Hall in 1903); Burke, Horwood & White; and Sproatt & Rolph. The winning design by Sproatt & Rolph was a collegiate Gothic building organized into a cruciform plan.

Constructed of Georgetown gray, Credit Valley ashlar with Indiana limestone trim, the building's primary axis runs north–south, with the main entrance at the north end. The soaring men's reading room occupied the west wing. A secondary entrance facing Queen's Park is surmounted by a large statue of Queen Victoria made of Bath stone by the Bromsgrove Guild of Worcestershire, England. The Birge-Carnegie served as Vic's main library until 1960, when the E. J. Pratt Library was opened. (In recent years, the library at Birge-Carnegie housed the United Church of Canada's archives and the Victoria University archives.)

Between 1928 and 1929, Sproatt & Rolph developed a comprehensive master plan to provide buildings for the new Emmanuel College on the grounds of Victoria. This included a joint administration, library, and classroom building, student residences, and a chapel for Emmanuel College, all designed in the

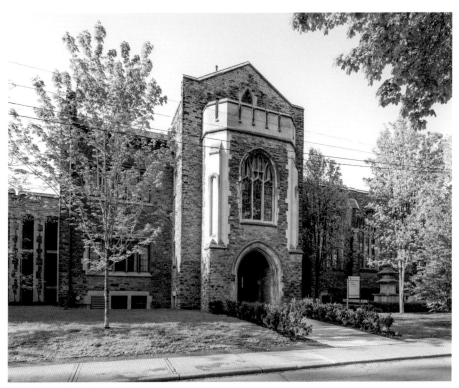

Birge-Carnegie, main entrance

collegiate Gothic style, adding strong urban edges to the emerging Vic quadrangle. As part of their vision, Sproatt & Rolph made preliminary drawings for what would have been an astonishing chapel at the northeast corner of Queen's Park. Due to the Great Depression, only parts of the master plan were eventually realized.

In 1931 the Emmanuel College building was added to the south end of the Birge-Carnegie Library, incorporating a much more modest chapel than originally proposed. Faced in the same Credit Valley stone as the library, the college has hidden roofs and longer, lower lines that make it appear more modern than the abutting building. The second-story Emmanuel College Library is especially splendid with grand, perpendicular tracery windows facing west. Walls of Indiana limestone meet a handsome floor made of inlaid travertine terrazzo, and a massive fireplace anchors the south end of the room. Arcades along the east side frame eight mezzanine study alcoves. A family of eight beautifully crafted wrought-iron chandeliers bring sparkle to this magnificent space.

To the north of Birge-Carnegie and Emmanuel College is the Korean Pagoda Garden, which honors Dr. Sang Chul Lee, chancellor of Victoria University from 1992 to 1998. At the center of the garden is a stone monument constructed in the Republic of Korea, given by the alumni of Yonsei University College of Medicine to commemorate three early Canadian medical missionaries that served people on the Korean peninsula.

39   E. J. Pratt Library

Gordon Adamson & Associates, 1960

Renovation

Shore Tilbe Irwin and Partners with Kohn Shnier Architects, 2004

Originally called the Victoria College Library, the building was renamed in 1967 to honor the poet E. J. Pratt. Austere and minimal on the exterior, the library underwent an interior renovation in 2004 that moved it into the twenty-first century. The new spaces created by Kohn Shnier Architects are carefully proportioned and enlivened with pattern and color. Rows of large white ceiling discs hover overhead, dramatic red walls appear, and venturing up the light-drenched central stair becomes an event—a climb rewarded at the top by the display of an ornate chair that belonged to Sir John Graves Simcoe, first lieutenant governor of Upper Canada from 1791 to 1796.

E. J. Pratt Library and the Lester B. Pearson Garden for Peace and Understanding

E. J. Pratt Library, reading room

Built into the slope that rises to Victoria College, the library's lower floor has continuous glazing on three sides. The east side overlooks the restful Lester B. Pearson Garden for Peace and Understanding, designed by landscape architect Paul Ehnes. Pearson, a 1919 Vic graduate, was chancellor from 1952 to 1959 and Canada's fourteenth prime minister. He helped define Canada's modern foreign policy and was awarded the Nobel Peace Prize in 1957.

Seven years after the E. J. Pratt Library was finished, Northrop Frye Hall was completed to the west. Designed by Gordon Adamson & Associates, it pairs with the library to make a set of "bookend blocks" that frame the south approach to Victoria University.

40 Isabel Bader Theatre

Lett/Smith Architects, 2001

This understated, dignified building faces Charles Street, filling a gap that existed along the north edge of Vic's main quadrangle. Interestingly, it roughly achieves what President Burwash had imagined a hundred years earlier when he called for "the library and residence meeting in the north to form a quadrangle opening to the sunny south."

Constructed of exposed concrete, Owen Sound limestone, stucco, and wood, the theater's cubic forms blend easily with the Birge-Carnegie Library to the west and Burwash Hall to the east. The acoustically superb five-hundred-seat auditorium is used for plays and film screenings, and as a general-purpose

Isabel Bader Theatre

classroom. The building resulted from a large donation from Alfred Bader, given to honor his wife, Isabel, a Victoria alumna.

41   Annesley Hall

George M. Miller, 1903

When the industrialist Hart Massey died in 1896, he made provision in his will for the construction of a women's residence at Vic, and in 1897 the Women's Educational Association was formed to make it happen. The new residence designed by George M. Miller opened in October 1903, providing forty-eight rooms, along with a dining room, gymnasium, and infirmary. The building was named for Susanna Annesley, the mother of the early leader of the Methodist movement, John Wesley.

Annesley Hall

Annesley Hall's Jacobethan Revival design merges the Jacobean and Elizabethan styles that were popular in nineteenth-century England. Miller imaginatively combined fancy, curved front-facing gables (which are also Dutch influenced), elaborate chimneys, and rectangular windows with small leaded panes to create this lovely residence, intended at the turn of the twentieth century to be "a home of high moral tone in an atmosphere of refined social culture."

42 Goldring Student Centre
Wymilwood (original building)
Fleury & Arthur, 1953
Addition
Moriyama & Teshima Architects, 2010

In 1925 Agnes E. Wood donated her Queen's Park mansion, Wymilwood, to Vic as a center for female students, and it served that role until 1953, when the new coed student union opened one block to the east. The mansion was subsequently named Falconer Hall in 1952, and it is now part of the Faculty of Law. The name

Wymilwood, precursor to the Goldring Student Centre

Wymilwood was transferred to the new modernist student union, and gateposts from the mansion (without their original stone spheres on top) can still be seen in front of the union.

One of the building's authors, Eric Arthur, was then professor of architecture at the University of Toronto, well known as both a preservationist and promoter of progressive architecture. In the case of Victoria University, it seems that Arthur was not wearing his preservationist hat. He and his firm partner, William Fleury, launched a master plan for Vic in 1950 that emphasized athletic fields, parking lots, and new dormitories—a scheme that called for the eventual demolishing of two magnificent historic structures: the central Victoria College building and the architecturally intriguing Annesley Hall.

The construction of a new student union—Wymilwood—was central to Fleury & Arthur's radical approach and formed stage one of their master plan. Stage two was the addition of an angular, three-hundred-seat auditorium attached to the west, and stage three called for a large L-shaped dormitory atop and extending north and east from the cafeteria, requiring the tearing down of historic Annesley Hall. (This unrealized master plan explains why Wymilwood is awkwardly connected to

Annesley Hall. It was supposed to be a temporary arrangement.) Thankfully, the central Victoria College building and Annesley Hall were spared the wrecking ball. Only the student union and Margaret Addison Hall, a semblance of the dormitory proposed in the master plan, were built.

When it opened in 1953, Wymilwood was a spirited modernist work, offering a gentle, domestic-scaled environment conducive to student life. Fleury & Arthur set the building back from Charles Street to create a sunken, south-facing terrace extending from a coffee shop. On the upper floors, common rooms, a reading room, and a music room were carefully detailed and included period lighting fixtures from Canada, Denmark, England, Italy, Sweden, and the United States. The folded-plate roof over the cafeteria was also of the period, giving the building a light, airy feeling.

The good bones of Wymilwood, an important Toronto modernist building, have been admirably preserved, including the original wood entry doors, terrazzo-paved lobby, and graceful main stair. Supported on a semicircular masonry wall, the spiral stair of reinforced concrete is a superb piece of 1950s design, with small red spheres dancing up and down the balusters. But as a social union, by the turn of the century, Wymilwood could no longer fulfill all the needs of Vic's students, and a major addition to the north and east by Moriyama & Teshima Architects, along with restoration work on the 1953 building, was completed in 2010.

Named to honor Vic graduates Blake Goldring and his sister Judy Goldring, whose major gift helped make the project possible, Wymilwood plus the addition now constitute the Goldring Student Centre, accommodating student clubs and study spaces, a café, the Office of the Dean of Students, and the Office of Alumni Affairs and Advancement. At the heart of the new architectural composition is the Wendy Marion Cecil Atrium, recognizing her service as Vic's chancellor from 2010 to 2016. The atrium overlooks a large courtyard, defined and enriched by the walls of five surrounding buildings, built over the course of a century.

The 2010 addition with its quirky, protruding panels of roughly hewn stone respects but avoids slavishly imitating the original building—an approach that would surely have pleased Arthur.

43 Margaret Addison Hall
Gordon Adamson & Associates, 1959

In the late 1950s, as a result of the post–World War Two baby boom and increasing enrollment of women, Vic needed more residence space. Fleury & Arthur's 1950 master plan had called for a new L-shaped dormitory north of Charles Street, integrated with Wymilwood. Margaret Addison Hall seems to have evolved from that vision, even though it is located further to the northeast and stands alone.

Named after the university's first dean of women, the six-story, boomerang-shaped building included sixty double rooms and eighty single rooms for women, along with music and typing rooms and a room in the basement for storing evening dresses and crinolines. Its main floor included a suave, cylindrical, wood-paneled

Margaret Addison Hall

library. The residence hall was affectionately referred to as "six stories of glory with a twist in the middle."

Now coeducational, the "boomerang" has a much improved setting as a result of the landscaped courtyard created by Moriyama & Teshima Architects' 2010 addition to the nearby student union.

44   Rowell Jackman Hall
Keith Becker Architects with Kuwabara Payne McKenna Blumberg Architects, 1993

Situated between Charles Street West and St. Mary Street at the easternmost edge of the Vic campus, Rowell Jackman Hall is an apartment-style coeducational residence. The primary six-story volume is clad in oversized orange bricks; two more stories are stepped back and clad in neutral brown steel panels. This stepped configuration and material application generate a background building that responds to and respects the scale of its urban context.

45   Lillian Massey Department of Household Science
George M. Miller, 1912

Although the title gracing the west-facing portico indicates otherwise, this outstanding building owned by Victoria University is no longer the home of courses in the domestic sciences for women. The south half houses the University of Toronto's Department of Classics, Centre for Mediaeval Studies, and other academic divisions, while the north half is leased by the clothing retailer Club Monaco.

Known first as the School of Household Science, the building was sponsored by Lillian Massey Treble, a daughter of Hart Massey (after whom Hart House would later be named). Degrees in household science were first offered by the university in 1902. Massey Treble contributed c$500,000 toward the building, which George M.

Lillian Massey Department of Household Science

Miller designed in the classical tradition, appropriately employing the feminine Ionic order. The building's main facade fronting the Royal Ontario Museum is templelike with four Ionic columns, bracketed to the left and right by sets of three engaged columns. The secondary north facade (now the entrance to Club Monaco) has four engaged Ionic columns between pedimented end pieces.

The building's main, marble-faced stair hall is worth visiting. It presents fine Pre-Raphaelite stained-glass windows showing women tending to household tasks and men hunting and harvesting.

46   McKinsey Building
Taylor Hariri Pontarini Architects, 1999

Constructed on land owned by Victoria University (with a future option for Vic to take over the building for academic purposes), this three-story structure houses the Canadian headquarters of McKinsey & Company, an international consulting firm.

Taylor Hariri Pontarini Architects took a holistic approach and engaged in an unusually large agenda for the 75,000-square-foot (6,970-square-meter) project—conducting research on the workplace, urban design, architecture, landscape, interior design, and furniture design—leading to a rigorous resolution that makes it one of the most admired places in downtown Toronto.

The zigzag floor plan responds to the immediate urban conditions. At the south the building is tight to the street and offers an elegant canopy, while on the west it embraces a courtyard. The east edge is intentionally less adventurous, facing a condominium tower and accommodating a ramp down to the parking level. The north end of the building has a secondary entrance from Sultan Street.

Taking cues from the many stone-clad buildings at Victoria University (and further south, at St. Michael's College), the McKinsey Building features gray Owen Sound stone, rough cut for the ground floor and smooth cut for the upper two floors. Set into the stone walls are generously sized windows with frames made of mahogany and operable ventilation units. The large areas of glazing bring natural

McKinsey Building

light deep into the working environment. The heart of the building is a three-story informal meeting place called "the hive." Here and throughout the project there is a sense of warmth provided by fireplaces, marble counters, Oriental rugs, and cherry-wood furniture—a kind of collective "big house."

THE UNIVERSITY OF ST. MICHAEL'S COLLEGE

Founded in 1852 as a Roman Catholic boys' school, by 1853 St. Michael's College functioned under the Congregation of St. Basil as a high school, *collège classique*, and minor seminary. (The Congregation of St. Basil, also known as the Basilian Fathers, was founded in France in 1822 and moved to Canada in the early nineteenth century. It was a community of priests, students for the priesthood, and lay associates.) St. Michael's College has been at its current location on Clover Hill since 1856. Today it has nearly 4,500 full-time students and is the largest Catholic post-secondary educational institution in English-speaking Canada. Its graduate Faculty of Theology is one of the largest theology schools in North America.

The tight cluster of fifteen buildings constituting St. Michael's stretches from Queen's Park to Bay Street, merging at the college's northwest corner with Victoria University and at its southwest corner with Regis College, a part of the Toronto School of Theology. It is an architecturally diverse campus, employing a broad range of building materials, such as limestone, copper, yellow brick, red brick, and concrete. To some extent the rolling, terraced, and wooded landscape holds this mélange of styles and materials together. Only one vehicular route, St. Joseph Street (Marshall McLuhan Way), cuts through the campus, allowing pedestrians and bicycles to prevail.

47   St. Basil's Church and Odette Hall

William Hay, 1856

Southeast wing

William T. Thomas, 1862

North extension

Architect unknown, 1878

Southern extension and tower

A. A. Post, 1887

Steeple and spire

Arthur W. Holmes, 1895

Odette Hall renovations

Carlos Ott Partnership, 1996

In 1853 Captain John Elmsley, owner of the country estate Clover Hill, donated four lots to the Basilian Fathers on the condition they build a parish church; later that year the Basilians purchased four additional lots from him, reflecting their grander aspirations. The architect William Hay proposed a large complex of Gothic-style buildings around a quadrangle, including St. Basil's Church. It was a complete, picturesque vision, set amid pastures and wooded hills. (See Introduction, page 18.) Tenders were let for the church and one wing of the college, and both opened in 1856. The parish was growing rapidly, however, and within a year more space was needed.

Hay's total vision was never realized. Instead, the church and college proceeded to expand piecemeal, with work completed by numerous architects over a sixty-six-year period. A southeast addition to the college wing opened in 1862; together with the original wing it is now known as Odette Hall, named in honor of art patron Louis L. Odette. There, one finds the college's extensive collection of modern religious art.

The college undertook large extensions in 1873 and 1903 (both demolished in 1971). In 1878 the original five-sided apse of the church was demolished; the sanctuary was extended fifty feet (15.2 meters) to the northeast; a new entrance, narthex, and tower were added in 1887; and in 1895 a slate-covered steeple and spire were completed (replaced with copper in the 1950s). In 1922 a plaster vaulted ceiling was installed in the sanctuary.

Despite this topsy-turvy history, St. Basil's has miraculously survived and remains as a beautiful, solemn place of worship in Toronto's downtown. After he died in 1863, Captain John Elmsley's body was buried in St. Michael's Cathedral, but his heart was buried separately, per his request, in the west wall of St. Basil's

marked by a white marble plaque. One must wonder what he would make of the complex sequence of building that has gone on for more than 150 years on his beloved Clover Hill.

48   Brennan Hall

Arthur W. Holmes, 1937

Addition and renovation

Brennan & Whale, 1968

Renovation

Gow Hastings Architects, 2018

Brennan Hall, St. Michael's central common space, was the second building at the college by architect Arthur W. Holmes. An accomplished ecclesiastical architect, Holmes trained in the office of the prominent British architect George E. Street and, after arriving in Toronto in 1886, devoted virtually all of his career to serving the Roman Catholic Church in the Toronto region.

For Brennan Hall, Holmes again used Credit Valley limestone with robust patterns and textures, which he had used so effectively two years earlier for Teefy Hall and the Pontifical Institute of Mediaeval Studies. The main entrance to Brennan Hall is on axis with Elmsley Place, and an attractive dining hall is located east of the entrance on the second floor.

ABOVE: Brennan Hall
OPPOSITE: St. Basil's Church and Odette Hall

TOP: Elmsley Hall
BOTTOM: Elmsley Place

49   Elmsley Hall

Brennan & Whale, 1955

This midcentury men's residence hall has a low wing facing St. Mary Street and a five-story main wing running south, terminated by a cubic power plant. At the south end, the architecture becomes richer, with the power plant and its chimney, a pedestrian underpass beneath a vehicular service bridge, and a series of south-facing, terraced flower gardens forming an interesting composition. The slightly concave south face of the bridge-underpass further underscores the subtle relationships among the building components and the landscape.

Elmsley Hall and the attached power plant are faced in Credit Valley limestone—from rough cut to striated to smooth—which was the dominant building material at St. Michael's from the 1930s through the 1950s.

50   Elmsley Place

Bellisle House, 1 Elmsley Place

Langley & Langley, 1896

Addition

J. P. Hynes, 1910

McCorkell House, 2 Elmsley Place
(joined to Sullivan House, 96 St. Joseph Street, 1890s)

M. B. Aylesworth, 1892

Additions

Burke, Horwood & White, 1897, 1903

Phelan House, 3 Elmsley Place

Langley & Langley, 1897

Windle House, 5 Elmsley Place

Attributed to John M. Lyle, 1897

Gilson-Maritain House, 6–8 Elmsley Place

A. Frank Wickson, 1901

One-block-long Elmsley Place—a verdant enclave of historic houses serving as administrative offices and residences for faculty and students—is a charming world of its own. The plan for this minisubdivision—Toronto's first subdivision—was registered in 1890 by Remigius Elmsley, son of Captain John Elmsley, who in 1853 had donated land from his Clover Hill estate for St. Michael's College and St. Basil's Church. Remigius Elmsley's own house, built in the 1870s, originally stood northwest of where Brennan Hall stands today. Between 1892 and 1901 a street called

Elmsley Place was created, and six large fashionable houses were built on "villa lots," five of which remain. (Willison House was demolished in 1962.)

The houses are all constructed of red brick, but their architectural styles vary. From 2007 to 2008, the firm of Goldsmith Borgal & Company Ltd. Architects completed extensive preservation and restoration work on the houses along the west side of Elmsley Place, and thoughtful landscaping complements this impressive project.

51 Teefy Hall and the Pontifical Institute of Mediaeval Studies
Arthur W. Holmes, 1936

An architectural drawing by Arthur W. Holmes published in 1929 shows a proposal for a long continuous building in the collegiate Gothic style facing Queen's Park and stretching from Victoria University at the north to St. Joseph Street at the south. Presumably because of the Great Depression, the extraordinary project was not realized. Instead, in 1936 St. Michael's College completed this pleasing building, which includes residences for men—the More, Fisher, and Teefy houses—along with the prestigious Pontifical Institute of Mediaeval Studies, founded in 1929.

Wings of the U-shaped stone structure extend toward Queen's Park, forming a lovely forecourt, from which a covered passageway leads to a peaceful quadrangle behind the building. The Credit Valley limestone that Holmes specified for the building is noteworthy because it was the first use of this material at St. Michael's

Teefy Hall

College. (Five buildings were clad in this type of stone in the nineteen-year period between 1935 and 1954.) It presents an array of wonderful patterns and textures, inviting close examination and touch, and we can sense the great craftsmanship it required. There is something appropriately suggestive of "the mediaeval" here, and it seems regrettable that this material vocabulary was not continued after 1954.

52 Carr Hall

Ernest Cormier with Brennan & Whale, 1954

Carr Hall, a classroom and office facility, is the third building completed for St. Michael's College by the Montreal-based architect Ernest Cormier, who lived from 1885 to 1980 and was one of Canada's most accomplished architects. Carr Hall has a prominent location at the northeast corner of Queen's Park Crescent East and St. Joseph Street, forming a quadrangle with Teefy Hall and the houses on the west side of Elmsley Place.

Named for Father Henry Carr, a leader of Roman Catholic religious education in Canada and cofounder, with Professor Etienne Gilson, of the Pontifical Institute of Mediaeval Studies, the building is modest, even austere; there are some surprises, though, including the abstract west facade, which has a grid of square windows, and a sculpturally inventive tower. The patterned, textured stone is nearly identical to that of neighboring Teefy Hall. While Carr Hall is essentially modern in style, it sits comfortably with the much older buildings around it.

Carr Hall

53   Sam Sorbara Hall

Carlos Ott Partnership, 2001

Thirty-two years passed between the completion of the John M. Kelly Library in 1969 and the 2001 opening of St. Michael's College's next building project, Sam Sorbara Hall. This resulted in a lot of speculation among the university community about what design direction St. Michael's would take after the three-decade lull in construction.

The site selected for the new men's residence was a particularly difficult one on the south slope of Clover Hill, a stone's throw from the historic St. Basil's Church and Odette Hall. The site was also adjacent to three historic houses on Elmsley Place. The college opted for a historicist approach: the postmodern Sorbara Hall mimics characteristics of St. Basil's and Odette Hall with its yellow brick, steeply sloped roofs, and dormer windows. Unlike the 1950s Cormier-designed buildings at St. Michael's, which fuse contextual considerations with spare, utilitarian modernism (and, in the case of Carr Hall, considerable formal invention), the thin historicism of Sam Sorbara Hall is uninspiring. Although it appropriately defers to St. Basil's Church, it lacks the kind of deeper resonance and criticality that could have brought the architecture of Sam Sorbara Hall and St. Michael's College into the twenty-first century.

54   Cardinal Flahiff Basilian Centre

Ernest Cormier with Brennan & Whale, 1949

Addition

Brennan & Whale, 1959

Addition and alterations

John J. Farrugia, 1979

During the late 1940s and early 1950s, St. Michael's College engaged Ernest Cormier to design three buildings: a boys' school, St. Basil's Seminary (now the

Cardinal Flahiff Basilian Centre), and Carr Hall. The school, completed in 1948, was located at the edge of the city's tony Forest Hill neighborhood and employed materials and elements found in Cormier's masterwork, the main pavilion of the University of Montreal, created between 1924 and 1943.

Cardinal Flahiff Basilian Centre

The boys' school's distinctive tower is strongly reminiscent of the imposing tower above the entrance of the University of Montreal's main pavilion.

Immediately following the boys' school, Cormier completed St. Basil's Seminary on the college's main campus. E-shaped in plan, the design is typical of Cormier's calm, careful modernism, incorporating yellow brick and handsome stone detailing. The center wing of the E houses a simple chapel, stacked above a dining hall. Although spare and utilitarian—the interior walls are unadorned concrete block with simple color banding—the chapel has thoughtful touches, such as a patterned terrazzo floor.

In 1979 the front of the seminary was drastically altered. The heavy-looking concrete addition and accompanying piers are unfortunate, serving as a reminder of the less appealing aspects of 1960s and 1970s Brutalism, when some architects misunderstood and misapplied Corbusian notions.

55 John M. Kelly Library
John J. Farrugia, 1969

During the 1960s and 1970s, many architects ran wild with the structural, sculptural, and textural possibilities of reinforced concrete, and the John M. Kelly Library is an aggressive example. Architect John J. Farrugia designed the floor plates as a concrete, waffle-slab system, which is exposed in the lobby ceiling. The battered

John M. Kelly Library

concrete walls on the eastern part of the building's base have a ridged, highly textured surface—the "corduroy" kind favored by the American architect Paul Rudolph. Above the battered wall is a three-story zone of concrete hoods that contain windows and catch the sunlight in dramatic ways. Indeed, the John M. Kelly Library is a tour de force, and visitors should examine it not just from the front on St. Joseph Street but on all sides, including the rear laneway elevation.

56 Muzzo Family Alumni Hall

Mathers & Haldenby, 1930, 1946
Renovations
John J. Farrugia, 1983

Muzzo Family Alumni Hall

The Muzzo Family Alumni Hall was originally a two-story structure housing the Ontario Research Foundation Laboratories. Although it is an unobtrusive building that is easy to pass by, its hybrid design—with one foot in the classical tradition and another stepping into modernism—is worth a second look. The long east elevation, which is rhythmically marked by fluted but abstracted two-story pilasters, is the most attractive. The "square-within-square" spandrel panels between the windows are made of Monel Metal, a material that became popular during the streamlined modern era from the late 1920s until the early 1950s. Two floors were added to the building in 1946.

THE MANSIONS ON QUEEN'S PARK CRESCENT EAST

Toronto's Queen's Park was opened by the Prince of Wales in 1860, and soon the adjacent region to the east became a fashionable area for the city's establishment to build town villas. Formidable brick houses in the latest architectural styles, with elegant coach houses behind, lined Queen's Park Crescent East. In 1981 the Province of Ontario transferred most of the properties on the east side of Queen's Park, between Wellesley Street West and St. Joseph Street, to the University of Toronto. Fortunately, most of these mansions have been preserved and now serve various academic purposes.

57 47 Queen's Park Crescent East: Toronto School of Theology
David B. Dick, 1892
Additions
Curry, Sproatt & Rolph, 1906
Renovations
Moffat Kinoshita Partnership, 1983

Exuberant and full of verve, this house was built for Reuben Millichamp, partner in Millichamp, Coyle & Co., wholesale distributors of cloth, blankets, and furs. The complex, rhythmic integration of architectural components is impressive, from the sophisticated manner in which the house turns the southeast corner, to the charm of small details, such as the terra-cotta panel of hollyhocks above and to the left of the front door.

In 1921 the property was acquired by the province and housed the Ontario Railway and Municipal Board, and in 1929 the Ontario Research Foundation occupied the house. Following renovations in 1983, it became the home of the Toronto School of Theology (TST), which is affiliated with the university. The TST, with its seven member and three affiliated schools, is the largest ecumenical center for theological education in Canada.

58 43 Queen's Park Crescent East
Beaumont Jarvis, 1896
Coach house and stable
attributed to George W. Gouinlock, 1903
Renovations
Larkin Architect Limited, 2009

This late-Victorian mansion has an ornate oriel window and a bargeboard with distinctive geometric tracery. The house was commissioned by Lieutenant Colonel James Mason, who participated in the Fenian raids and the North-West Rebellion and, after military service, became a banker and manager of the Home Savings & Loan Corporation. In 1918 ownership passed to Colonel H. D. Lockhart Gordon. The house was occupied by the Multicultural History Society of Ontario from 1980 to 2007. The building now accommodates offices for the Toronto branch of the Jesuits in Canada.

59 39 Queen's Park Crescent East
George W. Gouinlock, 1903; porte cochere, 1912

This house, constructed for Sir William T. White, general manager of the National Trust Company, abounds with architectural details, from the five brick chimneys thrusting skyward to the scalloped seashell at the central dormer. The front hall contains a fireplace with a finely crafted oak mantle and surround. In recent years

TOP: Toronto School of Theology
BOTTOM: 39 Queen's Park Crescent East

TOP: Regis College (Christie Mansion)
BOTTOM: Fontbonne Hall and Chapel

this fine building was occupied by the Faculty of Law, and it is now a swing space for various administrative divisions.

60 39A Queen's Park Crescent East: Marshall McLuhan Centre for Culture and Technology

George W. Gouinlock, 1903

Once a rear service building for the mansion at 39 Queen's Park Crescent, this little coach house is the unlikely home of the world famous McLuhan Program in Culture and Technology. In the early 1960s, Marshall McLuhan was a professor in the English department at St. Michael's College and was receiving attractive offers from foreign universities. In 1963, to retain him, the presidents of the University of Toronto and St. Michael's College created the Centre for Culture and Technology as a base for McLuhan's research. They developed ambitious plans for a new building to house the center but could not find sufficient funding. McLuhan commented, "We shall concentrate upon achieving an intellectual identity rather than a physical one," and the center moved into the former coach house in 1968.

McLuhan died in 1980, but his legacy and work have been carried on by the McLuhan Program in Culture and Technology, which became part of the University of Toronto's Faculty of Information Studies (now Faculty of Information) in 1994. Today the program aims at using McLuhan-inspired thinking and perception tools to investigate the effects of new human processes on culture and society.

61 29 Queen's Park Crescent East: Regis College

Christie Mansion

Gordon & Helliwell, 1882

Reconstruction and Additions

Gordon & Helliwell, 1899

Addition and alterations

Darling & Pearson, 1910

Renovations

Larkin Architect Limited, 2009

The first house on this corner site was completed in 1882, a decade before the Ontario Legislative Building to the southwest. It was designed by the prominent Toronto firm Gordon & Helliwell for William Mellis Christie and executed in the late-Victorian style with ornate gables and porches. Christie, who had immigrated from Scotland in 1848, was the cofounder of the extremely successful Christie, Brown & Company, makers of baked goods. In 1899 Gordon & Helliwell radically transformed and enlarged the original house (it is unclear how much of the 1882 house was actually kept), this time employing the Tudor style.

Christie's widow died in 1909, and the house was inherited by their son, Robert Christie, who commissioned Darling & Pearson to add to the house and make alterations. The result is known today as the Christie Mansion. From the imposing porte cochere, one enters a vestibule leading to a stunning long hall on the right with a barrel vault decorated with plaster ropes of flowers and fruit. Beyond are other handsome rooms, including the south-facing solarium by Darling & Pearson. Robert Christie lived there with his family until his death in 1926. In his will, he left the sale of the mansion to the discretion of his trustees, who sold it to Leonard Smith, who, four months later, sold it to the Sisters of St. Joseph. They then converted it to a residence for female students and in later years linked it to buildings they constructed to the east at 90 Wellesley Street West. In 2008 the University of Toronto purchased the property and leased it to Regis College, a member of the Toronto School of Theology. Regis College converted the former mansion into a classroom, study, and office facility while retaining its architectural grandeur.

62   90 Wellesley Street West
Mary Hall
Gordon Adamson & Associates, 1954
Fontbonne Hall
Gordon Adamson & Associates, 1956

Formerly owned by the Sisters of St. Joseph, this complex of buildings was purchased by the University of Toronto in 2007. Regis College leases parts of the complex for their library, chapel, and student lounge. Most of the buildings are now occupied by the Faculty of Music.

Together, Mary Hall (1954) at the rear and the Fontbonne Hall (1956) facing Wellesley Street West form a small midblock courtyard. The main east–west block of the 1956 portion has a thoughtfully designed pattern of windows, combining fixed and operable units. Most noteworthy in the complex is the simple chapel, which has four decorative glass windows designed by Karel Versteeg representing Faith, Hope, Charity, and the Tree of Life.

The North Campus

BLOOR STREET WEST

VARSITY BLUES

TORONTO

HOSKIN AVENUE

ST. GEORGE STREET

The North Campus

The north campus generally constitutes the area from Hoskin Avenue on the south to Bloor Street West on the north, and from Queen's Park (Avenue Road) on the east to St. George Street on the west. A 1923 Goad's *Atlas of the City of Toronto* map showing the University of Toronto campus reveals how underdeveloped this part of the campus once was. The section south of Hoskin Avenue already had some twenty-five university-owned buildings at that time, while north of Hoskin there were only six University of Toronto structures: Trinity College, three student residence buildings to the west of Trinity (now the Munk Centre for International Studies), the Dominion Meteorological Building (now the Munk School of Global Affairs), and Varsity Stadium, which had a grandstand along the west side. Both sides of St. George Street between Hoskin and Bloor were still solidly lined with private homes in 1923, but Taddle Creek was already gone, its former path shown by a faint dotted line, presumably indicating what we enjoy today as Philosopher's Walk. The map shows mostly open space in what is now the north campus, a reminder that this area has changed dramatically, filling in rapidly with buildings over the past ninety-five years.

Some sizeable open spaces have survived, though, and historical, social, and spatial continuity exists through the preservation and renewed use of places like Philosopher's Walk, Trinity College's playing field, and Varsity Stadium. Even though some of the private residences along St. George were demolished and the remaining ones have been converted for institutional use, a pleasant north–south public lane now runs through what was once their backyards, linking buildings, courtyards, and quadrangles.

63   Philosopher's Walk

Landscape master plan

Michael Hough, 1962; ENVision–The Hough Group Limited, 2004

Queen Alexandra Gateway

Chadwick & Beckett, 1901

Bennett Gates

ENVision–The Hough Group Limited, 2006

Shaded by a canopy of mature beech and oak trees, Philosopher's Walk winds from Bloor Street West to Hoskin Avenue through a shallow ravine in which Taddle Creek formerly flowed. This lovely meandering route is marked at the north end by the historic Queen Alexandra Gateway and at the south end by the Bennett Gates.

Taddle Creek once ran from glacial Lake Iroquois down to the Don River and Lake Ontario, entering Toronto's harbor near what is now the city's Distillery District.

Ojibway peoples fished and hunted along this route and knew the creek as Ziibiing. With the settlement and expansion of Toronto in the eighteenth and nineteenth centuries, people used Taddle Creek in new, and sometimes damaging, ways. In 1859 a dam was built to create McCaul's Pond east of University College, and this unnatural intervention led to the stream's pollution. From the 1850s to the 1870s, to deal with contamination, most of Taddle Creek was incorporated into the city's sewage system and covered over.

Interest in taming the Taddle Creek ravine can be documented as early as January 17, 1852, when the Council of King's College set aside about six acres for a botanic garden, shown in an 1852 sketch plan running southward, about one hundred yards (91.4 meters) wide, in the same location as today's Philosopher's Walk. But it was not until the early twentieth century that the walk evolved as a linear urban park, and nobody knows for certain how or when its formal name was assigned. In his 1917 "Preliminary Plan for the Landscape Improvement and General Expansion for the University of Toronto," landscape architect Bryant Fleming devoted a full page to what he referred to as the university's "valley" without ever mentioning Philosopher's Walk. A student club that existed from the 1890s to the 1950s, the Philosophical Society of the University, met in the 1920s at Wymilwood (now Falconer Hall), which is located along the walk, so some speculate that this is the origin of the name of Philosopher's Walk. Fleming recognized the potential of this distinctive part of the campus, stating in his 1917 report that

> this entire valley should be given very careful consideration, as it is one of the
> most important and interesting landscape features of the university grounds.
> It should be improved and maintained upon strictly naturalistic park lines, formality
> being strictly prohibited in its development, except insofar as the development
> of the courts and quadrangles of the adjacent buildings is concerned.

Fleming also called for "a good architectural entrance gateway" to the valley "between McMasters [now the Royal Conservatory of Music] and the Museum." Forty-five years passed before this was accomplished, when the Queen Alexandra Gateway was moved here in 1962. Twice relocated, the gateway originally stood at the intersection of Bloor Street West and Queen's Park (Avenue Road), marking the northern entrance to the park. It is named after Princess Alexandra Oldenburg, who came to England from Denmark as the wife of Edward VII, and was built to commemorate the 1901 visit of the Duke and Duchess of Cornwall and York. The lampposts, mounted atop the stone gateposts, have exquisite ironwork that serves as a fitting introduction to the naturalism of the ravine below.

In 2006 the Bennett Gates were added at the south end of Philosopher's Walk, honoring Avie Bennett, a leader in real estate development and publishing. The huge pineapples carved out of stone that top the gateway were rescued from a gate designed by Mathers & Haldenby that formerly stood facing College Street between the FitzGerald Building (1926) and the botany greenhouses constructed in 1932.

As the city densifies, this "fine natural valley," as Fleming called it, is increasingly treasured by Torontonians.

64 University of Trinity College

Darling & Pearson, 1925

East and west wings

George & Moorhouse, 1941

Chapel

Sir Giles Gilbert Scott, 1955

North wing

Somerville, McMurrich and Oxley, 1961

Quadrangle landscape

gh3 (Diana Gerrard and Pat Hanson), 2007

Trinity College was founded in 1851 by John Strachan, the first Anglican bishop of Toronto and first president of King's College, and it provided instruction in divinity, law, medicine, and the arts. The original college was located on Queen Street West, well beyond the town limits and far from the temptations of city life. Trinity federated with the University of Toronto in 1904 and opened a new building on the main campus in 1925, designed in the collegiate Gothic style by the noted architects Frank Darling and John A. Pearson. The Trinity campus now consists of the main Trinity College building facing Hoskin Avenue, the Gerald Larkin Academic Building and adjoining George Ignatieff Theatre, St. Hilda's College, and the University of

Trinity College, illuminated at night, 1927

Toronto's Munk Centre for International Studies, home of Trinity's John W. Graham Library. The college has 1,800 undergraduate students and some 140 graduate students in its Faculty of Divinity, Canada's oldest Anglican theological school.

In the early 1920s, Darling & Pearson conceived of Trinity College as two quadrangles extending northward from Hoskin Avenue to what are now the Trinity playing field and the Varsity Centre. However, by 1925 only a portion along Hoskin and two short wings running northward had been completed; it took from 1941 to 1961 to finish the other three sides of the Trinity quadrangle. (The second quadrangle was never realized.) The quad is the social crossroads of Trinity College and was given a contemporary update by the architecture and landscape design firm gh3, who created an imaginative new carpet for the space composed of stone tracery and grass that repeats the Greek letter *chi* (also the character that represents Christ in Greek).

The gothicized interior of Trinity College is just as spectacular as its exterior. The second floor of elegant Seeley Hall was originally intended to be a reading room but was used as the college's chapel until 1955. Strachan Hall, the dining facility that forms the bulk of the west wing, includes historic portraits and a large tapestry woven in Flanders that depicts the Queen of Sheba at the court of King Solomon. A grand private residence with a baronial stair hall at the east end of the 1925 wing provides splendid quarters for Trinity's provost. But the pièce de résistance is the college's chapel, designed by Sir Giles Gilbert Scott, who was the architect of Liverpool Cathedral. Executed in the Perpendicular Gothic style and opened in 1955, the chapel was one of the last works by this renowned English architect. Exhilarating in its extreme verticality—the chapel soars forty-seven feet (fourteen meters) to the bosses that ornament the vaulting—the building is also remarkable for the authenticity and integrity of its traditional masonry construction. The chapel's exquisite stained glass and decorative works add to its aura, including a bronze grille in the west transept designed by Scott that leads to the Lady Chapel.

65 Gerald Larkin Academic Building

Somerville, McMurrich and Oxley, 1961; George Ignatieff Theatre, 1979

This multiuse student commons for Trinity, named for Gerald Larkin, president of the Salada Tea Company from 1922 to 1957, was designed by the same architects, completed in the same year, and faced in the same stone as the north wing of the neighboring Trinity College building. Its most engaging architectural feature is a covered arcade with a subtly vaulted ceiling running along its south side. Three-story-tall, closely spaced

ABOVE: Gerald Larkin Academic Building
OPPOSITE: Trinity College, entrance

limestone fins cover the full length of the south facade, forming a screen at the arcade level. The horizontally exaggerated arcade and vertically exaggerated fins combine to create a visceral sense of the Gothic style, appropriate to Trinity.

66 St. Hilda's College

North wing

George & Moorhouse, 1938, 1960

South wing

Rounthwaite, Dick and Hadley Architects, 1982

Saint Hilda's College

St. Hilda's College received its charter in February 1890 to provide higher education for women, in affiliation with Trinity College; in 1938, after occupying various locations around the city, it settled on Devonshire Place. During the 1920s and 1930s, the University of Toronto strongly favored, and sometimes mandated, that new buildings be Georgian in character, so it is not surprising that St. Hilda's followed this pattern. Inside the classicized front entrance portal, a stair rises a half level to a central foyer, which leads to Cartwright Hall, now used for lectures. It was originally St. Hilda's theater before the George Ignatieff Theatre was added to the Gerald Larkin Academic Building across the street.

67 Munk Centre for International Studies

Eden Smith & Sons, 1909

Renovation and additions

Kuwabara Payne McKenna Blumberg Architects, 2000

David Bosanquet Gardens

Martin Lane Fox, 2000

Named after Canadian businessman Peter Munk, this hub for interdisciplinary academic research on global issues is located on the Trinity College campus and houses more than forty centers and programs, along with Trinity's John W. Graham Library. The pleasing U-shaped building focuses on the formal David Bosanquet

Munk Centre for International Studies

Gardens, designed by the well-known English landscape gardener Martin Lane Fox and among the university's most elegant outdoor rooms.

The three buildings that are now linked to form the Munk Centre were originally built in 1909 as separate residence halls for men and were then considered state of the art. That year's August issue of the magazine *Construction* noted that

> the red New Brunswick stone and red pressed brick dormitories were successfully planned with all three…similar in design, construction, and arrangement. They are composed around a quadrangle, which has a roadway forming the line of demarcation on its open side. The general architectural effect is derived from straight and broad lines, perfect proportions, simple surfaces, and a well-balanced door and window arrangement.

In fact, the architect of these long, slender buildings, Eden Smith, became well known in Toronto for designing progressive housing with a strong sense of community, exemplified by his projects for the Toronto Housing Company: Spruce Court, built in 1913, and Riverdale Courts, constructed in 1914. These provided affordable accommodations for working-class people and signaled an important beginning for the involvement of both Toronto and Ontario in public housing.

In 2000 Kuwabara Payne McKenna Blumberg Architects knit together the three former residence halls with an enclosed arcade (similar to the one at Woodsworth College). They extended two east–west wings westward toward Devonshire Place, creating light-filled meeting rooms faced in pink-gray granite on the exterior. Slender steel finials provide a subtle vertical thrust at these end rooms and reference the ornament of Massey College across the street.

68   Massey College

Thompson, Berwick & Pratt (Ron Thom, project architect), 1963
Renovations
Shim–Sutcliffe Architects, 1998–2017

If there is a most loved modern building on the St. George campus, it is surely Massey College, located at the northwest corner of Hoskin Avenue and Devonshire Place. On the surface, the explanation for the accolades is simple: the image Massey College presents is architecturally unthreatening, and its textures, intimate spaces, and ornamentation generate feelings of warmth and security. But the story of this small institution and its success is considerably more complex.

Massey College, a gift of the Massey family and the Massey Foundation, is an interdisciplinary residential college with a community consisting of 145 junior fellows (60 resident and 85 nonresident), senior fellows, senior residents, and the master (the chief administrative officer). Plans to create Massey College were considered as early as 1957 but not fully formalized until 1960, when Vincent Massey organized a national design competition. The committee for the competition included Vincent Massey's son, Hart, and his nephew Geoffrey, both of whom were architects and supporters of modernism.

Ron Thom, then a partner in the Vancouver-based firm Thompson, Berwick & Pratt and not well-known beyond the West Coast, submitted the winning design. It included a total of five residences, each with their own internal staircase, in the east, west, and north wings of a quadrangle building on the constricted site (150 × 300 feet, 46 × 91 meters); these were clustered near the master's lodge, library, common room, and dining rooms at the south end, along with a gatehouse. The chapel and a round room for meetings of the College Corporation were located at the northwest corner. The architect anchored the composition with a tall clock tower at the south end of the quadrangle, near the main entrance. (See Introduction, page 36.)

Prince Philip, Duke of Edinburgh, laid the cornerstone on May 25, 1962, and the building opened in 1963 to both fanfare and controversy. For many modernists, it was too traditional, and for many traditionalists, it was too modern. Indeed, Thom's very personal creative approach avoided stylistic labels and fused modernist and traditional sensibilities. On the one hand, he designed a quadrangle-type building as the competition committee had requested, inspired by the colleges

Massey College (ABOVE) and its Ondaatje Hall (OPPOSITE)

of Oxford and Cambridge; on the other hand, he created highly abstract, shifting planes (as seen in the college's perimeter walls along the street edges and in the clock tower), recalling the work of the Dutch modernist W. M. Dudok as well as the de Stijl movement of the early twentieth century. Permeating the whole design were strong influences from the American architect Frank Lloyd Wright, whose principles for an organic architecture had inspired Thom, filtered through his own experience of the naturalism of British Columbia. Furthermore, Thom had the audacity to add ornament to Massey College's design at a time when the minimalist International Style, which promoted a sleek, industrial look, was most popular. In retrospect, it is not surprising that Thom, sometimes affectionately called "Frank Lloyd Thom," struck nerves in Toronto, where he moved in 1963 and set up his own practice, eventually delivering major projects, such as the remarkable Trent University (1965–73) in nearby Peterborough, Ontario.

The story of Massey College would be incomplete without mentioning some of its superb interior spaces. The junior common room, located at the building's south end, is simultaneously compressive (it has a relatively low ceiling) and expansive (stepping down in section to large windows that face the quadrangle on one side and a narrow, walled courtyard on the other). The space exudes warmth. Located directly above is the main dining hall, Ondaatje Hall, a mysterious, lantern-like room. It hovers slightly above the rest of the college, gently announcing its importance. Here, Thom masterfully and magically manipulated natural light, making the hall one of the greatest rooms in the university. Nearby is a diminutive private dining room, where the College Charter is exhibited along with the Nobel Prize in Chemistry, presented to the college by Professor John Polanyi, recipient of the medal in 1986 and one of the founding fellows of the college.

Over the past two decades, a series of thoughtful, almost seamless renovations have been completed by Shim-Sutcliffe Architects. Their most recent project at Massey College is an elegant presidential suite, which includes custom-designed furniture. The suite is offered to University of Toronto presidents as transitional quarters when they complete their term.

69   Newman Centre of Toronto

Attributed to David Roberts, 1890

Ballroom addition

George M. Miller, 1901

St. Thomas Aquinas Church

Arthur W. Holmes, 1927

Among the grand homes that lined St. George Street in the nineteenth and early twentieth centuries, 89 St. George Street, which is now the Newman Centre of Toronto, was one of the most spectacular. It was built in 1890 for Wilmot D. Matthews, whose family fortune came from the grain trading business. A hybrid of the Richardsonian Romanesque and Queen Anne Revival styles, the red-brick house

Newman Centre of Toronto

is anchored at its southwest corner by a three-story cylindrical volume, echoed at the rear of the house by a second, somewhat smaller cylinder topped by a covered porch. In addition to red brick, the house's material palette also includes Credit Valley sandstone walls, a slate roof, and unglazed terra-cotta decorative elements. The building's many gables have elaborately carved vergeboards and scalloped wood shingles.

The Newman Centre of Toronto (formerly the Newman Foundation), which operates under the umbrella of the Archdiocese of Toronto and fosters dialogue between the Roman Catholic Church and the modern world, purchased the Matthews family's house in 1922. Admirably, the house has since been treated well, including the interior, which contains some of the finest late nineteenth-century rooms in Toronto, featuring wood-paneled walls, basket-weave oak floors with edge banding, coffered ceilings, plaster moldings, stained glass, and elaborate hardware. The outstanding vaulted ballroom was added to the building's south end in 1901, for the wedding of the Matthews's eldest daughter; it includes a highly sculptural brick chimney.

Soon after it bought the house, the Newman Foundation tore down a coach house at the rear of the property and during 1926 and 1927 constructed St. Thomas Aquinas Church, which is designed in the style of fifteenth-century Gothic architecture, with exterior walls of broken-face Credit Valley limestone and ashlar Indiana limestone, and a roof of gray slate and copper. Inside, we find arch-braced trusses and an exposed ceiling of dark-stained British Columbia fir.

Joseph L. Rotman School of Management interior (ABOVE) and exterior (PREVIOUS)

70   Joseph L. Rotman School of Management

Zeidler Partnership Architects, 1995

Addition

Zeidler Partnership Architects, 2006

John Downey House

Architect unknown, 1889

Canadian School of Missions (addition to Downey House)

Arthur McKenzie Brydonj, 1930

South addition and renovations to Downey House and Canadian School of Missions

Kuwabara Payne McKenna Blumberg Architects, 2011

Named in honor of Joseph L. Rotman, past chairman, CEO, and founder of Clairvest Group, the university's business school known as Rotman is housed in a cluster of connected buildings facing St. George Street. The 1995 north building by Eberhard Zeidler, one of Toronto's best-known architects, is difficult to categorize. Some of its architectural aspects are fairly normal and polite, such as the lower red-brick portion, which relates comfortably to the historic houses along St. George Street and the Innis College Student Residence next door (also designed by Zeidler). An attractive three-story multipurpose atrium rises at the heart of the north building.

This sense of the familiar is short-lived, though, because parts of the building seem to have broken loose—bending inward, folding outward, jagging upward— making it look like an agitated mouse-gray iceberg. Shard-like zinc and glass forms protrude as elongated dormers and sculptural skylights. One of Rotman's most memorable spaces is the faculty and staff lounge, which juts from the third floor at the northwest corner and reads as an amalgam of Victorian, modernist, and deconstructivist sensibilities.

In 2011 the Rotman completed an ambitious addition to the south, designed by Kuwabara Payne McKenna Blumberg Architects, providing space for the Desautels Centre for Integrative Thinking, the Lloyd and Delphine Martin Prosperity Institute, and other divisions, allowing the Rotman to double its enrollment. Extending south toward the Newman Centre of Toronto and west to the existing pedestrian lane, the south addition gave identity to a parcel of the campus that had been ill-defined for several decades. The addition is composed of four "boxes": a large five-story primary volume set back from St. George Street and clad in an elegant, blue-black, taut curtain wall; two smaller volumes clad in black glass; and a fourth, more perfunctory volume at the rear.

The interior of the south addition is welcoming and warm. Visitors are greeted by a comfortable lounge with a fireplace and an adjacent café overlooking St. George Street. To the left, a fabulous, generously scaled, lipstick-pink stair sweeps visitors upward. The project incorporates the historic John Downey House and the marvelous chapel on the second floor of the 1930 Canadian School of Missions. The former chapel, which has a beautiful ceiling, is now the Rotman's meeting house for PhD students.

71   Innis College Student Residence
Zeidler Partnership Architects, 1994

Serving Innis College, located directly across St. George Street, the U-shaped student residence has more than eighty apartment-style bedroom units. Within the U is an informal courtyard, contained at the open end by a semicircular fountain. The main entrance to the six-story building is marked by a large steel arch with an abstracted keystone (also made of steel), above which are stacked bay windows with steel articulations. The volumetric and material complexity displayed here is representative of that found throughout the building. Architect Eberhard Zeidler wanted

Innis College Student Residence

the residence to relate in scale, texture, and color to the numerous Victorian and Edwardian houses along St. George Street, and in this sense the postmodern design is successful. A year later, Zeidler completed the Joseph L. Rotman School of Management directly to the south, and the two buildings share a pleasant forecourt with a family of exuberant glass canopies.

72   Woodsworth College

Kuwabara Payne McKenna Blumberg Architects in association with Barton Myers Associates, Inc., 1992

119 St. George (Alexander McArthur House)

David B. Dick, 1892

Alterations

Francis S. Baker, 1911

Kruger Hall

Allward & Gouinlock Architects, 1947

Alterations

U of T Design and Engineering, 2009

Established in 1974 with a focus on part-time students in the Faculty of Arts and Science, Woodsworth College has more than 5,500 students, of which a majority are now full-time, coming directly from high school. The college was named for J. S. Woodsworth, an advocate for social justice and founder of the Canadian political party the Co-operative Commonwealth Federation, forerunner of the New Democratic Party.

Tucked discreetly behind three renovated mansions on St. George Street and organized around a long, narrow courtyard, Woodsworth College—designed by Barton Myers—remains one of the university's most thoughtfully and rigorously crafted projects of the past three decades. The new wings, arranged in an L shape, march along in a rational, disciplined manner, faced in custom-made, pinkish-orange brick rising from a base of gray granite. Myers used extensive wood detailing, along with elegant steel elements, to architecturally articulate and differentiate. The complex has numerous entrances, and the principal one at the south is marked by a distinctive tower sheathed in thin panels of pink onyx. Woodsworth College is reminiscent of the work of Louis Kahn—modern, but embedded in the classical tradition. This could be because Myers studied under Kahn at the University of Pennsylvania and worked with him following graduation.

As an infill, adaptive-reuse project, Woodsworth imaginatively incorporates the Alexander McArthur House (1892) and the officers' quarters for the Canadian Officers' Training Corp. (1941) that had been erected alongside the house. Now accommodating the college's administrative offices and various student functions, these buildings are the heart of Woodsworth. The renovated spaces, including Kruger Hall Commons, flow gracefully into a delightful skylit café, which is anchored at the south end by a monumental fireplace. The 1888 John R. Bailey House at

TOP: Woodsworth College, courtyard, looking northeast
BOTTOM: 119 St. George (Alexander McArthur House)

121 St. George Street (now the Centre for Industrial Relations and Human Resources) appears to be part of Woodsworth (and contributes walls and terraces along the west side) but is actually a separate division of the university.

One could argue that the second heart of the college is the Peter F. Bronfman Courtyard, an inviting gathering place surrounded by a gracious indoor-outdoor, cloister-like corridor. At the courtyard's northeast corner the architects included a distinctive octagonal boardroom. Following a long run of mediocre architecture in the 1970s and 1980s, the university took note of the exceptional Woodsworth project, which was guided by the college's vice principal and registrar, Dr. Alex R. Waugh. Woodsworth became a symbol of quality and a rallying point for both progressive architecture and the implementation of a new process for selecting architects. Consequently, in 1997 the university's Design Review Committee was established, which continues to advise on architectural design matters on the three campuses.

73   23 St. George Street

Burke and Horwood, 1900

The noted Toronto architect Edmund Burke designed this fantastic house, which was the home of Thomas M. Harris, a partner in Smith Brothers, a large carriage and wagon manufacturer, and his wife. The house now serves Woodsworth College and the Transitional Year Program. Noteworthy architectural features include the scalloped wood shingles on the front gable and the deeply recessed, arched entry, which is surrounded with beautifully carved red sandstone. Burke was also the author of the Student Commons building. (See Walk Five, pages 183–85.)

23 St. George Street

74   Woodsworth College Residence

Architects Alliance, 2004

The northern gateway of the University of Toronto's St. George campus is accentuated by the twenty-one-story Woodsworth College Residence, which provides accommodation for 371 students in apartment-like suites. The building's composition consists of a U-shaped, four-story podium from which a seventeen-story glass tower rises. The outdoor space formed by the podium, the Alex R. Waugh Courtyard,

Woodsworth College Residence

Munk School of Global Affairs

opens to the south and connects to the main Woodsworth College building, linking to an attractive new east–west walkway lined with a double row of birch trees.

The podium is transparent at its base and more solid from the second to fourth levels, where it is clad in yellow brick, divided into panels by vertical window slots that establish an irregular rhythm. The tower, wrapped in glass panels varying in shade and color, is more architecturally successful than the podium. Some of the tower's faces are rendered in a cheeky checkerboard pattern that recalls the populist side of mid-twentieth-century modernism, along with the work of the trailblazing Toronto modernist, architect Peter Dickinson.

75   Munk School of Global Affairs

Burke and Horwood, 1909

Restoration and south addition

Kuwabara Payne McKenna Blumberg Architects, Inc. with ERA Architects Inc., 2012

A small brass plaque on the iron fence in front of the Munk School of Global Affairs reads simply "Meteorological Office." Nearby, a larger plaque explains the story behind this mysterious title, which began when the British Army conducted meteorological and magnetic observations at the university in 1840. In 1853 Canada took over the program and built a new observatory, which became the headquarters of the Meteorological Service of Canada, providing a system of stations that by 1876 enabled the service to issue storm forecasts and warnings. In 1909 the meteorological service built its new headquarters (the Dominion Meteorological

Building), designed by Burke and Horwood, at 315 Bloor Street West. When the group moved in 1971, the university purchased the building to accommodate its admissions and awards services, and that group remained there for forty years.

The structure's heavily rusticated Miramichi sandstone facade gives it a rugged, fortresslike feel, while the upper-floor windows, with their delicately articulated mullions, lend an air of elegance. The volume's symmetrical composition is offset by a cylindrical, medieval-looking tower at the southeast corner, which originally had a domed observatory housing a telescope. The tiny transit house, located at the west side of the building and constructed at the same time as the meteorological office, is rotated slightly to be oriented due north.

During 2011 and 2012 the main building and the transit house were restored as the new home for the Munk School of Global Affairs, a component of the Munk Centre for International Studies, located one block southward. (See pages 148–49.) Made possible by a donation from gold-mining magnate Peter Munk and his wife, Melanie, along with c$25 million from the Ontario government, the Munk School of Global Affairs is a hub for Canada's conversation with the world and can be understood metaphorically as an "observatory," linking the school back to the building's original function.

76   Ontario Institute for Studies in Education (OISE)
Kenneth R. Cooper, 1968

Established by the Province of Ontario in 1965 as a center for graduate studies and research in education, the Ontario Institute for Studies in Education (OISE) symbolized the progressive 1960s institutionally and architecturally in Canada. Completed one year after the 1967 International and Universal Exposition (Expo 67) in Montreal, the OISE building displays the optimism of that bold venture. The institute, which became affiliated with the university in 1966 and fully integrated in 1996, serves some 3,300 graduate students and more than 7,400 continuing-education students.

OISE's narrow frontage on Bloor Street West disguises the immensity of this poured-in-place and prefabricated concrete building, which is best viewed from the east on Bedford Road or from the parking

Ontario Institute for Studies in Education

lot of the York Club to the west. From these vantage points, one can fully appreciate the two huge tower wings with their faceted, light-manipulating facades. A long, well-proportioned colonnade runs along the west side of the building, leading to the main entrance, the education commons, a five-hundred-seat auditorium, and an entrance to the subway. Brick, natural wood, and quarry tile warm OISE's interior, which displays modern art by Jack Bush, Sorel Etrog, and Kazuo Nakamura.

77 Factor-Inwentash Faculty of Social Work
Marani & Morris, 1950
Renovations
Dubois Plumb Partnership, 1999

In 1914 the University of Toronto created Canada's first school of social work. Now the Factor-Inwentash Faculty of Social Work, it is committed to social justice and to knowledge mobilization, supporting partnerships with more than three hundred community organizations.

The faculty's building at the northwest corner of Bloor Street West and Bedford Road epitomizes the conservative approach architects Marani & Morris held onto at a time when many Toronto firms fully embraced the wave of post–World War Two modernism that swept across North America. Completed in 1950 as an office building for Texaco, the structure is interesting in relation to Marani & Morris's design for the Bank of Canada (1958) on University Avenue. Both are classically composed (bilaterally symmetrical with an expression of base, middle, and top) and severely rational. However, the University of Toronto building lacks the deluxe materials and refinement of detail found in the Bank of Canada building. The School of Social Work (now the Factor-Inwentash Faculty of Social Work, named in recognition of philanthropists Lynn Factor and Sheldon Inwentash) moved into the former Texaco building in 1970. Dubois Plumb Partnership completed a series of handsome interior renovations in 1999.

Factor-Inwentash Faculty of Social Work

78 Varsity Centre for Physical Activity and Health

Stadium

Harkness Loudon & Hertzberg (engineers), 1924

Stadium master plan

Craig Madill and Loudon, 1929

Arena

Darling & Pearson with Harkness Loudon & Hertzberg as engineers, 1926

Stadium addition and renovations

Proctor, Redfern & Laughlin (engineers), 1950

New stadium

Diamond + Schmitt Architects in association with Ellerbe Becket Architects, 2006

Varsity Pavilion

Diamond + Schmitt Architects, 2010

The University of Toronto's Varsity Centre for Physical Activity and Health includes an entry pavilion, a 4,800-seat stadium, a four-hundred-meter eight-lane track, an artificial-turf field (with an air-supported polyester dome for winter use), and a four-thousand-seat hockey arena. This sports and recreation facility welcomes and encourages all levels of physical activity, from the high performance of competitive athletes to everyday casual exercise.

The site's history is worth recounting. Before 1898 the university's football team, the Varsity Blues, played in King's College Circle. When the sometimes rowdy games drew complaints, the Blues moved to a site at the location of today's Varsity Centre. In 1901 the first cinder track was created, along with a grandstand seating five hundred people, and in 1911 the university constructed Varsity Stadium. Built primarily of wood, it had a capacity of 7,200, soon increased to 10,500. A reinforced-concrete grandstand was constructed in 1924, raising the center's capacity to 16,000 people, and two years later the 4,000-seat Varsity Arena was added to the east.

In the late 1920s, James H. Craig and Henry Harrison Madill, in collaboration with engineering professor Thomas R. Loudon, designed a new horseshoe-shaped stadium, which would have made Varsity Centre the largest football stadium in Canada. But World War Two delayed the project, and the major renovation was not completed until 1950, with a capacity of only 21,767 rather than the hoped for 35,000.

By the mid-1990s Varsity Stadium had become run-down, but the land it sat on, particularly along Bloor Street West, was quite valuable. The university considered several grandiose scenarios including major commercial development along Bloor Street West, with a new stadium to the south. It was soon realized, though, that the site was too small for this grand vision. A subsequent imaginative, comprehensive plan for the site at Bloor Street West and Devonshire Place that included a new stadium, student housing, and modest commercial development also proved unworkable, as did a 2004 plan for a c$100 million complex that included a football stadium for the Toronto Argonauts.

Varsity Centre for Physical Activity and Health

The old stadium was finally demolished in 2002, and in 2006 the decade of debate over what to do with its site ended with the opening of the modest Varsity Centre, which features a 4,800-seat stadium with west-facing seating above a covered arcade that leads to the 1926 Varsity Arena. In 2010 a handsome new entry pavilion was erected at the south end of the site, also providing football changing rooms and a sports therapy facility.

79   Goldring Centre for High Performance Sport
Patkau Architects with MacLennan Jaunkalns Miller Architects, 2014
Academic Tower Addition
Patkau Architects with MacLennan Jaunkalns Miller Architects, expected completion 2021

The architecturally exhilarating Goldring Centre for High Performance Sport is part of the Faculty of Kinesiology and Physical Education. Designed by the celebrated Vancouver firm Patkau Architects in collaboration with Toronto-based sports facility specialists MacLennan Jaunkalns Miller Architects, 140,000 square feet (13,000 square meters) were packed into a sleek, bridge-like structure that spans the compact urban site. Included are basketball and volleyball courts, training and sports medicine facilities, faculty offices, research spaces, and a two-thousand-seat field

Goldring Centre for High Performance Sport field house interior (ABOVE) and exterior (OVERLEAF)

house. The architects placed the column-free field house below grade, made possible by huge steel trusses spanning north to south.

Along the east, front side of the building, one of the giant trusses supports a cable-hung, high-tensile glass wall, through which the public can see both the lower

View looking north from the top floor of the Academic Tower addition, Goldring Centre for High Performance Sport (architectural rendering)

field house and the upper Strength and Conditioning Centre. It is a place to see and be seen. Bringing together recreational athletes and Olympians to be, the Goldring Centre is one of the most innovative and elegant buildings completed by the university in the past decade. A multistory timber-frame Academic Tower will be added at the north end of the center, with completion expected in 2021.

80   Edward Johnson Building (Faculty of Music)

Gordon Adamson & Associates, 1961

Addition

Moffat Kinoshita Associates Inc., 1987

Established in 1918, the Faculty of Music offers academic studies (composition, ethnomusicology, music education, and music theory) and performance programs (conducting, early music, jazz, keyboard, and opera) and includes the Institute for Canadian Music and the Music and Health Research Collaborative. The faculty's main facility, the Edward Johnson Building, is set on a concrete plinth that rises from the bottom of the Philosopher's Walk valley. The building has a formal air about it, graced by twenty-four slender concrete columns around its perimeter. The structure was named for Edward Patrick Johnson, who was general manager of the Metropolitan Opera in

Edward Johnson Building

New York from 1935 to 1950 and also served as chairman of the board of the Royal Conservatory of Music. (See Walk Eleven, pages 336–37.) From the east, the three primary parts of the structure are evident: the main two-story concrete-and-glass volume, the brick-clad library hovering over the main part, and the brick stagehouse rising at the north. The main entrance is situated off-center within the eight-bay east facade and leads to a grand lobby with a pair of monumental light wells that pierce the ceiling and a third-floor lounge. These wells are capped by delirious skylights that look like enormous flowers whose eight "petals" are circular glazed units. From the lobby one enters the 815-seat MacMillan Theatre, designed for orchestral concerts and operas. On the lower floor, level with Philosopher's Walk, is the 490-seat Walter Hall, one of Toronto's finest small auditoriums, created for chamber music and recitals.

Although the Edward Johnson Building works well architecturally, its relationship to nearby buildings and streets is awkward, as it is sandwiched between Falconer Hall, McLaughlin Planetarium, the Royal Ontario Museum, and Philosopher's Walk. Unfortunately, its attractive front looks directly into the rear of Falconer Hall. With the forthcoming addition of a major cultural building on the planetarium site south of the Royal Ontario Museum, which will include a new recital hall for the Faculty of Music, the Edward Johnson Building will soon be recontextualized and given a proper setting.

FACULTY OF LAW

The progressive Faculty of Law offers JD, LLM, SJD, MSL, and GPLLM degrees in law, and it is consistently ranked by *Maclean's* magazine as the top law school in Canada. Among its graduates are a Canadian prime minister, two premiers of Ontario, two mayors of Toronto, and thirteen justices of the Supreme Court of Canada. A Faculty of Law was established in 1887, but no credit for its courses was given by the Law Society of Upper Canada, the governing body of the legal profession in Ontario. A strong undergraduate "honour law" program was established in the 1920s, but, again, no credit was given by the Law Society. Essentially, the Law Society provided on-the-job-training, complemented by law courses at Osgoode Hall. In 1949 the faculty created a blueprint for a modern law school, and the first class following the new program graduated in 1952. However, it would be 1957 before the Law Society finally accepted University of Toronto law graduates seeking admission to the Ontario bar on an equal footing with graduates of Osgoode Hall.

The faculty occupies three buildings in a treed setting between Queen's Park and Philosopher's Walk: the Jackman Law Building, Flavelle House, and Falconer Hall. The Fasken Martineau Building, on Spadina Avenue several blocks to the west, accommodates a number of programs, including the faculty's free legal services clinics and the professional legal education programs.

81 Flavelle House

Darling & Pearson, 1902

Library addition

Hart Massey and William J. McBain, 1961

Renovations and additions

Moffat Kinoshita Associates, 1989

Renovations

Taylor Hariri Pontarini, 2001

Flavelle House is an imposing mansion at the northwest corner of Queen's Park and was, until the opening of the Jackman Law Building in 2016, the heart of the Faculty of Law. Best described as Edwardian-Georgian in style, it was built for Sir Joseph Flavelle, who expanded his meatpacking business into Canada's first nationwide retail grocery chain.

The University of Toronto set up the residential neighborhood around Queen's Park in 1861, and homes for the wealthy appeared soon afterward. Flavelle chose Darling & Pearson—who were also the architects of the Canadian Bank of Commerce where Flavelle had been a director—to design his new home, Holwood, which was to have both the comfort and the charm of country homes he had admired in the south of England. The mansion consists of a main two-story wing and a three-story service wing set at an angle. A pedimented pavilion containing the main stair negotiates this obtuse angle. Darling & Pearson gave Holwood a grand portico supported by Corinthian columns finished in stucco, into which they set an elegantly framed door with slender Ionic colonnettes. (A duplicate portico faces west at the rear of the house.)

Within, Holwood's fine rooms have been preserved. To the right of the entrance, the front hall focuses on an elegant fireplace graced by a Jacobean oak mantel. The magnificent barrel-vaulted ceiling is decorated with four art nouveau angels by German-born Gustav Hahn. Flavelle died in 1939, leaving his home to the University of Toronto.

Over the years, wings were added to Flavelle House, dramatically changing the setting of the mansion. In 1961 an overtly modern structure designed by architects Hart Massey and William J. McBain was added on the sloping, wooded area to the south, housing a new law library and lecture rooms. The architects' idea was to keep the original mansion and new buildings separate and distinct from one another, which they achieved by creating a delicate, transparent glass link between the two. It was an extremely thoughtful solution, but, alas, the 1961 wing was later consumed by a bombastic, unsympathetic transformation in 1989. Needing more space and seeking comprehensive architectural renewal, the faculty launched an ambitious master plan in 2008. With the completion of the Jackman Law Building in 2016, the marvelous Flavelle House has been properly reintegrated and once again celebrated.

Jackman Law Building

82 Jackman Law Building

Hariri Pontarini Architects and B+H Architects, 2016

The Jackman Law Building is named for a graduate of the school, Henry "Hal" N. R. Jackman, who served as lieutenant governor of Ontario from 1991 to 1997 and made a major donation to the project. The design resulted from a long, complicated process that commenced with Hariri Pontarini Architects winning a 2008 international design competition to prepare a master plan for renewal. They proposed a 66,000-square-foot (6,132-square-meter) project that featured a crescent-shaped classroom and office wing overlooking Queen's Park, an updating of the outmoded library, and the creation of a unifying gathering space—a soaring atrium-forum incorporating the rear wall of the adjacent, historic Flavelle House.

      The building's volumetric distribution—a sort of triangular composition— stems from the transformation of preexisting wings and the shape of the site, bounded on the west by Philosopher's Walk, on the southeast by Queen's Park, and on the north by Flavelle House. The public face of the building presents a curve of narrow windows between heavy-looking stone fins set above a Wiarton limestone base. There are some attractive interior spaces, such as the central atrium with its dramatic stone wall and the light-filled, airy Bora Laskin Law Library overlooking Philosopher's Walk.

Jackman Law Building, atrium

83   Falconer Hall

Sproatt & Rolph, 1902

The lovely, Edwardian-style Falconer Hall, which houses part of the Faculty of Law, has had a complex history. Its multiple lives started in 1902 as Wymilwood, the home of the financier Edward R. Wood, vice president and managing director of Central Canada Loan & Savings, and his wife, Agnes. The Woods donated the house to Victoria University in 1925 as a women's residence. In 1949 ownership was transferred to the University of Toronto, and in 1952 the building was renamed Falconer Hall to honor the university's fourth president, Robert Falconer, as part of a plan to build a new women's athletic center on the site. Architects Fleury & Arthur drafted a plan for the athletic center, which was to preserve and reuse Falconer Hall as a women's social and meeting center. Early in 1955, the Woods' former coach house and servants' quarters were demolished to make way for the new building. However, the provincial government subsequently stopped the project, which it considered

Falconer Hall

too large and too close to the Ontario Legislative Building. A new site for the athletic center was found west of St. George Street, where the Women's Athletic Building was completed in 1959 (now called the Clara Benson Building).

From 1959 to 1961, Falconer Hall was briefly the home of the fledgling York University, before the Faculty of Law took over the building. It is primarily used for the graduate program in law, including staff and student offices. Falconer Hall will soon be reborn as part of the renewal of the area south of the Royal Ontario Museum that includes the Flavelle House, the Edward Johnson Building, and the former McLaughlin Planetarium site.

84   Centre for Civilizations, Cultures & Cities (CCC)
Diller Scofidio + Renfro and architectsAlliance, projected completion 2022

This academic and cultural project, to be located between the Royal Ontario Museum and the Faculty of Music's Edward Johnson Building, is in an early stage of development. Formerly the site of the Royal Ontario Museum's McLaughlin Planetarium, which closed in 1995, the land was sold to the university in 2009. The new Centre for Civilization, Cutures & Cities (CCC) facility will house the Department of History, the Department of Near and Middle Eastern Civilizations, a 250-seat performance hall for the Faculty of Music, and the School of Cities. The School of Cities, an initiative led by the President's Office—including participation by the Faculty of Arts and Science; the Faculty of Architecture, Landscape, and Design; the Faculty of Applied Science and Engineering; and the Joseph L. Rotman School of Management—will catalyze research, teaching, and outreach related to cities. As well, the CCC will create new and better connections to Philosopher's Walk.

The selection of New York–based Diller Scofidio + Renfro and Toronto-based architectsAlliance for the project is promising, because both firms are known for bold architectural statements and the making of thoughtful "social landscapes." Diller Scofidio + Renfro were the architects of the Boston Institute of Contemporary Art (2006) and the wildly successful High Line linear public park (2009–14) on Manhattan's West Side.

The Southwest Campus

The Southwest Campus

Up until the early 1950s, the university's central St. George campus extended north–south from Bloor Street to College Street and east–west from Queen's Park to St. George Street. With mounting enrollment pressures after World War Two, plans emerged to expand the campus west of St. George Street to Spadina Avenue. Although a planning committee report from 1949 supported this proposition, it was not until 1956 that a west campus designation was finally approved, identifying a thirty-three-acre area bounded by St. George Street, College Street, Spadina Avenue, and Harbord Street. In the meantime, however, two new university structures were built "beyond the border"—the Central Steam Plant in 1952 and the School of Nursing in 1953—signaling that the westward movement had already begun.

  The Plateau Committee, an advisory planning committee set up by the university's board of governors, envisioned that the new western precinct would be devoid of automobiles, full of green spaces, and designed for pedestrians. A January 1960 article on University of Toronto campus development in the *Journal of the Royal Architectural Institute of Canada* emphatically stated that "the exclusion of automobiles from campus areas is of prime importance" and also asserted that "all buildings on the West Campus would be simple and economical in construction and maintenance." The university imagined underground service access, and

Aerial view of the southwest campus (right) and One Spadina Crescent (center)

pedestrian overpasses and underpasses to allow students to move easily and safely across St. George Street from the old campus to the new, airy western side. There would be two large athletic fields and parking structures along Spadina Avenue to buffer the nascent Spadina Expressway. This grand vision, however, was laid to rest in 1957 due to funding problems, resulting in the patchwork planning of the past half century.

Nevertheless, campus master plans from the 1960s through the early 1990s slowly edged toward an emphasis on pedestrians, with one plan even calling for the complete removal of vehicles from St. George Street in order to unify the east and west areas as a "walking campus." The construction of the Earth Sciences Centre in 1989, which included the pedestrianization of Bancroft Avenue, the completion of the 1979 Warren Stevens Building, and the transformation of Classic Avenue into a benign service lane, went some distance toward realizing the dream of a landscaped and pedestrian-friendly west campus. It was not until 1996, though, when St. George Street itself was completely transformed under the leadership of planner and philanthropist Judy Matthews, that the university community started talking seriously again about the necessity for high-quality, pedestrian-friendly open space on campus.

With Matthews's prodding, in 1999 the university initiated a comprehensive open-space master plan, called "Investing in the Landscape," drafted by the landscape architecture firms Urban Strategies and Corban and Goode Landscape Architecture and Urbanism, along with Taylor Hariri Pontarini Architects. The plan started rethinking the southwest campus's fragmented landscape. In 2008 a community design charette studied the options for pedestrianizing Willcocks Street, leading to a pilot project launched in 2010 for the section between St. George and Huron Streets. Called Willcocks Common, it was a popular success, leading to the city's permanent closure of the block-long zone to cars in 2015. That same year the university commissioned landscape architecture firm DTAH to create the Willcocks Common Revitalization plan. The comprehensive design includes new paving and lighting, a grid of trees forming a canopy, and zones for gathering and activities.

The ambitious transformation of One Spadina Crescent for the John H. Daniels Faculty of Architecture, Landscape, and Design, completed in 2018, includes landscape renewal of the circle and pedestrian linkage with Russell Street, furthering the dreams from a half century ago of a green and pleasantly walkable campus west of St. George Street.

85 St. George Street, Wilson Gate, and Perly Rae Gate

Brown + Storey Architects and van Nostrand DiCastri Architects, with Corban and Goode Landscape Architecture and Urbanism, 1996

St. George Street, the busy public thoroughfare that runs north–south through the campus, had been problematic since World War Two. Widened in 1948 to accommodate more traffic at higher speeds, it was not only hazardous for students crossing from the old campus to the west campus, it was also unsightly. In the mid-1990s, the university, the City of Toronto, and urban activist-planner Judy Matthews set out to correct the situation by narrowing and calming the street; substantially widening sidewalks; and adding imaginative retaining walls, curbs, benches, planters, and bicycle racks, along with hundreds of trees.

This substantial undertaking had strong conceptual underpinnings. The project's architects and landscape architects devised a family of thick, angular concrete elements that are multivalent: they retain soil, protect trees, define circulation paths, and provide places to sit. At either end of the five-block-long area, these energetic concrete forms bend and increase in scale and are topped by conical steel "gateposts" to mark entrances to the campus. The south entry, called the Wilson Gate, honors Ann Elizabeth Wilson, who, along with her husband, former University of Toronto president Robert Prichard, was a strong supporter of the St. George Street revitalization. Similarly designed, the north Perly Rae Gate honors Arlene Perly Rae, journalist, arts patron, and wife of Bob Rae, who was premier of Ontario from 1990 to 1995.

As a result, the street not only has been transformed into a pedestrian-friendly corridor, it also has become a place—an elongated plaza of sorts—that finally binds the historic central campus to the west campus. In the past decade, thoughtfully landscaped tentacles have branched out east and west from St. George Street—including the Sir Daniel Wilson, Nona Macdonald, and Woodsworth College Walkways; the Davenport Chemical Research Building; the Lash Miller Chemical Laboratories Garden; and the Willcocks Common—generating further spatial connectivity and social interaction.

86   Koffler Student Services Centre

Alfred H. Chapman in association with Wickson & Gregg, 1908
Addition
Chapman & Oxley in association with Wickson & Gregg, 1930
Theater renovation
Irving Grossman, 1961
Renovation and restoration
Howard D. Chapman and Howard V. Walker, 1985

In 1905 the City of Toronto announced a national design competition for a new central reference library that was also to incorporate a branch library on College Street. Alfred H. Chapman's winning Beaux-Arts design features a grand entrance at the building's east end that rises up to the reference library on the piano nobile, balanced by a lesser entrance at the west end to the ground-floor branch library. The reference and reading room overlooked College Street through two-story windows set between Corinthian pilasters. The processional entry sequence moves memorably up and through the marble-lined entrance hall all the way to the third floor. In 1930 Chapman & Oxley completed a handsome addition along St. George Street.

Koffler Student Services Centre

The stately building was taken over by the university in the early 1980s and converted into the Koffler Student Services Centre, which also houses the university bookstore. Fortunately, the building's primary spaces were preserved and restored, although the bookstore functions have always seemed shoehorned into the historic spaces. A three-story postmodern concourse with seven pop art–like, mustard-colored arches was completed in 1985. In 2002 the center's north elevation was restored and carefully incorporated into the atrium of the new Bahen Centre for Information Technology.

87   Fields Institute for Research in Mathematical Sciences
Kuwabara Payne McKenna Blumberg Architects, 1995

Founded in 1991 as an advanced institute for research in mathematical sciences, the Fields Institute, known as "the Fields," is named in honor of John Charles Fields, professor of mathematics at the University of Toronto, who became well known for establishing the Fields Medal, often called the "Nobel Prize of mathematics."

The institute is set back from College Street to align with the Koffler Student Services Centre to the east, and the two buildings share a long, landscaped zone terminated by the Student Commons to the west. Clad in rusticated limestone and red brick, the Fields's public face projects decorum and good urban manners. Note the subtle game of chamfered corners at the southeast and southwest, which turn toward nearby buildings and create special corner rooms.

The exterior politeness continues inside, but with a few twists. On the second level, a helical stair and a wood-burning fireplace animate a three-story atrium. A Douglas fir ceiling plane hovers overhead, with natural light streaming in around the edges of this warm, communal space. At the rear, the communal area spills onto a terrace overlooking the Bahen Centre courtyard.

Fields Institute for Research in Mathematical Sciences, atrium

Fields Institute for Research in Mathematical Sciences

The second floor incorporates the James Stewart Library. Dr. James Stewart, a Toronto musician and author of calculus textbooks, was also a patron of great architecture, realizing his own 18,000-square-foot (1,672-square-meter) home, the internationally acclaimed Integral House (2009) by Shim-Sutcliffe Architects.

88   Student Commons

Burke, Horwood & White, 1909

North addition

Molesworth, West, and Secord, 1920

Addition and renovation

Kohn Shnier Architects, 2000

Renovation

superkül, 2018

If one looks carefully above the arched front entrance of the Student Commons, one will notice a horizontal stone plaque, now blank. It once had the inscription "Royal College of Dental Surgeons," revealing the structure's first use. The five-story brick building served dentistry students from 1909 until 1958; in 1961 the architecture department took it over, and it served as the home of the John H. Daniels Faculty of Architecture, Landscape, and Design until 2017.

Designed by the influential Toronto architect Edmund Burke, who was the principal author of the downtown department store for the Robert Simpson Company and the Bloor Viaduct, the building is essentially a turn-of-the-century, Chicago-inspired industrial structure with an overlay of Prairie Style motifs. The

Entry to the Royal College of Dental Surgeons, circa 1908-9

tripartite facades include a banded brick base, a middle section containing the main floor and mezzanine, and a more elaborate top section composed of loftlike spaces. These flexible, light-filled spaces first served as the dental school's laboratories and clinics before being adapted in the early 1960s into architecture studios. Originally, a simple classical cornice (now hidden) completed the composition. Four-story brick pilasters articulate the corners of the building, while engaged pilasters enliven the two upper stories. The top floor has small brick piers, topped with Prairie Style capitals. A handsomely sculpted portal frames the south entrance. In 2000 a sleek, cantilevered volume by Kohn Shnier Architects was added at the build-ing's southeast corner.

Student Commons (TOP) and an architectural rendering of the new west entry (BOTTOM)

The new Student Commons, administered by the University of Toronto Students' Union (UTSU), will operate as the first dedicated student amenity building on the St. George campus. It will emphasize twenty-four-hour accessibility, serving the university's diverse student community. The Student Commons will house multipurpose rooms, multi-faith prayer rooms, student club offices, computer labs, counseling spaces, a food and clothing bank, a used textbook store, and a bicycle repair training facility. The renovation by architecture firm superkül includes a new main entrance on Huron Street, an east–west interior bridge cutting through the ground floor, the addition of a seven-story circulation stairway, and an elevator at the east side of the building.

89 250 College and 33 Russell Streets

250 College Street

John B. Parkin Associates, 1966

33 Russell Street

Marani, Rounthwaite & Dick, 1969

Purchased by the university in 2017, these buildings are leased to the Centre for Addiction and Mental Health (CAMH), an institution that is fully affiliated with the University of Toronto. CAMH is Canada's largest mental health and addiction teaching hospital and also a major research center. In addition to its operations on the U of T's St. George campus, CAMH has a large campus on Queen Street West.

The building at 250 College Street is an imposing precast-concrete-clad tower attached to a low block to the north. It started life in 1966 as the province's Clarke

250 College Street

Institute of Psychiatry, the main teaching hospital for psychiatry at the University of Toronto. At the end of the 1960s two buildings were constructed nearby to house the Addiction Research Foundation at 33 Russell Street, completing the institute's College Street campus.

Among mid-twentieth-century corporate architectural practices in Toronto, the firm of John B. Parkin Associates looms large, having attained a status akin to that of Skidmore, Owings & Merrill in the United States. The commission to design the Clarke, as the CAMH was first known, came only a few years after the firm designed the university's Sidney Smith Hall in 1961. (See Walk Six, page 209.) If one ignores the entrance pavilion (a later addition) and the unsightly wing to the west, picturing the tower as a clean, ground-up extrusion of concrete, it remains an authoritative work of architecture. The scale of the three-story base, with its jazzlike rhythm of alternating elongated windows and concrete panels (the latter looking like disguised columns), is convincing. The disciplined wrapping of the tower's main body with precast concrete units and the slightly protruding concrete screen at its top (hiding mechanical equipment) add to the building's visual appeal.

The buildings at 33 Russell Street are another story. Here one finds a low concrete block linked to a squat brick tower, forming a mazelike territory of landscaped roofs, plazas, and service entries. The low building vaguely recalls Kallmann, McKinnell & Knowles's 1969 Boston City Hall (which in turn is indebted to Le Corbusier's 1960 Dominican monastery Sainte Marie de La Tourette near Lyon, France), and its overriding concrete frame is mildly interesting. But on the whole, the 33 Russell Street buildings are architecturally awkward and do little to reinforce Spadina Crescent, the important urban space that they join at the northwest.

90　215 Huron Street
Chapman & Hurst, 1959

In the late 1950s and early 1960s, the university was expanding rapidly and urgently needed a central servicing facility that included workshop and maintenance areas, storage, and physical plant administrative offices. Originally called the Superintendent's Building, it consisted of a ground floor with two levels of offices above. The unassuming,

215 Huron Street

utilitarian structure was an early example of a fast-track project—it was designed in a highly rationalized manner that allowed the ground floor maintenance and workshop area to be completed in four and a half months and put into operation while the two office floors, clad simply in precast concrete panels with long bands of continuous windows, were finished above. Additional office floors were added a few years later. Near the main entrance is a decorative concrete panel designed by Dora de Pedery-Hunt. The building currently houses numerous administrative divisions.

91 Anthropology Building
Basil G. Ludlow & Partners, 1963

Formerly the F. Norman Hughes Pharmacy Building, this modest brick-clad cube was renovated in 2007 by the university's Design & Engineering office as the new home for the Department of Anthropology. The symmetrical north elevation, politely aligned with the Central Steam Plant to the east, presents a matching

Anthropology Building

pair of recessed entrances on Russell Street, lined with sculpted blue and white ceramic units that mark the building as a child of the early 1960s. Between the two entries is a bronze sculpture modeled after cedar trees by the noted Canadian artist Walter Yarwood.

The most engaging architectural aspect of the building occurs at its inverted corners, where a splayed detail carefully exposes and articulates the brick cladding. Viewed from below, these corners read as negative columns.

92 Cody Hall (Department of Astronomy and Astrophysics)
Allward & Gouinlock Architects, 1953

Cody Hall was named in honor of John Henry Cody, university president. The building originally served as the School of Nursing. In retrospect, its location can be seen as a quiet but important factor in the university's aggressive westward expansion during the 1960s. In 1956 U of T President Smith stated in a letter that

Cody Hall

"in placing the Heating Plant [Central Steam Plant] and the School of Nursing west of St. George Street we have, in effect, made the decision to go west."

With its humanely scaled elevations, the building anchors the northwest corner of St. George and Russell Streets well, and many original materials and detailing survive in the main interior spaces. Surprisingly, conservative-looking Cody Hall was designed by architects Allward & Gouinlock Architects just five years after they completed the overtly modern Mechanical Engineering Building on King's College Road. (See Walk Two, pages 103–4.) Had they lost confidence in modernism, or were they simply the kind of firm that was adroit at working in a variety of styles? Whatever was the case, by the early 1960s Allward & Gouinlock Architects were once again in the modernist camp, as evidenced by their design for the Lash Miller Chemical Laboratories.

93 Lash Miller Chemical Laboratories and the John and Edna Davenport Chemical Research Building

Lash Miller Chemical Laboratories
Allward & Gouinlock Architects, 1963
John and Edna Davenport Chemical Research Building, renovations and additions
Diamond + Schmitt Architects, 2001
Garden
Phillips Farevaag Smallenberg in association with PMA Landscape Architects, 2005

The Lash Miller Chemical Laboratories originally comprised three components: a block-long, seven-story volume paralleling Willcocks Street; a one-story lecture hall at the corner of Willcocks and St. George Streets; and a two-story wing along St. George Street. The building's main section is clad in brown brick with a regular rhythm of windows framed by aquamarine steel panels below. Carefully designed areas of small aquamarine ceramic tiles provide secondary articulation on the energetic front entrance canopy's soffit and somewhat wacky garden element with a Swiss cheese–like pattern that hides exhaust ducts. On the exterior of the concrete lecture hall, the building announces its function through a display of three-dimensional chemical symbols.

Two decades ago, a major laboratory addition to the building was constructed atop the two-story wing along St. George Street. Using sympathetic materials and scale, the architects successfully blended new and old. The glass-enclosed, cantilevered stair at the addition's south end and the copper-clad, bowed-out element on its west facade give exuberance to the revitalized ensemble, which was named the John and Edna Davenport Chemical Research Building.

Like other buildings in the area, such as the McLennan Physical Laboratories and Sidney Smith Hall, the chemistry-building complex has moatlike recesses running along most of its edges in order to bring natural light to the basement level. While not particularly attractive or friendly, some of these recesses have nevertheless been imaginatively incorporated into the garden between the Lash Miller

Lash Miller Chemical Laboratories and garden

Chemical Laboratories, the Davenport Chemical Research Building, and the McLennan Physical Laboratories.

94   Burton Tower (McLennan Physical Laboratories)

Shore & Moffat & Partners, 1967

Now more than fifty years old, the fourteen-story Burton Tower and three-story wing to its north that constitute the McLennan Physical Laboratories are starting to feel historic, and certain aspects of this 1960s architecture are quite captivating. At first glance, the tower and its wing seem a bit brutish, and an insistent moat that wraps around the complex adds to their standoffish appearance. However, closer examination reveals a highly disciplined, if spare, modern architecture.

Sitting on a small elevated plaza, the tower is clad in stone and charcoal-brown brick, with glazing areas that are broken into carefully proportioned horizontal bands (which are repeated, in various subcompositions, throughout the project). Square in plan, the tower reveals its structural bays—four on each side—with cantilevered corners.

95 Earth Sciences Centre

Bregman + Hamann Architects with A. J. (Jack) Diamond, Donald Schmitt and Company, 1989

High Bay Facility

Barry–Bryan Associates, 2002

In the mid-1970s, the university announced intentions to construct a major facility for the departments of botany, forestry, geography, geology, and environmental studies. After more than a decade of planning, the 100,000-square-foot (9,290-square-meter) Earth Sciences Centre, consuming half the large urban block bounded by Willcocks, Huron, and Russell Streets, was finally realized. Although architecturally of its time in a mildly postmodern style, it does not look outdated today, thirty years after its opening. This is largely because it was designed to dissolve into the surrounding urban fabric. Several existing historic buildings were preserved and integrated into the project.

The center is organized around two major axes: a north–south axis, expressed as a covered colonnade; and an east–west axis, consisting of pedestrianized Bancroft Avenue. Adjacent to the intersection of the axes is a five-story elliptical volume containing an auditorium, library, and reading room. Laboratories,

ABOVE: Earth Sciences Centre
OPPOSITE: Burton Tower

classrooms, and offices are housed in linked linear buildings that form hard urban edges along Willcocks, Huron, and Russell Streets. The naturalized concept for a series of outdoor courtyards came from the landscape architect Michael Hough, aided by the expertise of the botany and forestry faculty and serving some of their research interests. At the heart of the Earth Sciences Centre is Bancroft Avenue, formerly a vehicular route connecting Huron Street to Spadina Avenue. Diamond Schmitt Architects transformed this street into an elongated urban space that now functions like a piazza.

The building's architecture speaks with a 1980s postmodern voice, employing steeply gabled planes, a variety of materials, and captivating bands of ocular windows, like large portholes, that hover somewhere between Georgian and moderne. The motifs and particular use of color and materials in the Earth Sciences Centre are highly abstracted, however, distinguishing this project from the saccharine overkill that frequently occurred in American postmodernism during the 1970s and 1980s.

96 Graduate Students' Union
Gordon & Helliwell, 1911

This small, spirited building was originally a private club, the Baraca Club, and at one time contained a swimming pool and a bowling alley, along with an open yard to its east, bordering the City (later Borden) Dairy service garage. The former club now houses the Graduate Students' Union, its pub, and Sylvester's Cafe. Large wooden brackets support an overhanging roof, and two graceful bay windows mark the lower front facade of the building.

Graduate Students' Union

Koffler House

97   Koffler House
Shore Tilbe Henschel Irwin Peters, 1990
Multi-faith Centre for Spiritual Study and Practice
Moriyama & Teshima Architects, 2007

Located at the west end of Bancroft Avenue, this postmodern structure was designed to house the Koffler Institute for Pharmacy Management, which moved in 2006 to the new Leslie L. Dan Pharmacy Building several blocks to the southeast. Architects Shore Tilbe Henschel Irwin Peters achieved a low-key contextualism by relating the institute's height and materials to nearby historic buildings and by gently curving its Spadina Avenue–facing facade toward Spadina Crescent and the Borden Buildings to the south. Sculptural orange-tan- and yellow-brick walls dance in and out, up and down. The building's design creates some surprising and exuberant moments—for example, at the upper northwest corner, the third-floor volume is indented to make a triangular space, into which juts a triangular bay window. Entering the building from Bancroft Avenue, one is immediately inside a soaring, light-filled rotunda space, topped by a dome and accented with bands of glass block. Its verticality is exaggerated by eight slender concrete columns that rise through the full three stories and support a ring of balconies.

In 2007 the 6,000-square-foot (550-square-meter) Multi-faith Centre for Spiritual Study and Practice was skillfully inserted into the building. Using a restrained palette of bare concrete, white onyx, and sapele (an African hardwood), Moriyama & Teshima Architects created a handsome sequence of sacred spaces appropriate for all faiths. The center's focus is a large meeting space that can

Faculty Club

be transformed into prayer and lecture areas. A small meditation room features a living wall of air-cleansing plants. Even the storage areas for religious tools and iconography—Buddhist scrolls, Christian crosses, Jewish Torahs, First Nations sweetgrass—are elegantly designed.

98 Faculty Club

Benjamin Brown, 1920

This Georgian Revival building started life as the Primrose Club (originally the Cosmopolitan Society), a private meeting place for Jewish business and professional men. (Women were eventually admitted.) Its designer was Benjamin Brown, one of Toronto's first Jewish architects, who was responsible for the design of several landmarks in the city, including the Beth Jacob Synagogue (1922), the Balfour Building (1930), and the extremely interesting Hermant Office Tower (1929), which stands at the southeast corner of Dundas Square. Brown and architect-partner Arthur McConnell merged existing attached homes at 37–39 Willcocks Street into the new structure for the Primrose Club, creating one of the city's most prestigious meeting places.

In 1959 the university's faculty union obtained the building, leading to the formation of the present-day Faculty Club, which features comfortable lounges, an elegant Wedgewood-blue dining room, and various meeting rooms. When the neighboring New College Residence was constructed in 2003, the Faculty Club created a delightful outdoor dining terrace along the west side of their building.

99 New College Residence

Saucier + Perrotte, 2003

This is the third student residence constructed for New College, joining New College I (Wetmore Hall) and New College II (Wilson Hall), which are located directly to the north across Willcocks Street. (See Walk Six, pages 238–39.) The nine-story "new New College," as the 2003 building is known, provides single-room accommodations for 277 students. It blends admirably into its physical setting, responding, chameleonlike, to its urban and immediate campus contexts.

The residence hall is made up of two parallel "bar" buildings with service cores between. The west-facing bar, along Spadina Avenue, is clad in red brick and has a staccato pattern of white-framed windows. A cubic void is cut into the bar, generating an outdoor garden room. The building relates comfortably to the small-scale, red-brick Victorian houses in the neighborhood across the street. The east-facing bar, which faces the university, is clad in zinc and has larger, regularly spaced windows. It also incorporates a cubic garden, reminiscent of the residential gardens in the sky favored by Le Corbusier. The residence's main entrance is tucked under and between the bars along Willcocks Street, where the differentiated conceptual logic of the two bar facades is momentarily revealed.

Between the New College Residence, the Faculty Club, and the Graduate Students' Union, a public pedestrian walkway, a dining terrace, and a courtyard announce the rear, campus-side entrance to the building. Underneath the unadorned lobbies, the architects inserted a beautifully proportioned multipurpose hall, the William Doo Auditorium.

100 North and South Borden Buildings

North Building

George M. Miller, 1900

South Building

George M. Miller, 1910

The quirky North and South Borden Buildings are in need of revitalization, but they have interesting histories as part of a complex of buildings that housed the City Dairy Company, which was owned by the Massey family, ambitious supporters of pasteurized milk production. The Massey's Dentonia Park Farm, established by Walter E. H. Massey in 1897 at the northeast edge of Toronto, was a model dairy farm that supplied raw milk to the City Dairy. The farm also produced poultry, eggs, and trout. George M. Miller, architect for the North and South Borden Buildings, designed numerous structures for the Dentonia Park Farm during 1907 and 1908, including the farmhouse, barns, workers' housing, and a water tower. The City Dairy was purchased by the Toronto division of the Borden Company around 1940.

The large North Borden Building contained production areas for butter and milk, cold storage, offices, and employee dressing rooms, while the South Borden

ABOVE: **North Borden Building**
OPPOSITE: **New College Residence**

Building was devoted to ice-cream making. Walking under the second-floor enclosed passageway that connects the two buildings, one discovers an outdoor service court, which, with its old brick walls on two sides and antiquated loading docks, still conveys a strong sense of history and place. The Borden Buildings now accommodate various university offices, divisions, and centers, including the visual studies department, and First Nations House, founded in 1992. The First Nations House has a birch bark canoe suspended from the ceiling. Made by students in the twelfth grade at Pelican Falls First Nations High School in Sioux Lookout, Ontario, the canoe (*wiigwaas chiimaan*) was donated to First Nations House in 2005 to honor Anishinaabe students who have gone on to higher education.

Unfortunately, the pair of curved, red-brick buildings has suffered some mindless renovations over the years, including the infill of two bays of the once lovely five-bay front porch of the North Borden Building. Nevertheless, the buildings still convey a sense of architectural grandeur. Note the upper portion of the North Borden Building with its two-story engaged brick columns and the wonderful egg-and-dart moldings on the South Borden Building. Seen today, the Borden Buildings are noteworthy from an urban standpoint. Their stage set–like front facades help shape the northeast portion of Spadina Crescent, the large circle in the center of Spadina Avenue. These scenographic buildings deserve to play an even stronger role in the campus and city's appearance and should be imaginatively rethought and rehabilitated.

101 John H. Daniels Building (Faculty of Architecture, Landscape, and Design), One Spadina Crescent

Smith & Gemmell, 1875
Renovation and addition
NADAAA with Adamson Associates Architects and ERA Architects, 2017

Among the places that clearly stand out in the 1878 color lithograph *Bird's-Eye View of Toronto* is the Presbyterian Theological School of Knox College, not only because it was a city landmark at the time, but also because it commands a unique circular piece of land right in the center of Spadina Avenue. (See *Bird's-Eye View of Toronto*, Introduction, page 11.) Now this distinctive building, along with a new addition to the north, is, fittingly, the home of the John H. Daniels Faculty of Architecture, Landscape, and Design. In 1890 the University of Toronto established the first architecture program in Canada, and now, with nearly 1,350 students, the Daniels Faculty is Canada's largest school for the integrated study of architecture, landscape architecture, urban design, and visual studies. The faculty also includes the Global Cities Institute, a research hub connecting students and researchers in engineering, political science, and social work with those in the Daniels Faculty.

This now revitalized island of creativity was first shaped by Dr. William Warren Baldwin in the nineteenth century as part of his vision for the wide avenue, which extended from his Spadina estate on a hill to the north, down to Queen Street at the south. Baldwin imagined the circle becoming a fine English garden, but the Presbyterians acquired the land and in 1875 constructed a building with a grand central tower, commanding the avenue. (See Introduction, page 15.) In 1915 Knox College moved to King's College Circle, and its former building became the Spadina Military Hospital for World War One veterans. It was sold to Connaught Laboratories in 1943, and the university purchased it in 1972. Over the next forty-five years, One Spadina Crescent hosted many users, including the Department of Ophthalmology, the Eye Bank of Canada, the Department of Anthropology, and the visual studies program.

The unique site and the prominence of the building attracted numerous development proposals over the years, some quite grandiose. At the end of the 1920s, when the Toronto Maple Leafs' owner Conn Smythe was deciding where to construct a new arena for his team, he and a group of businessmen proposed to tear down the existing building at Spadina Crescent and erect a sixteen-thousand-seat circular hockey arena, architecturally similar to the Olympic Arena in Detroit. But this grand notion did not fly, and in 1931 the Maple Leafs built their new home on Carleton Street instead. In 2007 a master plan was launched imagining One Spadina Crescent as the new home for art history and visual studies, but this vision never materialized. Another decade passed before the historically designated building from the Victorian era would finally be reborn as the new home of the John H. Daniels Faculty of Architecture, Landscape, and Design, named in recognition of the benefaction to the faculty by John H. Daniels and Myrna Daniels. Designed by the prominent

John H. Daniels Building, view from north

ABOVE: John H. Daniels Building, view from northeast
PREVIOUS: John H. Daniels Building, graduate studio

architects Nader Tehrani and Katherine Faulkner of Boston-based NADAA, the
faculty's impressive new home opened in 2017 and the surrounding landscape was
completed in 2018. The project has garnered numerous awards, including, in 2018,
a Best of Year Award from *Interior Design* and a Design Award from the American
Institute of Architects, New York Chapter.

Composed of the restored, historic building facing south and a large addition
to the north, the building has more than 120,000 square feet (11,230 square meters),
accommodating design studios, faculty offices, the Model Cities Theatre and
Laboratory, a four-hundred-seat multiuse hall, digital fabrication laboratories, an
architecture and design gallery, and the beautiful Eberhard Zeidler Library. An
interior, zigzag "street"—the Commons—runs east to west through the new addition
and includes a café. The grand, light-filled studio space for master's degree
students, facing north, is no less than spectacular.

Adding to the symmetrical, neo-Gothic structure, with its fanciful dormers,
towers, and turrets, presented a considerable challenge architecturally. The folded
walls, sloping roofs, and cheeky canopies of the north addition successfully recall
the geometries of the historic building, while the new north face—a bold, pleasantly
proportioned, Mies-inspired curtain wall of black steel and fritted glass—presents
an entirely modern face to the city. A new landscape of intriguing wavy mounds,
along with the south-facing Paul Oberman Belvedere, adds further drama to the
architectural ensemble.

Surrounded by a flow of automobiles and streetcars, the circular, island-like
site is tricky for pedestrians to access; inside, orientation and wayfinding can
be challenging for visitors. But these are minor concerns compared with the big

John H. Daniels Building, Eberhard Zeidler Library (TOP) and ground-floor corridor (BOTTOM)

picture—the imaginative revitalization of one of Toronto's most important landmarks, now a whirlwind of creativity and innovation.

In his book *The University of Toronto: A History*, Martin Friedland notes that, as part of the university's 1957 report proposing major westward expansion of the St. George campus, the authors of the report stated that "architecture should get a new building." Sixty years would pass before that finally happened.

The Northwest Campus

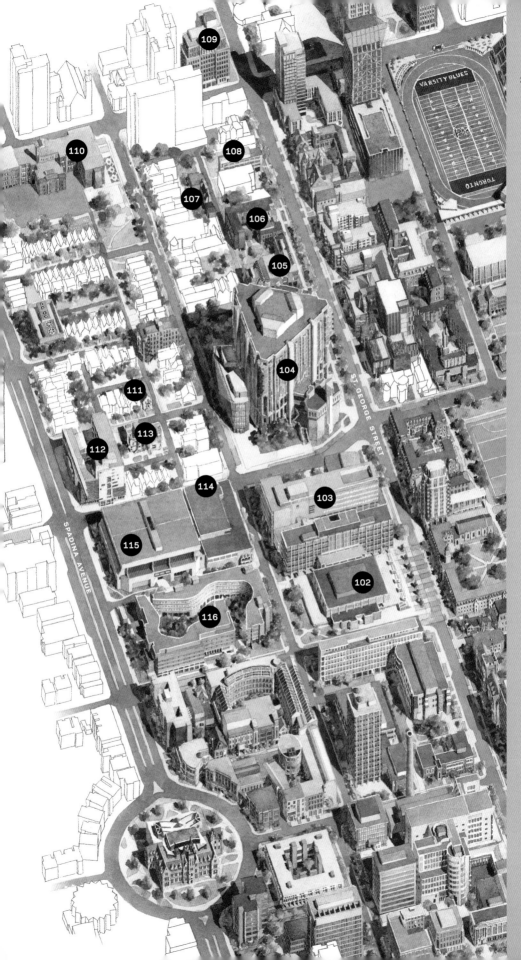

The Northwest Campus

About a third of the University of Toronto's northwest campus consists of shady, quiet streets lined with Victorian houses from the late nineteenth and early twentieth centuries, many of which are owned by the university and used for academic purposes or rented to students or faculty. This pocket of tranquility has largely survived despite aggressive growth in the mid-twentieth century, when both the university and the city had grandiose plans for the area.

In the 1950s and 1960s, the university did demolish entire residential blocks through eminent domain to allow the construction of huge projects, such as Sidney Smith Hall and the John P. Robarts Research Library on the northwest campus. In the mid-1960s, the city announced plans for the north–south Spadina Expressway, which was to extend down Spadina Road and Spadina Avenue, making a noisy wall of speeding traffic along the university's western edge. Following grassroots protests led by Jane Jacobs, the famous planning critic who had recently moved from New York to Toronto—and supported by civic leaders, downtown residents, and academics, such as Marshall McLuhan—further construction of the Spadina Expressway south of Eglinton Avenue was stopped in the summer of 1971. Walking along Spadina Avenue today, one can still see traces of reactions to the once impending expressway: some of the university's buildings from the 1960s, such as New College, turned their backs to the street as a defense against it.

Sidney Smith Hall

In recent years, the university has further densified the northwest campus with projects such as Graduate House, the Early Learning Centre, the School of Continuing Studies, the Department of Economics, and Robarts Common. In 2014, working closely with the Huron-Sussex Residents Organization, the urban design firm BrookMcIlroy and the University of Toronto completed the Huron-Sussex Neighbourhood Planning Study. The study provides a framework for enhancement and development of the area and foresees midrise intensification along Spadina Avenue and Harbord Street and low-rise infill housing within the community, fronting on active laneways, including the proposed Living Lane pathway that will extend from Washington Street. The collective vision, incorporating existing buildings and new construction, promises to preserve the northwest campus as the special, peaceful enclave that it has been for more than a century.

102 Sidney Smith Hall

John B. Parkin Associates, 1961

South addition

Beinhaker/Irwin Associates, mid-1980s

Infill and renovation

Ian MacDonald Architect, Inc., 2002 and 2004

In 1956 the University of Toronto's Plateau Committee, set up by President Sidney Smith, set out to double the university's enrollment, from twelve thousand to twenty-four thousand students. Soon after, a 1957 master planning committee proposed that "a centrally located arts building should be built on the west side of St. George Street" as part of the university's new west campus, leading to the construction of Sidney Smith Hall, named for the university's sixth president, who later became Canada's secretary of state for external affairs. The hall, known as Sid Smith, houses the Faculty of Arts and Science, which has more than twenty-five thousand students, making it the largest academic division in the university.

Opened in 1961, the building was uncompromisingly modern, consisting of a long, six-story slab with large windows; a floating, solid-looking volume extending southward from the slab structure; and two expansive concrete terraces to the east and west. Following the dictates of the west campus master plan, these elements were set on a plinth to provide a basement service level with some natural lighting. The building—whose steel-and-concrete structure was clad in stone, precast concrete, and brick—was a mid-twentieth-century essay on the flow of space and light. None of this seems radical now, but at the time Sid Smith was a trailblazer at the university, since the only other overtly modernist buildings on campus were the Mechanical Engineering Building (1948 addition), the Central Steam Plant (1952), the Women's Athletic Building (1959), and the Superintendent's Building (1959).

Sid Smith has been added to, renovated, and infilled over the years, forfeiting its stylistic purity but at the same time reducing the building's aloofness. With the addition of broad steps, the elevated terraces are now visually and socially integrated with the public sidewalks. Clad in corrugated stainless steel, thoughtful infill projects by Ian MacDonald Architect in 2002 and 2004 brought metallic sparkle to the building in the form of light-filled student lounges and meeting spaces.

103 Ramsay Wright Zoological Laboratories
Marani Morris & Allan, 1965
Centre for Biological Timing and Cognition
Stantec Inc., 2007

The Department of Zoology grew out of the Department of Biology and was established in 1916 by Robert Ramsay Wright, a noted biologist and the university's first vice president. The building named to honor him, known simply as Ramsay Wright, is one of the largest on the northwest campus, but its architecture is

Ramsay Wright Zoological Laboratories

unremarkable. With the exception of its confidently expressed stair towers, every-thing about it is so architecturally neutral that one can pass the building day after day and easily ignore it. Its primary, T-shaped volume runs east–west from St. George Street to Huron Street, with the north side and main lobby facing a lawn that runs along Harbord Street. An awkwardly shaped pavilion, linked to the main building and containing lecture halls and offices, is situated at the key intersection of Harbord and St. George Streets.

The 1965 complex is happily complemented by the silvery-green Centre for Biological Timing and Cognition addition at Ramsay Wright's southwest corner and by a zoomorphic silhouette of a moose. Titled *Mooseconstrue*, the steel sculpture was installed in 2001 on a grassy hill at the building's northeast corner by artist Charles Pachter. It is the positive, solid form leftover from the cutout negative-space moose sculpture Pachter made for the courtyard at nearby Graduate House.

104 John P. Robarts Research Library, Thomas Fisher Rare Book Library, and the Claude T. Bissell Building (Faculty of Information)

Warner, Burns, Toan & Lunde (design consultants) with Mathers & Haldenby (architects), 1971–73

Master plan for renewal and expansion

Diamond + Schmitt Architects, 2008

Portico enclosure

Diamond Schmitt Architects, 2010

Robarts Common

Diamond Schmitt Architects, expected completion 2019

The John P. Robarts Research Library (Robarts) complex presents itself as a modern monument, rising above and peering over the campus. As the institution's "treasury of knowledge," it has an unambiguous architectural authority appropriate to its role.

The Robarts holds 4.7 million books, making it the largest academic library in Canada. It is the main humanities and social sciences library of the University of Toronto Libraries system, which has forty-four libraries. The history of Robarts goes back to February 1962, when the university launched plans to add to its existing library, constructed in 1892 on King's College Circle. Architects Mathers & Haldenby produced preliminary sketches for an extension eastward and a square, seven-story tower to replace the much older portions of the library. Their proposal went no further, however, due to cost, space, and time issues. Instead, then pres-ident Claude Bissell persuaded the Ontario Ministry of University Affairs to make available a new, much larger site: an entire city block bounded by St. George Street, Sussex Avenue, Huron Street, and Harbord Street. President Bissell decided the new library would be the university's showstopping Canadian centennial project for 1967—even if it meant clearing the block of houses by eminent domain. A library school was added to the site's program, and in March 1964, Mathers & Haldenby presented a feasibility study for the new site "in the form of a six-storey rectangle running parallel to St. George Street, set on a broad podium." (It is little known that just one month later, John Andrews, the architect and University of Toronto professor who had designed Scarborough College, put forward a design for the library formed like a large amphitheater. Although not carried forward, Andrews's unorthodox proposal did propel President Bissell and the newly formed Library Committee in more exciting directions.)

In 1966 the Library Committee, led by chief librarian Robert H. Blackburn, went on a tour of six libraries in the United States, two of which were designed by the New York firm of Warner, Burns, Toan & Lunde (WBTL), which led to the university's decision to commission WBTL in association with Mathers & Haldenby. From the five different designs generated by WBTL, a scheme based on triangular geometry was chosen, both because it could provide a window in each of the one thousand study carrel rooms the program called for and because President Bissell wanted something bold and exciting.

Constructed of poured-in-place and precast concrete, the central Robarts rises fourteen stories, flanked by two lower volumes: the Fisher Rare Book Library at the southeast and the Faculty of Information Studies (now the Faculty of Information) at the northeast. (See Introduction, page 39.) A third, future volume was imagined at the west. The gray concrete exterior contrasts with warmer finishes inside, including African mahogany from Ghana. The use of wood is especially effective in the soaring central space of the rare book facility, which, in its moody darkness, is one of the most astonishing spaces on campus. The building's triangulated geometry is sometimes frustrating: climbing the strangely angular main entrance steps is a chore. But at other times, moving up through the library—through hexagonal and octagonal spaces and, finally, to rooms in the pointed prows that jut from the upper levels—is genuinely exhilarating.

When it opened in the early 1970s, the library complex was met with great hostility by some—it was even likened to George Orwell's Ministry of Truth as described in his book *Nineteen Eighty-Four*. Architect Ron Thom, designer of nearby Massey College, called it an "illustrated dictionary of architectural miseries," and scathing reviews continued to appear. What can be deduced from this storm of provocation? Why did the John P. Robarts Research Library spawn so much virulence? Perhaps its monumentality and slightly spooky "otherness" were the causes. It stands alone, proud, and aloof, serving as a harsh reminder of our miniscule place in the grand scheme of things—something we would generally prefer to forget.

Some of the aloofness will surely dissipate with the opening of Robarts Common, a new, five-story wing under construction to the west that, by comparison with the original 1971–73 structure, will feel softer and friendlier. The new pavilion by Diamond Schmitt Architects, providing 1,200 study spaces, will hover on piers above an existing service area. (The original master plan for Robarts, from the late 1960s, called for a four-hundred-seat auditorium in this location.) Although the design will not replicate the triangulated geometry nor the pervasive exposed concrete of the original structure, the new wing makes subtle overtures to it.

John P. Robarts Research Library

Innis College

105 Innis College

A. J. (Jack) Diamond & Barton Myers, 1975

Founded in 1964, Innis College, which offers a multidisciplinary program, is named for Harold Innis, who was a prominent University of Toronto political economist. With around 1,650 students, Innis is a small community, and its main building, finished in 1975, is similarly scaled. The structure is an early example of architect A. J. Diamond's expertise with renovation, urban infill, and the creation of courtyard spaces, evident in university projects such as his firm's Bahen Centre for Information Technology and Earth Sciences Centre.

Innis College consists of a renovated Victorian house and a series of linked orange-brick-clad additions that match the rhythm and scale of the nineteenth-century streetscapes along Sussex Avenue and St. George Street. These house-like volumes are interrupted by entrance areas with fully glazed roofs, making Innis College one of the brightest and most cheerful interior environments on campus. On the north and west sides, the building opens to a pleasant outdoor courtyard, now further enhanced by the adjoining courtyard of Max Gluskin House. The heart of Innis College is the town hall, a well-proportioned room that serves as a forum and also functions as a fully equipped cinema. In 1994 the college added a residence hall for its students directly across St. George Street.

Fisher Rare Book Library

106 Max Gluskin House (Department of Economics)
Hariri Pontarini Architects, 2008

150 St. George Street
Architect unknown, 1889

South wing
Allward & Gouinlock Architects, 1960

Home of the Department of Economics, Max Gluskin House efficiently links two restored historic buildings facing St. George Street with a new L-shaped wing along the north and west edges of the site. This complex, designed by Hariri Pontarini Architects, focuses on a sunny, south-facing courtyard. The old-plus-new strategy, and the resulting sophistication and warmth of the architecture, are reminiscent of Woodsworth College directly across the street, which architect Siamak Hariri was also involved with.

The oldest part of Max Gluskin House is the Victorian home built in 1889 for William Crowther, a partner in the firm of wholesale grocers Sloan & Crowther.

Max Gluskin House

In 1927 the house and a coach house at the rear were acquired by the China Inland Mission, an international organization formed to spread Christianity throughout China. The organization added a structure at the back of the house and connected it on the second floor to the coach house, allowing a driveway to pass underneath. The Canadian Medical Association purchased the site in 1955 and in 1960 completed a flat-roofed, Georgian Revival wing to the south. The complex was taken over by the university in the 1960s to house its Centre for Urban and Community Studies and, later, the Institute for Policy Analysis, before the Department of Economics moved into the building in 1982.

In composing the new Max Gluskin House complex on the constrained site, Hariri Pontarini Architects first performed some creative erasure, demolishing the coach house and eliminating the driveway. The two northern bays of the 1960s addition were torn down, opening up breathing room and providing transparency between the Victorian and Georgian Revival pieces. Now the St. George Street facade has a pleasing rhythm of old-new-old-new. Also noteworthy are the robust corten weathering-steel panels on the courtyard facades and the rugged brickwork on the wing along the western edge of the site, where Max Gluskin House meets bpNichol Lane.

107 Coach House Books

Architect unknown, circa 1890

The Coach House Books publishing house was founded in 1965 by Stan Bevington and, since 1968, has occupied a series of old coach houses on bpNichol Lane, named in honor of the Canadian poet Barrie Phillip Nichol (known as bpNichol). Coach House Books produces innovative and experimental books with small print runs that larger publishers would not take on, and it has published works by such illustrious figures as Margaret Atwood, bpNichol, Allen Ginsberg, and Michael Ondaatje. An eight-line poem by bpNichol is carved into the concrete lane alongside Coach House Books' offices, reading,

A
LAKE
A
LANE
A
LINE
A
LONE

Coach House Books

Although Coach House Books is not part of the university, this tiny place is such a literary landmark and so much a part of the northwest campus community that it would be wrong not to include it here. In 2008 the publisher won the Premier's Award for Excellence in the Arts, administered by the Ontario Arts Council.

108   School of Continuing Studies

Robert M. Saunders, 1958
Renovation and addition
Moriyama & Teshima Architects, 2004

In the 1970s the university transformed its former Department of Extension into the School of Continuing Studies. The school grew rapidly and now offers hundreds of courses and certificate programs to more than fifteen thousand people annually. To accommodate the expanding program, a preexisting modern office building, which was originally the St. George Medical Centre, was completely overhauled by Moriyama & Teshima Architects. They added a two-story, glass-enclosed lounge at the front to welcome people and connect with the community. This cubic room has a trellised sunshade wrapping around the east facade and the southeast corner, where it intersects a freestanding wall of stone. The most intriguing space in the renovated building is the double-height lounge-seminar room at its west end, where three unusual slit windows provide subdued natural light: a low horizontal one overlooks a tiny garden; a vertical one looks to nearby buildings; and a north-facing horizontal window opens to the sky.

109   Jackman Humanities Building

Marani, Lawson & Paisley, 1929
Jackman Humanities Institute
Kohn Shnier Architects, 2008

The university purchased this building in 2002 for use as teaching, research, and office space, and recently named it in honor of Hal Jackman, the twenty-fifth lieutenant governor of Ontario and former chancellor of the university. The ten-story

School of Continuing Studies

Jackman Humanities Building

structure, designed by architects Marani, Lawson & Paisley in 1929, combines Georgian and moderne influences in a stepped form reminiscent of Manhattan skyscrapers of the era.

Although the Jackman Humanities Building seen from Bloor and St. George Streets appears to be a huge, four-square block, it is actually L-shaped. Its more visible east and west sides are dressed in Indiana limestone and fully decorated, while the rest of the exterior is more plain looking. The main lobby off St. George Street is decked out in bronze and verde antique marble and embellished with fancy lighting fixtures. Practicality was also important to the architects, who incorporated state-of-the-art Otis-Fensom elevators, telephone systems, laundry chutes, and compressed air distribution systems into the design.

Kohn Shnier Architects transformed the tenth-floor penthouse into the Jackman Humanities Institute in 2008. The penthouse, along with the suave 1929 lobby, are the showpiece spaces in the building. The institute will bring together scholars from all the humanities branches, including architecture, fine arts, philosophy, and literature.

110 371 Bloor Street West

Darling & Pearson, 1910

Auditorium and east wing

Darling & Pearson, 1924

First west wing

Darling & Pearson, 1931

Second west wing

Marani & Morris, 1949

Spadina wing

Marani & Morris, 1958

Spadina wing renovations

DuBois Plumb Partnership, 1999

East addition

Diamond Schmitt Architects, 2017–ongoing

University of Toronto Schools (UTS) is the major tenant in this historic building owned by the university. UTS was launched in the early twentieth century as a one-thousand-pupil model school with two hundred teachers. It was to serve primary and secondary students and would include a technical school. When funding was not available for this ambitious plan, the technical school and lower primary grades were eliminated, and enrollment was limited to boys. (Girls were eventually admitted, starting in 1973.) Although the original grand vision was never implemented, UTS expanded numerous times over its hundred-year history. The school had a glorious start, followed by a gradual diminishment of spatial and material aspirations. Between 1910 and 1958, its architecture went from being inspiring to merely functional.

371 Bloor Street West, atrium (LEFT) and public space linking 371 Bloor Street West to Huron-Washington Parkette (architectural renderings)

371 Bloor Street West

The original, bilaterally symmetrical building, designed by Darling & Pearson and facing Bloor Street West, mirrored the ideals of the Faculty of Education, which set out in 1910 to establish a model environment for practice teaching. The building was (and still is) dignified, proud, and robust. The very first issue of the *UTS Monthly*, from February 1920, has a perspective drawing of the Georgian Revival brick building on the cover, revealing its architectural and institutional authority.

Over the years, 371 Bloor evolved into an E-shaped structure with a fine eight-hundred-seat auditorium at its center. Directly above is the library, whose furnishings and character have changed little since 1910. Equally interesting is the tiny gymnasium on the first floor, stacked above a ground-floor swimming pool, both part of the 1924 addition.

By the time wings were added in 1949 and 1958, Darling & Pearson were no longer involved, architectural ambitions had been ratcheted down considerably, and no-frills functionality prevailed. However, in 1999 the second and third floors of the west wing were renovated by DuBois Plumb Partnership, who provided handsome quarters for the university's Department of Sociology, signaling a reaffirmation of the original commitment to quality architecture established at 371 Bloor a century ago.

The university recently renewed its affiliation agreement with UTS and launched an ambitious master plan for renewal and expansion that will bridge the school's heritage and twenty-first-century aspirations. A new wing, linked to the existing building with an atrium, will be added at the southeast and will contain a seven-hundred-seat auditorium and double gymnasium. The design by Donald Schmitt, an alumnus of both UTS and U of T, also features a new link to the Huron-Washington Parkette, underscoring the desire for reciprocity between UTS, the university, and the community.

111 Studio Theatre

Maurice Klein, 1914

Renovations

Maurice Klein, late 1960s

This former church houses the Graduate Centre for the Study of Drama and includes a one-hundred-seat black box theater. Originally St. Paul's Lutheran English Church, the building was designed by architect Maurice Klein, who was just seventeen

Studio Theatre

years old when he signed the building permit for the church in 1913. From the 1930s to the 1960s, the church served a Russian Orthodox congregation. Following deconsecration in 1966, it was sold to the university.

Tyrone Guthrie, first artistic director at the Stratford Shakespearean Festival of Canada in Stratford, Ontario, and founder of the Guthrie Theater in Minneapolis, Minnesota, was subsequently invited to the university to comment on the possibility of making the former church into a theater. The idea gained momentum and, following renovations, the Studio Theatre opened on October 16, 1968.

112 Graduate House

Morphosis / Teeple Architects, Inc. (joint venture), 2000

In the 1990s the University of Toronto decided to significantly expand residential space for students on the St. George campus, given both the high cost of renting an apartment in downtown Toronto and the desire of the University of Toronto to create a stronger sense of community. Graduate House was the first building planned under that initiative, on a constricted site bounded by Harbord Street, Spadina Avenue, and Glen Morris Street. The city imposed height restrictions and also required a publicly accessible courtyard. The university and the School of Graduate Studies further increased expectations by calling for a student-oriented café at the new building's southwest corner and asking that it act as a "gateway" into the campus from the west.

An international competition open to invitees in 1998 was won by Los Angeles–based architecture firm Morphosis in a joint venture with Toronto's Teeple Architects. Their aggressively deconstructivist design generated immediate controversy, especially the proposed monumental gateway cantilever over Harbord Street, which Thom Mayne of Morphosis referred to as a "Pop-scale, two-story cornice." The cantilever's "borrowing" of public space over the sidewalk and street was what caused the biggest row, but the city strongly supported the project. Graduate House opened in 2000, and architecture critic Christopher Hume christened it Toronto's "first architectural landmark of the twenty-first century."

The dramatic building consists of efficient urban blocks composed around a central courtyard and reflecting pool, the latter graced by a humorous corten weathering-steel moose sculpture by artist Charles Pachter. Graduate House is clad in charcoal-colored precast concrete with a perforated aluminum skin draped over the north and east facades. A skew in the south block generates positive agitation and practically delaminates the facade into overlapping planes of texture. The tight packing of the structure accommodates over 420 graduate students in 120 apartment-type suites. Two-story units in the east wing are interlocked in section, similar to Le Corbusier's Unité d'Habitation (1946–52) in Marseille, France. The utopian approaches to housing that infiltrate this project seem to flow from a broad range of early twentieth-century sources, including that of the Russian avant-garde. For example, Graduate House shares a certain kinship with the Narkomfin

OVERLEAF: Graduate House

building (1928–29) in Moscow by Moisei Ginzburg, an icon of the early twentieth century, embodying progressive housing ideas. But it is the dramatically canti-levered tectonic element hovering over Harbord Street—simultaneously cornice, corridor, lounge, gateway, and sign—that gives the building its signature status. Here, "University of Toronto" is spelled out in giant ceramic-frit lettering on glass. (The final sculptural *O* is made of steel.)

Graduate House is a strong forerunner of later Morphosis-designed build-ings, such as the Caltrans District 7 Headquarters building (2004) in Los Angeles and the Albert Nerken School of Engineering (2009) at Cooper Union in New York, where overlapping planes and skins give the building an ethereal character. Graduate House went on to win design awards from the magazines *Canadian Architect* and *Progressive Architecture*, and from the Los Angeles Chapter of the American Institute of Architects. In 2005 Mayne won the prestigious Pritzker Architecture Prize.

Early Learning Centre

113 Early Learning Centre

Teeple Architects, Inc., 2003

Silvery and sculptural, this day care facility for one hundred children is a little gem. It primarily accommodates the children of University of Toronto faculty, staff, and students, from infants to junior kindergarten age. The center's three levels of integrated indoor-outdoor learning and playing areas are organized around a dramatic ramp that extends from the east-side car arrival and drop-off area to the second floor. Vertical slots thread through the structure, bringing natural light deep into the building and generating exaggerated views from one level to another. The experience of moving through the building is like climbing in a giant, fantastic tree house.

114 Clara Benson Building

Fleury, Arthur & Barclay, 1959

Clara Benson Building

The Clara Benson Building, originally known as the Women's Athletic Building, is part of the group of mid-twentieth-century buildings known locally as Toronto Modern. Indeed, its embrace of modernism was radical for Toronto in 1959. Built tight to the surrounding sidewalks, it had a surprising urbanity at a time when the university seemed to think of the new west campus with a suburban mentality.

Clad in brown bricks that range in color, the building's structural frame is periodically exposed, faced in tiny white and beige-gold ceramic tiles. Its structure is easily legible at the top of the long east elevation, and a varied pattern of fenestration suggests the functional layout of the athletic facilities within. At the southeast corner are projecting balconies, the south-facing one enlivened by a three-bay scalloped concrete canopy.

Clara Benson, the building's namesake, was a powerhouse at the University of Toronto for fifty years. She received a doctorate degree in chemistry from the university in 1903 (one of the first two women in Toronto to be awarded one), and from 1926 to 1945 was head of the Department of Food Chemistry in the Lillian Massey Department of Household Science. During World War Two, she set up a course that taught women in munitions factories how to measure the chemical properties of explosives. The Clara Benson Building was named to recognize her efforts to obtain better athletic facilities for female students. In 1998 it was linked to and integrated with the Warren Stevens Building to the west to create a larger, more flexible athletic center.

115 Warren Stevens Building

Prack & Prack (later Norman Dobell Associates Architects), 1979
Renovations
Oleson Worland Architects, 1998

The Warren Stevens Building embodies
the definition of *athletic*: it seems
physically powerful, large, and muscular
in build. In fact, no other building on
the St. George campus has the sheer
sense of mass displayed by this building.
Proudly exposing its reinforced-
concrete structure, this monolithic hulk
has plenty of architectural presence,
its seriousness only contested by the
smiles formed by the rounded corners

Warren Stevens Building

of its red steel window frames. To accommodate the enormous clear-span spaces
necessary for a fifty-meter Olympic-size pool and a five-lane, two-hundred-meter
indoor running track (the largest in Ontario), the building has a superstructure of four
huge steel trusses, each twenty-two feet (6.7 meters) deep, that carry loads to
the corners of the building, where concrete piers transfer them to deep foundations.

The Warren Stevens Building is a modernist machine, supporting athletic,
fitness, and recreational activities. However, its internalized nature causes it to
ignore the surrounding streets, particularly busy Spadina Avenue. The addition of
a coffee shop and outdoor café facing Harbord Street softened the building's
north urban edge.

116 New College

North building (New College I / Wetmore Hall)
Fairfield & DuBois, 1964
South building (New College II / Wilson Hall)
Fairfield & DuBois, 1969
Addition and renovation
Dunker Associates, 1999

Founded in 1962, New College comprises three structures: a pair of flowing,
spatially interlocking buildings from the 1960s designed by Macy DuBois of Fairfield
& DuBois, and a residence hall completed in 2003. (See Walk Five, pages 197–99.)
The two older buildings are indebted to the architect Alvar Aalto, who influenced
DuBois. The imaginative, thoughtfully designed complex immediately recalls Aalto's
masterful, curvilinear Baker House Dormitory (1948) at MIT. There are subtle
differences between the north and south buildings, which were finished five years
apart. The north building, Wetmore Hall, has rectangular columns and features a

series of concrete fins along the upper ribbon windows; it seems less refined than the later south building, Wilson Hall. This structure has round columns, no upper concrete fins, and metal-slat ceilings in its main public areas. Both buildings use robust materials—brick, slate, and wood—and have lovely period lighting fixtures, including the huge orange cylindrical lights in the D. G. Ivey Library in Wilson Hall.

DuBois gave the buildings logical, rectilinear facades along their street- and sidewalk-facing edges, contrasting these hard sides with soft, flowing facades facing inward, creating an interior S-shaped courtyard. This pair of buildings and their shared courtyard remind us of the talent of DuBois, who deserves elevation as one of Canada's finest twentieth-century architects.

In 2017 new landscaping was added along Willcocks Street, tying New College more closely to the evolving Willcocks Common pedestrian spine.

New College, Wilson Hall

The Medical and Health Sciences Precinct

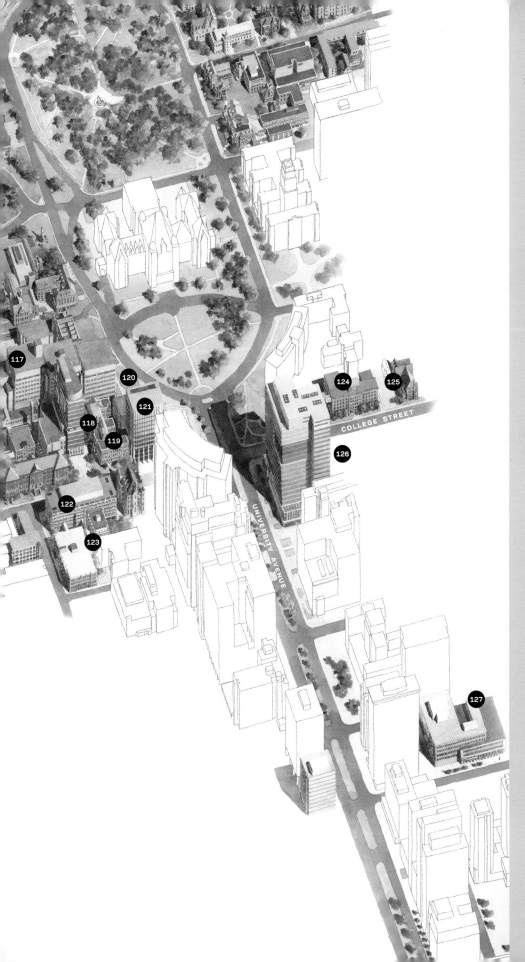

The Medical and Health Sciences Precinct

The University of Toronto's faculties of medicine, nursing, dentistry, and pharmacy are within a fifteen-minute walk of one another, threaded in and around an area at the southeast corner of the downtown campus known as Toronto's Discovery District. This neighborhood is bordered by Bloor Street, Dundas Street, Bay Street, and Spadina Avenue and includes University Avenue, which is lined with major hospitals. The Discovery District is the locus of the city's expanding biomedical industry, symbolized by the dynamic MaRS Centre.

Unlike universities such as Northwestern and Harvard that operate teaching hospitals and have easily identified medical precincts, the University of Toronto does not own or run any hospitals. Furthermore, only a few of the hospitals and centers affiliated with the university's health sciences programs are geographically within the medical and health sciences precinct. Most are scattered throughout downtown Toronto, the suburbs, and outlying areas. While many of these buildings are architecturally engaging, it is beyond the scope of this guidebook to include individual entries on them. A list of affiliated hospitals and centers is included below for those readers who want to explore one of North America's largest health sciences constellations.

Hospitals and Centers Affiliated with the University of Toronto:

FULLY AFFILIATED HOSPITALS AND RESEARCH INSTITUTES

Baycrest Health Sciences

Holland Bloorview Kids Rehabilitation Hospital

Centre for Addiction and Mental Health

Hospital for Sick Children

Mount Sinai Hospital

St. Michael's Hospital

Sunnybrook Health Sciences Centre

University Health Network:

· Toronto General Hospital

· Princess Margaret Hospital

· Toronto Western Hospital

· Toronto Rehabilitation Institute

Women's College Hospital

COMMUNITY-AFFILIATED HOSPITALS AND SITES

Humber River Hospital

Lakeridge Health

Markham-Stouffville Hospital

Ontario Shores Centre for Mental Health Sciences

Providence Healthcare

Royal Victoria Regional Health Centre

The Scarborough Hospital

Southlake Regional Health Centre

Rouge Valley Health System

West Park Healthcare Centre

Waypoint Centre for Mental Health Care

William Osler Health System

Walkway between the Terrence Donnelly Centre for Cellular and Biomolecular Research (left) and the Fitzgerald Building (right)

Medical Sciences Building

117 Medical Sciences Building

Govan Kaminker Langley Keenleyside Melick Devonshire & Wilson with
Somerville McMurrich & Oxley, 1969

The seven-story Medical Sciences Building (Med Sci) houses the Faculty of
Medicine, founded in 1843. It is one of the largest, and strangest, buildings on
campus, with a "shaggy-dog" precast concrete cladding that serves as a reminder
of the hallucinatory, anything-goes late-1960s era it was built in.

Med Sci is composed of deep, solid blocks so that little natural light
reaches the center of the building, reinforcing its highly internalized nature. Mazelike
corridors with beige concrete-block walls make the interior seem like a cross
between a no-nonsense high school and a low-cost hospital. In contrast, the exterior
surfaces command attention. Project architect Peter Goering convinced the university to devote public art funds allocated for the building to the fabrication of an artful
facade. Serving simultaneously as a rain-screen system (technically innovative at
the time) and a grand sculpture project, the precast cladding's surface was designed
by multidisciplinary artist Robert Downing, who, in association with his former
sculpture professor, Ted Bieler, worked collaboratively with Beer Precast Concrete.
(In addition to his imaginative contribution to the building's surfaces, Downing
executed two interior relief walls, and Bieler contributed both the *Wave* [1971] ground
sculpture in the courtyard and the vertical *Helix of Life* [1971], which stands near
the main entrance.) Downing was interested in the intersection of modern technology and spirituality, and was also deeply focused on what he called "organic
geometry." By the time he died in 1997, he had become a noted and notorious (for his
early LSD-imbibing days) artist in Canada.

Med Sci's eccentrically ribbed coat lends it an air of surreality, made even more bizarre by the presence of a fine statue of Robert Raikes, founder of the Sunday School Movement in England in 1780, which stands at the building's northeast corner. On the north face of Med Sci, Downing's obsession with organic geometry comes into full bloom. Here, robust Virginia creeper vines grow up six stories through the sculpted concrete, and cold abstraction and thriving greenery intertwine.

In 2005 Behnisch, Behnisch & Partner linked the Medical Sciences Building southward to the new Terrence Donnelly Centre for Cellular and Biomolecular Research with an attractive cafeteria. The architects cleverly captured a panel of Downing and Bieler's sculpted wall and integrated it into the east wall of the addition. This element and the shaggy walls beyond now seem curiously contemporary, showing how architectural tastes and criticism often come full circle. Indeed, it is not surprising that today's digitally savvy architecture students are fascinated by the building's sculpted relief patterns, which, fifty years later, match their own preoccupations with complex surface manipulation.

118 Terrence Donnelly Centre for Cellular and Biomolecular Research (Donnelly CCBR)

architectsAlliance and Behnisch, Behnisch & Partner, 2005

The cutting-edge research that goes on within the Terrence Donnelly Centre for Cellular and Biomolecular Research is as progressive as its design. The Donnelly CCBR, with its open, flexible, loftlike spaces, encourages interaction between the four hundred researchers from the fields of medicine, pharmacy, applied science and engineering, and arts and science that work there. The idea for this interdisciplinary research facility came from Dr. James Friesen and Dr. Cecil Yip, professors and colleagues in the Faculty of Medicine. (A plaque recognizing their contribution to the project is affixed to one of the ovoid seminar rooms on the main level.) In the late 1990s Friesen and Yip collaborated with the university's Design Review Committee to launch an international search for an architect, resulting in the selection of the innovative Stuttgart-based firm Behnisch, Behnisch & Partner, working closely with the Toronto firm architectsAlliance. The center was named to recognize the generous financial support of retired lawyer and businessman Terrence Donnelly.

A constricted but interesting site became available for the Donnelly CCBR when the university decided to close down Taddle Creek Road, which in the nineteenth century ran northwest from College Street to University College, but in recent years only extended one block north of College Street. University planners and the architects decided to set the building 170 feet (50 meters) back from College Street, thus generating a south-facing forecourt. The center was integrated with the Medical Sciences Building to the north and with two heritage buildings flanking the site: the Rosebrugh Building to the west and the FitzGerald Building to the east. The east facade of the nearby Mining Building also added positively to the

Terrence Donnelly Centre for Cellular and Biomolecular Research, interior

emerging open space. Landscape architect Diana Gerrard composed the forecourt as a series of energetic, sloping diagonals, rendered elegantly in black granite, pink-gray granite, and stainless steel. A figurative sculpture titled *Spirit of Discovery* (2005), by Veronica and Edwin Dam de Nogales, stands in a grove of birch trees at the west side of the forecourt.

Rising from this sunny, well-used public space, the elongated, transparent, twelve-story Donnelly CCBR embraces sustainable design principles. The tower of repetitive laboratory zones (recessed at the seventh floor to accommodate mechanical equipment and to scale the building down) has a double-skin facade on the south to help reduce heat loss and provide wind and acoustical modulation. This laboratory volume sits atop a public concourse that steps up to and connects with the Medical Sciences Building. A winter garden grows between the Donnelly CCBR and the Rosebrugh Building, and it is complemented on upper levels of the tower with three south-facing interior sky gardens that adjoin faculty-student lounges. The building is particularly spectacular at night, when it is glowing in its colorful nakedness, and a sense of the synergistic scientific work on molecular genetics comes alive.

119 FitzGerald Building

Mathers & Haldenby, 1926

This red-brick building was constructed in the mid-1920s to house the School of Hygiene, which was dedicated to public health and preventive medicine. It was later named in honor of Dr. John Gerald FitzGerald, one of the fathers of the progressive provincial and federal health care programs that now exist in Canada. In recent years the FitzGerald Building contained various divisions of the Faculty of Medicine and Faculty of Dentistry. These divisions will be vacating in 2018, and the future of this building is envisaged as central administrative space for the university.

The FitzGerald Building originally faced Taddle Creek Road, later closed. Now, even in its somewhat demoted status in the shadows of the Donnelly CCBR and the Leslie L. Dan Pharmacy Building, it contributes significantly, along with the Mining and Rosebrugh Buildings, to the shaping of the Donnelly CCBR forecourt. Though stylistically different, these buildings form an ensemble that proves old and new can fit together successfully.

A mildly Georgian structure with an E-shaped footprint, the FitzGerald Building is typical of the low-key, conservative architecture of Mathers & Haldenby. Attractive stone carving, delicate glasswork, and bracketed lamps enliven the entrances. Inside, a fine lobby sports a marble floor, a handsome chandelier, and a wall inscription from the nineteenth-century English biologist and agnostic Thomas Henry Huxley, on the importance of a liberal education and a directive for individuals "to respect others as himself."

FitzGerald Building

C. David Naylor Building

120 C. David Naylor Building

Mathers & Haldenby, 1931

Formerly the Tanz Neuroscience Building, in 2015 this noble structure was named the C. David Naylor Building, honoring the university's fifteenth president. Dr. David Naylor, a distinguished scholar and medical innovator, served as president from 2005 to 2013. While designed by the same architects as the nearby FitzGerald Building, the C. David Naylor Building is more architecturally ambitious. Originally the university's Botany Building, it had elegant greenhouses extending from its south face. (Completed in 1932, they were designed by Mathers & Haldenby in association with Lord & Burnham, a company that specializes in greenhouse structures.) The greenhouses were removed during 2003 and 2004 to make way for the new Leslie L. Dan Pharmacy Building, and major portions were reconstructed in Allan Gardens, a public park twelve blocks to the east, where they now serve as the Children's Conservatory.)

The stone-clad Naylor Building is handsomely proportioned and, with its angled front elevation facing Queen's Park, polite in urban disposition. It is a curious architectural hybrid: while it is generally Georgian Revival in style, it also incorporates modern steel-casement windows. Inside, the building is humble, featuring a petite octagonal lobby faced in Tyndall Stone from Manitoba and a floor of inlaid marble.

The respect commanded by the Naylor Building is evident in Foster + Partners' concept for the Leslie L. Dan Pharmacy Building directly to the south. The firm admired the 1930s building and drew and extended southward an imagined horizontal line at the height of the Naylor Building's parapet, which determined the height of the Pharmacy Building's grand lobby's ceiling and became the starting point for the cubic volume of laboratories above. The two buildings now sit comfortably side by side, sharing a pleasant courtyard between them. The building currently houses various medical divisions, including the Tanz Centre for Research in Neurodegenerative Diseases, created through a gift in 1987 from land developer Mark Tanz and his family.

121 Leslie L. Dan Pharmacy Building

Foster + Partners with Moffat Kinoshita Architects, Inc. (later Cannon Design), 2006

By 2000 the Province of Ontario was facing a critical shortage of pharmacists. With this news, the University of Toronto's Faculty of Pharmacy set out to double its enrollment and expand its research agenda. Leslie L. Dan, a 1954 graduate of the school, made a significant gift for an ambitious new facility that was named

Leslie L. Dan Pharmacy Building

Leslie L. Dan Pharmacy Building, atrium

in his honor. Tailor-made seems an apt description for the building, because it both admirably fits its teaching agenda and has been crafted like a fine English suit by London-based Foster + Partners, the architects responsible for this restrained yet bold structure facing Queen's Park.

      Its prominent site, flanked on the north and west by historic buildings, already had a set of much-loved greenhouses dating from 1932 that presented challenging preservation issues. Technologically past their prime, the greenhouses were no longer useful to the university, and the most architecturally significant portions were relocated to the city's Allan Gardens.

      Even with the greenhouses gone, a very small site was left for the 167,000-square-foot (16,500-square-meter) Pharmacy Building. Lord Norman Foster and his team devised a simple, three-volume scheme that maximizes use of the available land by placing two large lecture halls in an underground volume and setting a laboratory/office "glass cube" on slender concrete columns atop a transparent five-story atrium. The architects cleverly aligned the bottom of the elevated, glass-clad cube with the cornices of the adjacent historic buildings. The Pharmacy Building's rationally knit-together spaces, profusion of natural light, and precise detailing create an impressive place.

Two wonderfully mysterious, ovoid forms float above a coffee shop and seating area in the grand lobby. These pods, which seem to defy gravity, were constructed as "steel baskets" and suspended by steel rods. They contain seminar rooms and have student and faculty lounges carved into their tops. At night, computer-programmed lighting bounces off the pods and the lobby's soaring glass walls, presenting a theatrical display for passersby.

The Pharmacy Building's generosity of scale and overall aesthetic clarity enable it to play a significant role at the junction of University Avenue and College Street. Its stately concrete columns and elegant, fritted-glass cladding relate well to the materials employed in the nineteen-story Ontario Power Building to the south. With the completion in 2013 of the twenty-story, glass-clad west tower of the MaRS Centre diagonally opposite, the Pharmacy Building participates in a distinctive, three-tower urban composition at this key Toronto intersection.

122 Health Sciences Building

Page & Steele Architects, 1961
Renovations
Stantec, 2006

A decade ago, with few sites available for new construction and open space becoming more desirable on the St. George campus, the University of Toronto began to acquire major buildings around its periphery for future teaching and research purposes. When the Education Centre at the southeast corner of College and McCaul Streets became available in 2003, the university purchased the 200,000-square-foot (18,580-square-meter) structure.

Renovated and renamed the Health Sciences Building, it now houses the Lawrence S. Bloomberg Faculty of Nursing and an array of departments from the Faculty of Medicine, including the Dalla Lana School of Public Health. The facility promotes collaboration with many of the university's affiliated teaching hospitals and research institutes.

Designed for the Toronto Board of Education by the prominent British-Canadian architect Peter Dickinson (while a partner at Toronto's Page & Steele Architects), the eight-story Education Centre was a strong example of midcentury modernism that provided a comfortable environment for innovative research and training in education. It would also be one of *Mad Men*–era Dickinson's last works. He died of cancer in 1961 at the age of thirty-five.

The building's concrete structure is clad in Indiana limestone and Deer Island gray granite from Georgia; the main entrance is surfaced in mirror-finished stainless steel; and the suave two-story foyer sports Loredo Chiaro marble walls

Health Sciences Building

and a travertine floor. But there is much more to celebrate here than the handsome 1960s material palette. The north and south facades, which, in their rhythmic fenestration patterns, are reminiscent of piano keyboards, richly engage light and shadow. A mechanical penthouse enclosed in translucent glass glides coolly above these sculpted faces. Glazed in metal sashes with fixed, cast-wire glass between precast concrete fins, the penthouse is among the most attractive in Toronto.

The original Education Centre included a number of distinctive interior murals created by Stefan Fritz and Merton Chambers, and a lovely exterior relief by Elizabeth Hahn—an ambitious program of art intended to express the ideals and prominence of the city's educational system. Fortunately, the university preserved these spirited works in the new spaces of the Health Sciences Building, along with the delightful auditorium designed by Dickinson.

123 263 McCaul Street
Charles H. Bishop, 1916

Auditorium and boardroom restoration and renovation
Robyn Huether Architect, 2017

Among the university's hidden architectural gems is the original Toronto Board of Education Administration Building, a grand Beaux-Arts edifice designed by Charles

H. Bishop, who served as architect for the Toronto Board of Education from 1888 until 1919 and is credited with the design of more than fifty schools in the Toronto area, many of which still stand today.

The Toronto Board of Education Administration Building in its original location on the south side of College Street, October 20, 1957

The building fronted on College Street until 1959, when it was moved south to make way for the new Education Centre. Now the century-old Toronto Board of Education's building is a kind of lonely island—hard to find and difficult to access—and its original grand entrance sits high above a service ramp, absent its front steps. The building's old address plate, "155," still hangs next to the front door. Above the original entrance, a magnificent porch and window composition is marked by Ionic columns.

Today, 263 McCaul Street houses various divisions of the Faculty of Medicine, such as the Life Course and Aging Institute, and Health and Well-being Programs and Services. In 2017 the Faculty of Medicine admirably restored the former Toronto Board of Education's auditorium, a handsome century-old space that now serves as a classroom.

124 Banting and Best Site

Banting Institute

Darling & Pearson, 1930

Best Institute

Mathers & Haldenby, 1954

Master Plan for Development

Weiss/Manfredi Architects with Teeple Architects, Inc., 2018

Known as Banting and Best, these two unremarkable red-brick buildings will soon be razed to enable phased development of the properties making up 92–112 College Street. Phase One proposes an approximately thirteen-story tower for research at the west, where the Best Institute now stands. Later phases will include a twenty-one-story tower on the Banting Institute site to the east. The university intends to create new and vibrant research facilities, significantly expanding the medical and health sciences precinct.

The existing buildings are named in recognition of the two individuals who discovered insulin. The Banting Institute, which housed various medical departments until 2008, is named for Sir Frederick Banting, the Nobel Prize–winning Toronto surgeon and scientist who successfully developed insulin with Dr. Charles H. Best in the laboratory of Dr. John James Rickard Macleod between 1920 and 1922.

(The 1923 Nobel Prize in Physiology or Medicine was shared between Banting and Macleod.) Considering that the building was designed by the famed Toronto firm Darling & Pearson, its architecture seems rather matter-of-fact. This could be because the firm's leading light, Frank Darling, died in 1923, and architects with less talent took over. Whatever the reasons for its underdeveloped design, the building served a broad range of university uses from 2008 to 2018.

Directly west of the Banting Institute sits the Best Institute, an appropriate pairing, considering that the building's namesake is Dr. Charles H. Best, who worked together with Sir Frederick Banting to develop insulin in the 1920s. Architects Mathers & Haldenby oriented the Best Institute's principal symmetrical facade westward, toward the grand mall of Queen's Park. A portrait of Best by the noted artist Cleeve Horne graced the front lobby, and nearby hung a small landscape painting by Best, who was also an amateur artist.

125 Joint Centre for Bioethics
Smith & Gemmell, 1883

Originally built as the Zion Congregational Church (by Smith & Gemmell, the architects who designed the original Knox College [now the Daniels Building], and the Church of the Redeemer at the northeast corner of Bloor Street West and Avenue Road), the building's steep, slate-tiled roof, Gothic windows, and sturdily crafted doorways speak of the faith and hope of two centuries ago. The university acquired the building in 1965.

Offices and meeting rooms have been awkwardly shoehorned into the former church to house the Joint Centre for Bioethics, but the soaring central space still exists, and among the makeshift partitions one can still glimpse the patterned brick walls, lovely wood beams and brackets supporting the roof, and colorful stained-glass windows. This former place of worship still holds many traces of history and will be retained as part of the comprehensive redevelopment of the Banting and Best site to the west.

126 The MaRS Centre
Darling & Pearson, 1912
East tower (Medical Discovery Tower), South Tower, and renovations
Adamson Associates Architects, 2005
West Tower
Bregman + Hamann, 2013

Located on College Street directly across from the university's Banting and Best Institutes and adjacent to Toronto General Hospital, the MaRS Centre is the world's largest urban innovation hub, comprising 1.5 million square feet (139,354 square meters). The MaRS Discovery District, as it is known administratively, supports a broad spectrum of research, including biotechnology, engineering, advanced

MaRS Centre, west tower

information technology, and nanotechnology. Founded in 2000 and funded by government, industry, and private initiatives, the MaRS Discovery District is not part of the university but is strongly affiliated with it. The architecturally ambitious MaRS Centre consists of the historic Toronto General Hospital building—its central set piece—and three sleek new additions, including "bookend" tower blocks to the

Toronto General Hospital (now part of the MaRS Centre) and view of College Street from the west, 1920

east and west of the former hospital building. An attractive atrium links the four structures.

The Toronto General Hospital complex originally consisted of eleven buildings spread over nine acres with landscaped gardens and lawns at its center, and at one point it was the largest private hospital in North America. It was also considered one of the most modern hospitals in the world and for decades was the site of collaborative research with the university, spawning such medical breakthroughs as the artificial kidney and the pacemaker. The iconic central portion facing College Street, designed by Darling & Pearson in an eclectic Renaissance style, contained the hospital's administration building, which was flanked on one side by the surgical wing and on the other by the medical wing.

The magnificent Administration Building (1912) and the wings facing College Street were preserved and integrated into the new MaRS complex. Its beautifully proportioned domed cupola rising above the central entrance was restored, as were facade materials, including terra-cotta and Roman-length brick. Up close, take note of the surprising color range of the bricks, presenting golden to bronze-purple flecks.

The metallic Toronto Medical Discovery Tower (2005) to the east defers to the central heritage building, while the twenty-story west tower, opened in 2013, is more ambitious architecturally. The MaRS Centre's front lawn along College Street draws inspiration from the hospital's original landscape plan and includes portions of the beautiful iron fence that once ran the full length of the block.

In 2006 the MaRS Centre received a Heritage Toronto Award, adding to the well-deserved attention that this vibrant innovation center has received.

127 Dentistry Building

Allward & Gouinlock Architects, 1959

Addition

Allward & Gouinlock Architects, 1985

The Faculty of Dentistry is located near the many teaching hospitals that stretch along University Avenue. Founded as the School of Dentistry by the Royal College of Dental Surgeons of Ontario in 1875, it affiliated with the University of Toronto in 1888 and is the oldest dental school in Canada. The country's first female dentist, C. L. Josephine Wells, graduated from the school in 1893.

In 1909 a new building was completed for the Faculty of Dentistry at the northeast corner of College and Huron Streets. (See Walk Five, pages 183–85.) The school remained there for fifty years, moving to a new, buff-brick, International Style building on Edwards Street in 1959. Originally U-shaped, with a dominant five-story wing along the south and lower three-story wings on the east and north, the building's courtyard was filled in with a major addition at the north and west sides in 1985. Inside the Faculty of Dentistry, a vast two-

Dentistry Building (TOP) and its clinic (BOTTOM)

story clinic on the east side of the second floor is filled with a sea of dental examination chairs. A long horizontal band of windows floods the room with natural light.

Visitors arriving in the south lobby of Canada's largest dental school are greeted by a huge and colorful, but rather unsettling, mural on the subject of pain, executed in 1978 by artist Carmen Cereceda.

The Museum and Gallery Walk

The fervent urban life encircling and infiltrating the University of Toronto's downtown (St. George) campus is one of the institution's greatest assets. Reciprocity abounds: the university shares its spaces and opportunities with surrounding neighborhoods, while the city simultaneously influences the university. Within this dynamic context are scores of stimulating cultural destinations, including great museums and galleries.

Toronto has a long tradition of collecting and exhibiting art. In 1847 the municipal government sponsored the first annual exhibition of the Toronto Society of Arts. The Art Museum of Toronto was founded in 1900 (renamed the Art Gallery of Toronto in 1919, then the Art Gallery of Ontario in 1966). Then the Arts & Letters Club of Toronto was established in 1908.

Similarly, the University of Toronto has valued, collected, and supported the visual arts over the course of several centuries. King's College (1827–50), the forerunner of the university, had a museum that included art in one of its buildings on Front Street. University College collected portraits of its faculty, the earliest signed one dated 1874. After World War One, these portraits, along with a growing body of other art, led to the establishment of the university's oldest collection, the University College Collection; the Hart House Collection was launched in 1922; and from 1912

Royal Ontario Museum,
University of Toronto

ABOVE: Postcard showing the Royal Ontario Museum, which opened in 1914
PREVIOUS: Arcade, Art Museum at the University of Toronto

to 1968, the University of Toronto operated the Royal Ontario Museum, the largest museum in Canada, with which it continues to maintain close ties. The university operates a progressive art museum on the St. George campus and lively galleries at both the Mississauga and Scarborough campuses. In addition to these venues, in 2018 the university opened its new gallery for exhibiting architecture and design in the Daniels Building at One Spadina

Art Museum at the University of Toronto, north entrance

Crescent. As well, the three campuses are populated with inspiring outdoor sculpture. The university offers master's programs in visual art and in curatorial studies, the latter tied closely to the Art Museum at the University of Toronto. Indeed, art remains central to the cultural life of the university, along with the institution's outreach to and collaboration with neighboring art institutions.

The university's art museum is at the core of a tight downtown zone, twenty blocks long and seven blocks wide—from Bloor Street West on the north to King Street West on the south, and from John Street on the west to Gould Street on the east. Within this zone, there is a network of sister museums and galleries: the Bata Shoe Museum, the Royal Ontario Museum, the Gardiner Museum, the Art Gallery of Ontario, the Ontario College of Art and Design University Galleries System, the Textile Museum of Canada, the Ryerson Image Centre, and the arts space 401 Richmond Street West. These are extraordinary loci of culture that present and interpret visual arts, from those of Canada's aboriginal peoples and the Group of Seven to internationally acclaimed contemporary artists and designers. The array of work collected, exhibited, and critically interpreted by these institutions is broad and offers Torontonians and visitors opportunity for thought and reflection.

Many of the museums and galleries in this walking tour are housed in distinctive buildings, some designed by acclaimed architects and firms such as Frank Gehry, Diamond Schmitt Architects, Kuwabara Payne McKenna Blumberg Architects, Daniel Libeskind, Raymond Moriyama, and Will Alsop. Others are nearly invisible, including the university's own art museum, deeply hidden within Hart House and University College. The museum's invisibility is perhaps explained in part by two factors: the University of Toronto choosing not to get into the museum business in a major way again, following the separation between the university and the vast Royal Ontario Museum in 1968, so that it could attract its own funding from the provincial government and the private sector; and the fact that the art museum's permanent collection is very small, consisting of around seven thousand works, making bricks and mortar less important. Whatever the explanation for the museum being essentially invisible, it deserves to have a more dynamic presence and more significant role within the university, Toronto, and Canada. This tour examines the Art Museum at the University of Toronto together with nine distinctive neighboring places that celebrate the visual arts, some of which have major permanent collections. Other important art centers in downtown Toronto, located beyond this tour of museums and galleries, include the Power Plant and the Museum of Contemporary Art Toronto Canada.

128 Art Museum at the University of Toronto, 7 Hart House Circle and 15 King's College Circle

The art museum comprises two galleries: the Justina M. Barnicke Gallery (JMB) at Hart House and the University of Toronto Art Centre (UTAC) at University College. These two galleries are a mere fifty yards (45.7 meters) apart. The JMB was founded

Emily Carr, Canadian, 1871–1945. *Kitwacool Totems*, 1928. Oil on canvas, 109.5 x 69.5 cm. Donated by the graduating class of 1929, Hart House Collection

in 1983 in response to the growing, historically renowned Hart House art collection (launched in 1922), with the mandate of producing a year-round program of contemporary art exhibitions. UTAC was founded in 1996 to develop and administer the three major collections within the wider university: the University College Collection, the Malcove Collection of Early Christian and Byzantine Art, and the University of Toronto Collection. In 2014 UTAC and the JMB were federated to encourage synergy and growth, generating a newly branded Art Museum at the University of Toronto.

This art museum conglomerate is best known for the numerous Group of Seven paintings and sketches in its collections. Founded in 1920, the Group of Seven (Franklin Carmichael, Lawren Harris, A. Y. Jackson, Franz Johnston, Arthur Lismer, J. E. H. MacDonald, and F. H. Varley) had romantic leanings and

Lawren Stewart Harris, Canadian, 1885–1970. *Isolation Peak*, 1929. Oil on canvas, 107.3 x 128 cm. Purchased by the Art Committee with income from the Harold and Murray Wrong Memorial Fund, 1946; Hart House Collection

Ken Lum, Canadian, born 1956. *Untitled [Language Painting]*, 1987. Oil and enamel on panel, 161.6 x 213.36 cm. Gift of Lonti Ebers, University of Toronto Art Collection

are best known for their spiritual, sometimes mystical interpretation of Canadian forests and lakes. The museum also has outstanding contemporary pieces by such important Canadian artists and collectives as General Idea, Kent Monkman, Lisa Steele, Arnaud Maggs, Luis Jacob, and Liz Magor, to name a few. In 2009 the Barnicke Gallery was chosen to represent Canada at the fifty-third Venice Biennale with the exhibition of Canadian artist Mark Lewis, and in 2017 the Art Centre hosted the exhibition *It's All Happening So Fast: A Counter-History of the Modern Canadian Environment* loaned from the prestigious Canadian Centre for Architecture in Montreal.

129 The Royal Ontario Museum, 100 Queens Park

Darling & Pearson, 1914; Chapman & Oxley, 1933; Moffat Moffat & Kinoshita, 1984
McLaughlin Planetarium
Allward & Gouinlock Architects, 1968
Michael Lee-Chin Crystal Studio
Daniel Libeskind with Bregman + Hamman Architects, 2007
Renovation
Hariri Pontarini Architects, 2018

The Royal Ontario Museum (ROM) is the largest museum in Canada and one of the world's preeminent centers for the exhibition and study of art, world cultures, and natural history. Its collection contains more than six million items. Established in 1912 by the province's Royal Ontario Museum Act, ROM was operated by the University of Toronto until 1968. It is now an independent institution yet maintains close ties with the university and is located at the northeast corner of the St. George campus.

Darling & Pearson's master plan for the ROM had a rectangular plan with two huge rectangular courts carved out of the massive volume. About a quarter of this

The Royal Ontario Museum

Beaux-Arts-inspired design was realized in 1914, along the western edge of the site. (See page 250.) In 1933 Chapman & Oxley completed a large T-shaped addition, fronting on Queen's Park, which gave the museum an overall H shape. Following this, Darling & Pearson's master plan was abandoned: the area they had imagined to

Cree (Nehiyawak), Canadian Plains region horse mask, circa 1900. Beaded cotton cloth; belonged to Walter Ochopowace, Plains Cree. The Royal Ontario Museum

be a grand south court was filled in with a curatorial building, and their proposed grand north court was used for a gallery addition terracing down to Bloor Street. This 1984 infilling was the most extensive of hundreds of incremental edits to the original intentions and clarity of Darling & Pearson's vision. The original architect's design was amended with the insertion of mechanical rooms, the covering of windows, and the division of galleries, which led to visual and spatial confusion.

Architect Daniel Libeskind's 2007 redesign of the ROM reordered the piecemeal changes of the past seeral decades (including the 1984 north addition), restoring much of the clarity of Darling & Pearson's and Chapman

& Oxley's designs. In the cityscape, Libeskind's bold and highly sculptural addition on Bloor Street—named the Michael Lee-Chin Crystal for the principal donor—commands attention. Libeskind originally proposed to sheath about half of the building with glass or a translucent material; yet, due to climatic and curatorial conditions, the transparent surface glazing was reduced to about 20 percent, a change that greatly undermined the architect's intent. However, Libeskind's interior spaces are dramatic, particularly the soaring Hyacinth Gloria Chen Crystal Court, which completes Darling & Pearson's conceptual intent for the north court. Topped by two shard-like skylights, the crystal court is a monumental space, and it has become one of the city's great rooms—a coveted venue for receptions, experimental art installations, and cultural performances.

Frank Lloyd Wright, American, 1867-1959. Table and side chairs designed for the Imperial Hotel, Tokyo, Japan. Oak, oilcloth, designed circa 1915-21, made circa 1925-45. The Royal Ontario Museum

The ROM's 2017–18 Welcome Project retained the north Bloor Street entrance (added by Libeskind in 2007) while restoring the ROM's main axial historic entry, which faces east. The rejuvenation, by Hariri Pontarini Architects, reconfigured the historic 1933 rotunda space and added a new café, outdoor amphitheater, and additional plazas. The project has improved the ROM's functionality and made it a more welcoming place to visit.

Among the ROM's forty galleries is the Gallery of Modern Design, which displays objects by twentieth-century European and American designers. Here you can see exquisite pieces by the likes of Charles and Ray Eames, Arne Jacobsen, Jacques-Émile Ruhlmann, and Frank Lloyd Wright. Equally rewarding is the Daphne Cockwell Gallery of Canada: it displays *First Peoples*, a permanent exhibit created with the advice of Native advisors and displaying more than a thousand artifacts representing the culture and traditions of Canada's First Peoples.

130 Bata Shoe Museum, 327 Bloor Street West

Moriyama & Teshima Architects, 1995

The Bata Shoe Museum is the brainchild of Sonja Bata, wife of Thomas J. Bata, whose father, Tomas Bata, established the Bata Shoe Company in the Moravian town of Zlin (in the current day Czech Republic) in 1894. Between 1931 and 1939 the Bata company expanded widely throughout Europe, Asia, Africa, and the Americas.

Bata Shoe Museum

Ottoman Empire Turkish nailins, nineteenth century. Worn by women in Turkish bathhouses. 26 cm height. Image © 2018, Bata Shoe Museum, Toronto

Canadian Sandals, twentieth century. Sandals belonging to Pierre Elliott Trudeau (1919–2000), prime minister of Canada from 1968 to 1979 and from 1980 to 1984, who said he had worn them "while bumming around the world" in 1948 and 1949

It adhered to progressive planning, emulated Ebenezer Howard's garden city ideals, and aggressively embraced modern architecture for its factories, offices, stores, and workers' housing. The prominent Canadian architect John C. Parkin designed Bata's world headquarters in Don Mills, Ontario, completed in 1965 and recognized as one of Toronto's most important midcentury modern buildings. The Bata building was demolished in 2007 to make way for the c$300 million complex containing the Aga Khan Foundation, Ismaili Centre, and a park, which all opened in 2014.

Trained in Switzerland as an architect herself, Sonja Bata commissioned Raymond Moriyama to design the five-story Bata Shoe Museum, which contains some 13,000 artifacts spanning 4,500 years of footwear history. The museum fits neatly into a tight urban site with three floors above ground and two below. The building's canted walls and glass-shard elements suggest influence from the Museum of Modern Art's 1988 exhibition *Deconstructivist Architecture*. Perhaps it is also meant to evoke an opening shoebox. Inside, a multilevel spatial cut contains the main stair and provides a clear view to the three-story faceted glass wall designed by Lutz Haufschild on the south facade.

A place that is good for the sole, the Bata's extensive permanent collection includes footwear worn by Elton John, Marilyn Monroe, Madonna, Elvis Presley, and Canadian prime minister Pierre Trudeau, to name a few.

131 Gardiner Museum, 111 Queen's Park
Keith Wagland, 1984
Renovation and additions
Kuwabara Payne McKenna Blumberg Architects, 2006

George and Helen Gardiner opened the Gardiner Museum in 1984 to house their collection of ancient American artifacts and European pottery and porcelain. Located on Victoria University lands, it was redesigned a decade ago by Kuwabara Payne McKenna Blumberg Architects, who strived to "give this great small museum an intimate monumentality," as Bruce Kuwabara stated. Rising from a series of terraced platforms, the hovering limestone-clad

Roseline Delisle, Canadian, 1952-2003. *Septet 4*, 1999. Purchased with the support of the Canada Council for the Arts Acquisition Assistance Program, Gardiner Museum

Gardiner Museum

building consists of a composition of cubic volumes, accented by a bold screen of limestone louvers. The interior spatial sequence is gentle, flowing up to a third-floor gallery for temporary exhibitions, a pleasant restaurant, and a terrace with wonderful vistas of Queen's Park, the Royal Ontario Museum, the University of Toronto, and the downtown skyline.

In scale and character, the museum negotiates between the austerity of the neoclassical Lillian Massey Department of Household Science on the north and the Queen Anne–style Annesley Hall on the south. The three now sit together comfortably, demonstrating how historical and contemporary buildings can be successfully related.

The permanent collection includes ancient American ceramics, Italian Renaissance pottery, seventeenth-century English pottery, and eighteenth-century European porcelain. In recent years the Gardiner Museum has imaginatively expanded its mandate to include a wider range of concepts, artifacts, and exhibitions related partially, but not exclusively, to clay. For example, in 2016 the museum presented the exhibition *True Nordic: How Scandinavia Influenced Design in Canada*, which included not only ceramics but also furniture, glassware, and textiles.

132   Art Gallery of Ontario (AGO), 317 Dundas Street West

Darling & Pearson, 1918, 1926
Addition
Darling, Pearson & Cleveland, 1935
Additions
John C. Parkin, 1974, 1977
Additions and renovations
Barton Myers with Kuwabara Payne McKenna Blumberg Architects, 1993
Additions and renovations
Gehry International Architects, 2008

In 1910 Harriette Boulton Smith left her historic home, The Grange, and seven acres of property to the Art Museum of Toronto, which gave most of the area to the city for a public park. A year later, the Art Gallery of Ontario (AGO) engaged the noted firm of Darling & Pearson to develop a design for a new museum to the north, to augment The Grange. Frank Darling generated a grand Beaux-Arts scheme of some thirty galleries organized around three interior courtyards; by 1918 a small fraction of the project had been built. A second phase, incorporating a sculpture court (Walker Court), was completed in 1926, and in 1935 Darling, Pearson & Cleveland added two more galleries.

The museum's collections and programs expanded dramatically over the next few decades, and major additions and renovations were undertaken in the mid-1970s and early 1990s. By the mid-1990s it was clear that the AGO once again lacked sufficient facilities and, equally important, architectural clarity. In the fall of 2002,

Art Gallery of Ontario

with the promise of major gifts and support from Kenneth Thomson, a Canadian businessman and art collector, the AGO announced the appointment of Toronto-born Frank Gehry's firm, Gehry International Architects, to design its ambitious Transformation AGO project, which concluded six years later.

In this redesign of the AGO, Gehry made three bold moves: he recentered the main entrance on the historic Walker Court and bent this entrance axis vertically with a sculptural, upward-spiraling staircase; he added a six-hundred-foot-long (183-meter-long) glass-skinned sculpture promenade overlooking Dundas Street; and he built an enormous blue titanium-clad boxlike volume, housing contemporary galleries above the historic Grange and overlooking Grange Park. Although the project has scores of other reworkings, it is these three moves that provided the underlying strategies allowing Gehry to spatially, sculpturally, and programmatically transform the institution. For Gehry, who grew up in the neighborhood surrounding the AGO, it was an intensely personal project. In the fall of 2005, he shared with me his first memory of the AGO, which he had visited as a child with his mother, Thelma Goldberg:

> It was my first time in an art museum. I think I was eight years old, and my mother took me. There was snow on the ground, and we were wearing galoshes. I remember a fence and a driveway and iron gates. The building was set back from the street, and you walked right into the Walker Court.…When the AGO hired me I saw right away that the circulation had become confusing. The original building had been added to piecemeal. My sense was, if we were going to redo the AGO, you could solve the confusion by centering the main entrance on the historic Walker Court.

Many aspects of Gehry's AGO design can be traced to his early work in Los Angeles from the 1960s to the early 1980s—projects such as Loyola Law School, the Geffen Contemporary at MOCA (formerly the Temporary Contemporary), and Gehry's own residence in Santa Monica of 1978. These were less spectacular projects—before the Guggenheim Museum Bilbao and the Walt Disney Concert Hall—that had a toughness and elemental quality that reappears in the AGO. Underlying zoomorphic preoccupations and interest in the primitive that have surfaced throughout Gehry's career are also present, from the fish-skeleton, ship-hull quality of the sculpture promenade along Dundas Street to the orgiastic stairs that curl up and down through the project. Moreover, Gehry's

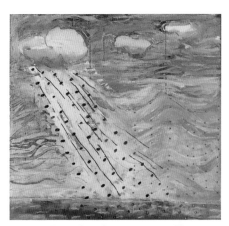

Paterson Ewen, Canadian, 1925–2002. *Flag Effect*, 1974. Acrylic on gouged plywood, 229.5 × 244.8 cm. Art Gallery of Ontario, reproduced by permission of Mary Alison Handford

grand sense of history and time, along with his sensitivity to art, have brought to the AGO both new complexity and new clarity, reorchestrating ninety years of architectural good intentions.

During 2017 and 2018, the AGO embarked on a major initiative called Look Forward to rethink the display of its permanent collection of more than ninety thousand art objects. (In the past, only about four thousand

Henry Moore. British, 1898–1986. *Draped Seated Woman*, 1957–58. Plaster. Art Gallery of Ontario, reproduced by permission of the Henry Moore Foundation

of these have typically been on view at any one time.) The AGO plans to increase the display space for the permanent collection by 50 percent, a total of 70,000 square feet (6,500 square meters), and to promote new curatorial approaches.

The AGO and the Ontario College of Art and Design visually frame the lovely Grange Park to the south. In 2017 the park was renovated, and an AGO Henry Moore sculpture, *Large Two Forms* (1969), was relocated from the corner of Dundas and McCaul Streets to become the park's centerpiece.

133   Ontario College of Art and Design University (OCADU), 100 McCaul Street

Horwood & White, 1921

Central building

Govan Ferguson Lindsay Kaminker Langley & Keenlyside, 1957

South wing

Govan Ferguson Lindsay Kaminker Langley & Keenlyside, 1963

North wing

Govan Kaminker Langley Keenlyside Melick Devonshire Wilson, 1967

Sharp Centre for Design

Alsop Architects with Robbie Young + Wright, 2004

Rosalie Sharp Pavilion

Bartolotto Architects, 2015

Addition and renovation ("Creative City Campus")

Morphosis and Teeple Architects with Two Row Architect, expected completion, 2021

Established in 1876 as the Ontario School of Art and incorporated as the Ontario College of Art in 1912, today's Ontario College of Art and Design University (OCADU)

Ontario College of Art and Design University

is Canada's largest university of art and design. Noted alumni include Jack Bush, Olivia Chow, Greg Curnoe, Garry Kennedy, Bruce Mau, Doris McCarthy, and Michael Snow. Its first building was designed by Horwood & White in close collaboration with the painter and, at the time, principal of the college, George Reid. Completed in 1921 in the Georgian style, it was constructed on a site provided by the Art Gallery of Toronto (now the Art Gallery of Ontario). This original building remains at the northeast corner of Grange Park.

In recent years, OCADU has become a hothouse of innovation. The institution's newfound vitality was spurred by the 2004 construction of the Sharp Centre for Design, named for Isadore Sharp, founder of the Four

Gord Peteran, Canadian, born 1956. *INBOX*, 2009. Portal-entryway to the Anniversary Gallery, Ontario College of Art and Design University, made of recycled tree trunks and contributed artifacts from more than 150 artists associated with the university and its history. Permanent collection, Ontario College of Art and Design University

Seasons Hotels and Resorts chain, and his wife, Rosalie Sharp, an OCADU alumna. The building was designed by one of England's most inventive architects, Will Alsop. When his pixelated box on stilts for OCADU was completed in 2004, it stirred tremendous controversy. But such a colorful tour de force turned out to be the exact shock that OCADU needed to kick it into the twenty-first century.

The leggy pavilion recalls Archigram's visionary project *Walking City* (1964)— a dynamic concoction that exudes youthful vitality. Alsop's elevated box is, in a 1960s sense, a happening. It feels as though it could start prancing across Grange Park to have a chat with the giant blue, titanium-clad box that Frank Gehry perched atop the Art Gallery of Ontario—a sister volume that Gehry orchestrated, urbanistically, to relate to and converse with Alsop's big black-and-white box.

In 2017 OCADU launched its Creative City Campus project, which proposes about 55,000 square feet (5,110 square meters) of new space and about 95,000 square feet (8,826 square meters) of renovated space. Designed by Los Angeles–based Morphosis and Toronto-based Teeple Architects, the bold initiative will include renovation and expansion of the university's library, new studio and classroom spaces, a student commons, and the construction of an Indigeneous Visual Culture and Student Center. Talking about the forthcoming OCADU project, Morphosis's Thom Mayne, who designed Graduate House at the University of Toronto in 2000, comments,

> We're interested in dialogue and transparency and conversation, buildings that promote conversation and in the end promote inquisitiveness. Do people like or dislike our building? I don't care. I care about whether it makes people think differently about what architecture can be. I'm interested in architecture that operates on your brain and raises questions about what it means to make buildings today.

OCADU's Galleries System has nine exhibition spaces for the display of art, design, and digital media. Exhibitions include work by OCADU students and by internationally renowned professionals—artists, designers, and researchers innovating for the twenty-first century.

134 The Textile Museum of Canada, 55 Centre Avenue

The Textile Museum of Canada is in an unassuming building nestled between the Ontario College of Art and Design University and Toronto City Hall. It might be easily overlooked, yet it is well worth a visit. Once inside, riches pour forth: textiles spanning two thousand years and two hundred global regions. The permanent collection of more the thirteen thousand artifacts includes fabrics, ceremonial cloths, garments, carpets, and quilts. The museum develops temporary exhibitions and also presents traveling exhibitions. Among the most fascinating traveling exhibitions was the 2015 show *Artist Textiles: Picasso to Warhol*, from the Fashion and Textile Museum in London.

Otomi, Hidalgo, Mexico, early twentieth century.
Bag. Gift of Dr. Howard Gorman, Collection of
the Textile Museum of Canada

Innu, Sept-Iles, Quebec, Canada, late nine-
teenth to early twentieth century. Hat.
Gift of Greta Ferguson, Collection of the
Textile Museum of Canada

Turkmen, Afghanistan, mid-twentieth century. Camel flank decoration.
From the Fitzgerald Collection, Collection of the Textile Museum of Canada

Ryerson Image Centre

135   The Ryerson Image Centre (RIC), 33 Gould Street
Diamond Schmitt Architects, 2012

The Ryerson Image Centre (RIC) is part of Ryerson University's School of Image Arts. Housed in a former brewery warehouse, the RIC has become one of the world's foremost institutions for research, teaching, and exhibiting photography and related media. Its Peter Higdon Research Centre contains the Black Star Collection of more than 292,000 photographs, dating from 1910 to 1992, from the New York–based Black Star photo agency. Emphasizing fine art photography and photojournalism, RIC maintains an exhibition program of the highest quality.

The renovated building, designed by Don Schmitt of Diamond Schmitt Architects, is one of downtown Toronto's most exquisite small structures: three stories wrapped in a double-skin of glass with integral LED lighting. At night the building transforms, becoming a programmable, dynamic work of art. It is a three-dimensional photograph of sorts. At certain times, the building can be "played," using a smartphone app.

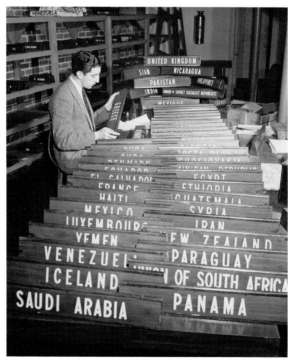

Unknown photographer. *[Preparations for the second part of the United Nations General Assembly]*, March 1949. Gelatin silver print. The Black Star Collection, Ryerson Image Centre

Wendy Snyder MacNeil, American, 1943–2016. *Andrew Ruvido and Robyn Wessner*, 1981–82. Platinum palladium print on tracing vellum. Wendy Snyder MacNeil Archive, Ryerson Image Centre

Robert Burley, Canadian, born 1957. *Kodak Image Centre, Building 7, Kodak Canada, Toronto*, 2006. Chromogenic color print. Collection of the Ryerson Image Centre

401 Richmond

136 401 Richmond, 401 Richmond Street West

John Wilson Siddall, 1899

Master plan, additions, and renovations

Margaret Zeidler, coordinator, 1996–ongoing

Sometimes referred to as "a village in a box," 401 Richmond is an urban community of artists, designers, architects, inventors, and entrepreneurs. It is imaginatively housed in a heritage-designated industrial building, the former MacDonald Manufacturing Company. Creative types share affordable work spaces, galleries, retail shops, a day care center, and a café.

Margaret (Margie) Zeidler purchased the building in 1994 and lovingly shaped the 401 vision. Trained as an architect at the University of Toronto, Zeidler, who is founder, president, and creative director of 401 Richmond, became passionate about the preservation of historic buildings and the development of community diversity. She has coordinated numerous additions and renovations at 401, inspired by the urbanist Jane Jacobs, who once said, "Old ideas can use new buildings, but new ideas need old buildings." This beehive of creativity supports numerous art galleries. Moreover, 401 Richmond has become a model of intelligent, imaginative urban development.

401 Richmond interior with Gordon Rayner, *Colour Swirl*, 1968. Permanent collection of 401 Richmond / Zeidler Family

University of Toronto Scarborough (UTSC)

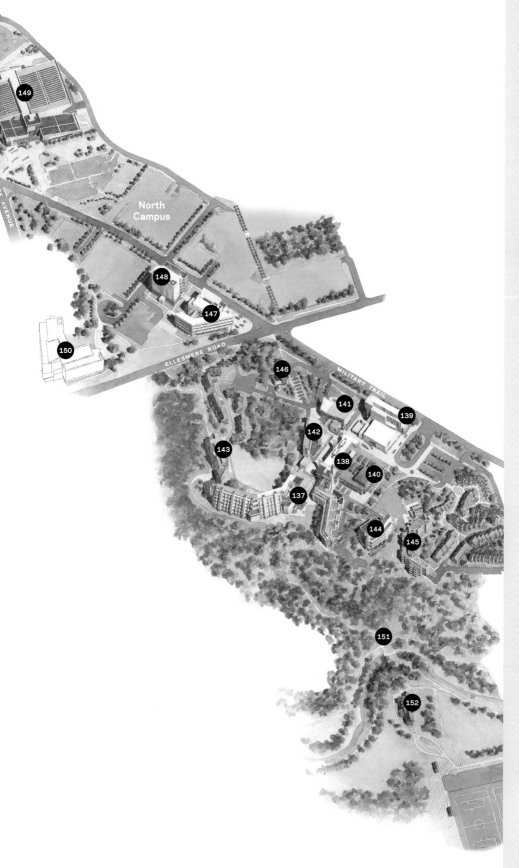

North
Campus

149

148

147

150

ELLESMERE ROAD

AVENUE

146

MILITARY TRAIL

141

139

142

143

138

140

137

144

145

151

152

University of Toronto Scarborough (UTSC)

Located twenty miles (thirty-two kilometers) east of the university's downtown (St. George) campus, the University of Toronto Scarborough was established in 1964 as Scarborough College, beginning with evening classes held at a local high school. The first building, designed by architect John Andrews, opened in January 1966. Today UTSC boasts more than thirteen thousand students enrolled in almost two hundred undergraduate and graduate programs. Nearly one in five students takes advantage of work-study opportunities in UTSC's co-op program. As revealed by the juxtaposition of on-campus housing for only about 760 students but with 2,740 parking spaces, it is largely a commuter campus. However, car culture does not entirely dominate, and students enjoy an increasingly pedestrian-friendly 350-acre campus in one of Toronto's most dramatic natural landscapes, the Highland Creek Valley.

The sprawling suburban area known as Scarborough is inhabited by more than 635,000 people and was a separate municipality until 1998, when it was amalgamated into the City of Toronto. Elizabeth Simcoe, wife of the first lieutenant governor of Upper Canada, Sir John Graves Simcoe, chose the name Scarborough for the precinct in the eighteenth century because the geological features along Lake Ontario reminded her of the limestone cliffs in Scarborough, England.

It was surely both the raw power of the Highland Creek Valley landscape and the reality of the cold north that inspired architect Andrews to sculpt his bold, megastructural vision for the campus, originally known as Scarborough College and changed to University of Toronto at Scarborough in 1972. Australian-born

Postcard showing the Scarborough College building, which opened in 1966

Andrews had been a finalist in the 1958 international design competition for Toronto City Hall, and, although Viljo Revell's scheme was selected instead of his, he stayed in Toronto to work with the firm of John B. Parkin Associates, the associated architects for the new city hall. During the early 1960s, when he was working on Scarborough College, Andrews was a professor of architecture at the University of Toronto. Together with colleagues Michael Hugo-Brunt, a planner, and Michael Hough, a landscape architect, he developed a master plan for the new college in six weeks. Andrews and his team designed a linear, concrete building with a stepped, pyramidal cross section and a system of internal pedestrian streets as the connective tissue. The first phases of the Scarborough College building—the Humanities and Science Wings—were completed in late 1965 and included a 6,000-square-foot (560-square-meter) television studio to develop and transmit closed-circuit lectures. In *The University of Toronto: A History* (first edition, 2002), Martin Friedland explains this unique experiment in pedagogy:

> One distinctive plan of Scarborough College was the plan to make wide-spread use of television for teaching purposes. This was not an afterthought but was built into the design of the college. "Scarborough was planned as a TV-college," the sociologist John Lee has written, "in a way which at that time was original in North America." Carl Williams had promoted the use of television in the extension program, and the first dean at Scarborough, the zoologist William Beckel, had successfully used the medium in his own teaching. Half the classes were to be taught using video-taped lectures. The use of television, it was thought, would save money and help ease the problem of finding enough staff members to teach the courses.

But this brave experiment failed, in part, because as Friedland notes, "Students—particularly in the second half of the 1960s—were not willing to accept either the lack of interaction with lecturers or what in most cases were second-rate productions compared to what they were seeing on television at home."

Nevertheless, the building itself was an astonishing essay in form, space, and light, and it became an international destination for architecture students and architects. Although not universally loved, Andrews's sculpturally powerful design branded Scarborough College, and the institution continues to wrestle with this, at times enthusiastically respecting and extending Andrews's legacy and at other times seeming to flee from it.

The fact remains that Scarborough College is one of Canada's most important modern buildings, and it propelled Andrews into national and international spotlights. Indeed, it can easily be argued that Scarborough College, along with Moshe Safdie's Habitat structure for Expo 67 in Montreal, is one of the two iconic works of twentieth-century Canadian architecture that continues to resonate internationally.

Enrollment on the Scarborough campus grew rapidly during the 1990s, reaching a population of five thousand students, and in 2000 the university commissioned the Toronto firm of Baird Sampson Neuert to develop a comprehensive master plan for future expansion. Barry Sampson of Baird Sampson Neuert revealed a deep understanding of Andrews's organic principles of flexibility and growth, while also accepting the realities of several unsympathetic additions that had been inflicted on the campus over the three decades since the original Andrews buildings. An intelligent new master plan resulted, which the university generally followed between 2000 and 2008—a period of rapid expansion—although with mixed results architecturally. The increased densification and attention to landscape during this period were admirable; however, one might question the overly diverse palette of building materials and colors—charcoal brick, orange-tan brick, yellow brick, copper, green-glass curtain wall, among many others—which undermined visual coherence during that period. Moreover, many of the buildings constructed between 2000 and 2008 seem groundless instead of embedded in and seeming to grow from the earth, as Andrews's original buildings do so convincingly.

By 2008 various factors led the university to rethink the future of the campus: continued enrollment growth, ecological/environmental responsibility, public transit challenges, and an opportunity to host parts of the Toronto 2015 Pan Am & Parapan Am Games. UTSC worked with Urban Strategies to develop a bold vision, and a new master plan was adopted by Governing Council in 2011. The fifty-year "blueprint" for the campus seeks to integrate growth seamlessly with the surrounding urban fabric of Scarborough and rapidly expanding Toronto. Construction of the large sports center for the 2015 Pan Am & Parapan Am Games at the intersection of Morningside Avenue and Military Trail was funded by the federal government, the City of Toronto, and the University of Toronto. A lion's share of the funding was provided by the UTSC students, whose vision for the campus and broader community was supported by a levy in 2010. The sports center jump-started the development of the new north campus. An important aspect of the UTSC vision is the construction of extensive housing on the north campus, serving students, faculty, and staff. Diverse housing options and associated retail, along with the hoped for construction of a Light Rail Transit line, will lead to a vibrant, twenty-four-hour campus community.

The University of Toronto Scarborough's new emphasis on connectivity, outreach, and integration with the surrounding city is a fundamentally different vision from the original Scarborough College megastructure by Andrews of fifty years ago—a kind of northern climate, organic fortress that focuses inward. As laudable as UTSC's new, outward-looking vision is academically and socially, it has yet to find strategies via architecture, landscape, and urbanism that will bring visual cohesion and a strong identity to the evolving campus. Four proposed landscape initiatives hold great promise in terms of binding together the currently disparate parts and providing a distinctive institutional identity: the Military Trail pedestrian spine, the north campus commons, the south campus commons, and the enhance-ment and reconnection of the Highland Creek ravine. If done boldly and imagina-tively, these major open-space projects could give the campus a strong identity like it once had, when Andrews created Scarborough College. The University of Toronto Scarborough deserves to regain a vigorous sense of *place* to inspire students for the daunting challenges of the twenty-first century.

Humanities Wing

THE SOUTH CAMPUS

The UTSC south campus is bounded by Ellesmere Road, Military Trail, and the surrounding Highland Creek ravine to the southwest. The iconic reinforced-concrete Scarborough College building was completed here in 1965, on the edge of the ravine. Since then, the south campus has been incrementally filled in with academic and residential buildings in a broad range of materials, becoming village-like and pedestrianized. Although infilling will continue on the south campus, most new construction will be on the new north campus.

137 Humanities and Science Wings

John Andrews Architects with Page & Steele Architects;
Michael Hough, landscape architect, 1966

Conceived as part of a larger megastructural master plan for Scarborough College, the two wings were built in just over twenty-four months, starting in 1963 and ending in January 1966. The Science Wing runs east–west along the ridge of the Highland Creek Valley, with the Humanities Wing running north–south. The two connect at an "elbow" consisting of a four-story central meeting place and a large outdoor patio, providing a framed view of the valley and river below. Tucked into the hillside, the wings vary from five to six stories, and the complex is connected by a linear pedestrian street that protects against winter harshness and, like a small village, encourages socializing.

John Andrews was the driving force behind the willful design, but the role of Michael Hough, the university's campus landscape architect at the time, was

significant. Hough started analyzing the site before Andrews became fully engaged, and he brought a progressive environmental perspective to the project. Hough maintained that the new buildings should protect the existing slope and prevent erosion, and he brought in climatologists and other experts to ensure an environmental approach. Then president Claude Bissel also fully endorsed the environmental emphasis.

Andrews's forms are highly sculptural and masterful in their composition. The long horizontals are marked near the center elbow by the vertical thrust of the power plant chimneys, reminiscent of Italian Futurist architect Antonio Sant'Elia's visionary Citta Nuova project of 1914. (See photo of power-plant chimneys, page 273.) Just as the Futurists embraced the industrial world and emphasized audacity and energy, so did Andrews half a century later. Together, the Humanities and Science Wings read as a giant educational machine charging through the landscape, spinning out knowledge. Like Sant'Elia, Andrews loved the brute authority of industrial reinforced concrete, and there is little escape from it in his design, both inside and outside. Thankfully, the floors of the internal street and the collective spaces are paved in terra-cotta-colored English quarry tile. These handsome floors—along with fine-scaled wood paneling on some ceilings and walls, and abundant natural light flowing from skylights—humanize the great machine.

In its composition and treatment of volume, Andrews's work at Scarborough is ambitious, to say the least. The pyramidal stepped forms respond locally to program, with classrooms, laboratories, auditoria, offices, and stairs given strong sculptural expression. The west-facing side of the Humanities Wing presents an array of stacked auditoria with sloping walls that look almost Mayan, while the south facade of the Science Wing is arranged in descending terraces knit together by two monumental sloping service ducts. To the university's credit, it has preserved these important mid-twentieth-century buildings and, when changes became necessary, made modifications with care, such as the elegant glass mechanical penthouse enclosure designed by Jon Neuert of Baird Sampson Neuert Architects.

Andrews once claimed that "only architecture that meets the needs of people endures." In his understanding, these needs comprised, on the one hand, notions of monumentality and energy and, on the other, a range of rather everyday human activities, such as casual street encounters. Andrews gave Scarborough a brilliantly inspiring and enduring work of architecture. At the same time, and somewhat ironically, the buildings' "mega" quality and the insistent gray roughness of the exposed concrete have not met certain psychological needs; this has caused the university to construct, in recent years, smaller-scaled, more inviting structures on the Scarborough campus. But most of these lack the inspirational aspect—the sheer daring—of the Andrews buildings.

Looking at the south campus as a whole, it is regrettable that Andrews's clear vision has been so compromised. Walking along the ravine side of the Humanities Wing, one encounters a sculpture titled *A Tall Couple* (1966) by Louis Archambault, originally commissioned for Expo 67 in Montreal, then donated to Scarborough

Science Wing, central meeting place

College by the House of Seagram. If one pauses near this fine sculpture, with Andrews's structure rising above and the landscape rolling dramatically down to the river below, it is hard to deny the enduring spiritual presence of this remarkable building.

138 Recreation Wing (R-Wing)

John Andrews International Pty. Ltd, 1973
Library Addition
John Andrews International Pty. Ltd., 1982

Seven years after John Andrews's Humanities and Science Wings opened and in accordance with his master plan, a third wing, the Recreation Wing, was added to the northeast on essentially flat land. The new wing provided athletic facilities and additional classrooms and offices. In 1982 a library was added to the R-Wing—the Vincent W. Bladen Library, named in memory of a former member of Scarborough's economics department. (This library was renamed the UTSC Library in 1999 and later absorbed into the new Academic Resource Centre in 2003.)

   With the addition of the new wing in 1973, Andrews's composition became Y-shaped, extending the original ridge buildings to the campus's entrance on Military Trail. The R-Wing connected to the Humanities Wing under the podium level and via an enclosed bridge on the second floor, adjacent to the power plant chimneys. The bridge created a framed view and a strong east–west visual corridor. In 2003, with the visual axis to the east strengthened by the construction of Joan Foley Hall, the Academic Learning Centre, and the Management Building, the overhead bridge was removed.

   Although the new wing religiously followed Andrews's master plan, the R-Wing had little of the conceptual, spatial, and material rigor of the original buildings. Drastic budget reductions during design development—as well as the fact that, by the early 1970s, Andrews had started establishing a practice in his native Australia and was less focused on Toronto—dragged the project down, with the result that it felt more like a suburban high school than a dignified place of higher learning. Little by little, with new buildings constructed around it, the R-Wing became, rather fortunately, buried in the center of the campus. A large portion of the R-Wing is known today as the Bladen Wing (B-Wing), recalling the former Bladen Library.

139 Highland Hall

Perkins and Will Architects, 2018

With the completion of Highland Hall, the campus will have an inviting, bold new face along Military Trail. The five-story building, incorporating a former nondescript gymnasium, will house social sciences departments, faculty and administrative offices, lounges, study spaces, a student commons, and a flexible great hall that can be used for banquets and examinations. Composed of stacked, offset, twisted volumes clad in brushed aluminum, the upper two floors of the structure's west end will hover dramatically over a grand porch leading to a landscaped walkway into the campus.

Highland Hall (architectural rendering)

140 Academic Resource Centre (ARC)

Brian MacKay-Lyons in association with Rounthwaite, Dick and Hadley Architects, Inc., 2003

Designed by Halifax-based architect and urban designer Brian MacKay-Lyons, the low-slung, Academic Resource Centre (ARC) includes the renovated UTSC Library, the Informatics Commons, the Doris McCarthy Gallery, and a five-hundred-seat lecture theater. It merges smoothly with the former Vincent W. Bladen Library within B-Wing and contributes significantly to the formation of the east–west pedestrian walkway that runs from the heart of the campus east to Joan Foley Hall and the residences to the south.

MacKay-Lyons used a tartan grid as the basic ordering device for the ARC, both for space planning and the building structure. It is akin to Louis Kahn's concept of "served and servant" spaces, wherein circulation and support systems are relegated to secondary zones, freeing up large, flexible areas in between. The architect applied this system rigorously in the ARC, extending linear strips of the tartan

south, beyond the building, to generate an elegant courtyard. Viewed against the horizontal copper cladding that has turned an inviting chocolate-brown color, the white birch trees populating the courtyard are a lovely sight.

Besides the spatial geometry of the tartan grid, the ARC's interior displays an intentionally frugal material vocabulary of concrete floors and unpainted concrete-block walls, warmed with wood furnishings and fittings. MacKay-Lyons's architecture consistently shows conceptual clarity and economy of means, but here the architect also made a concerted effort to link it with the boldness and toughness of John Andrews's legacy. The Academic Learning Centre has a strong, organic sense of place. Simply stated, it fits.

Academic Resource Centre, exterior (ABOVE) and interior (PREVIOUS)

141 Student Centre

Stantec Architecture Ltd., 2004

Entering the campus at the entrance on Military Trail, one is struck by the dramatic structural cantilever and the soaring butterfly roof of the Student Centre. This three-story, 48,000-square-foot (4,460-square-meter) building was funded primarily by a 2001 UTSC student levy. Students pledged over c$20 million for the Student Centre—at the time the largest single financial commitment to the University of Toronto in its 174-year history.

Student Centre

The Student Centre houses offices of student organizations and student affairs, the health center, a support center for women and trans people, a food court, a restaurant/pub, two multifaith prayer rooms, the campus radio station, study areas, and retail stores. It is uncompromisingly modern—overtly optimistic and ready to fly.

A lot of spatial and topographical maneuvering was required for the tight site, which had to absorb the campus's main shipping and receiving ramp leading underground along the center's east edge. A lawn slopes down to a basement-level pub and outdoor deck at the northwest corner. To the south, the Student Centre reaches out toward the Arts and Administration Building with two building wings. If somewhat erratic in composition and material palette, the architectural gymnastics do contribute to the building's social liveliness. Visually, there seems to be something for everyone. Indeed, the building has become a real hub of student activity.

Environmental sustainability played an important role in the design, and the architects worked closely with the student stakeholders to explore innovative techniques to minimize environmental consequences through efficient use of energy and resources. The building was imaginatively designed to reduce energy consumption, and eighteen tons of steel were reused from demolition at the Royal Ontario Museum. The project achieved a LEED Silver rating from the LEED (Leadership in Energy and Environmental Design) program and received a Canadian Green Design Award in 2005 from the City of Toronto.

142 Arts and Administration Building

Montgomery Sisam Architects, 2005

The most refined of the three buildings constructed at the core of the south campus between 2003 and 2005 is the unassuming yet substantial Arts and Administration Building. Situated behind the Student Centre and thoughtfully linked to it by an elegant pergola along the east side, the yellow-brick Arts and Administration Building is angled on the west to form a kind of prow. This prow, which faces the entrance driveway into the campus with a huge double-height window,

Arts and Administration Building, main stair (ABOVE)
and exterior (OVERLEAF)

signals one of the building's roles, which is to serve as a visitor's center. For most newcomers to the campus, the Arts and Administration Building is the point of orientation and welcoming.

And this role it serves well. Within a plan configuration and detail system that seem partly inspired by the original John Andrews–designed buildings and partly derived from Montgomery and Sisam Architects' long-standing interest in the work of the architect Alvar Aalto, there is a sense of flow, comfort, and ease. At the south end of the building, located at the very heart of the campus, is a hand-somely designed volume containing the institution's seat of governance, the Council Chamber. This is a tall, grand room with vertical wood-slot paneling, generous amounts of natural light, and brown leather chairs. If the former Andrews-designed Council Chamber in the Humanities Wing was quirky in its castle-like extreme, the new Council Chamber is the opposite: calm and dignified.

The slender courtyard formed between the Arts and Administration Building and the Bladen Wing, designed by Janet Rosenburg Associates, represents land-scape architecture at its best, with subtly angled walkways, gracious and varied plant material, and pleasant night lighting that make this little place a gem.

143 Science Research Building

Moriyama & Teshima Architects, 2008

The Science Research Building is connected to the northwest end of John Andrews's 1966 Science Wing. The facility houses sixteen laboratories, offices for faculty and research assistants, and a 235-seat lecture hall. Resulting in part from strong

Science Research Building

Science Research Building, horizontal sun shades

prodding from the university's Design Review Committee, the location, footprint, and materials of the Science Building are sympathetic with and extend Andrews's original megastructure. With its generosity of scale, long bands of horizontal windows, horizontal sun shades, and charcoal-color zinc cladding, the building makes a positive impression in the campus landscape. Sweeping to the north, it also contributes to the positive shaping of an emerging grand west lawn—the future South Commons. Unlike the Social Science Building, which remains physically unconnected to the Humanities Wing and thus seems adrift, the Science Building reads as a familial architectural extension and demonstrates respect for Andrews's vision.

144 Social Science Building
Kuwabara Payne McKenna Blumberg Architects, 2004

Similar to most buildings constructed on the Scarborough campus over the past fifteen years, the Social Science Building (originally called the Management Building) was done on a modest budget that makes the John Andrews heyday seem very distant. The masonry and glass curtain-wall structure has a slightly cranked plan that inflects toward and attempts to relate to the nearby Humanities Wing. However, the exterior barely resonates with Andrews's Scarborough College building, and only inside is there a sense of connection to the spirit of the 1960s megastructure. The primary interior move is a spatially exhilarating, four-story atrium that provides a sense of community for students. Natural light flows down through the space, enlivening the concrete structure, charcoal-color masonry block walls, polished

Social Science Building

concrete floor, and cherry paneling. A dignified multipurpose room opens southward to an outdoor courtyard, and from here one can enjoy the insistent horizontals of the elegant south elevation, which is the most successful face of the building.

The Social Science Building's front door faces onto the east–west pedestrian spine of the campus, and there is an attempt to anchor the building along this spine with a grand stair tower. Unfortunately, this undistinguished tower, clad in charcoal-color masonry units, competes uncomfortably with the glass-enclosed, axial tower of Joan Foley Hall further to the east.

The promise of the Social Science Building is that, someday, an infill structure will link it to the west with the Humanities Wing, thereby allowing the lovely atrium to be understood as not just an entity in itself but, rather, as a continuation of the Andrews-designed pedestrian street system.

145 Joan Foley Hall
Baird Sampson Neuert and Montgomery Sisam Architects, 2003

This 231-bed, apartment-style student residence was named in honor of the first female provost at the University of Toronto (and UTSC's first female principal), Joan E. Foley, who began her teaching career in psychology in 1963. Since 1993 the university has presented the annual Joan E. Foley Quality of Student Experience Award to a student, faculty, or staff member.

The four-story structure rambles along the crest of the ravine and includes a sculptural, glazed tower, which visually anchors the eastern termination of the

Joan Foley Hall

campus's east–west pedestrian spine. Clad in orange-tan brick and generous amounts of glass, Joan Foley Hall is exuberant in plan configuration while expressing simplicity in elevation. A bold and well-composed mechanical penthouse atop the southern wing is worth noting. Clustered apartments are cleverly distributed to maximize natural light from corner windows. Environmental responsibility and sustainability played an important role in the design, and the building is energy efficient.

On a campus that is dominated by commuting students, Joan Foley Hall is a welcome example of the kind of pleasant residential life that is possible at UTSC.

146 N'sheemaehn Child Care Centre
Michael H. K. Wong Architects Inc., 1990

Conveniently located near the campus's main entrance, the economically designed N'sheemaehn Child Care Centre was built to serve both the local community and

the university. Service and storage spaces wrap around a central open-plan hub. The center's indoor spaces are thoughtfully linked to generous outdoor play areas, the whole being nestled in the wooded surroundings.

N'sheemaehn Child Care Centre, outdoor play area

147 Instructional Centre

Diamond Schmitt Architects, 2011

The Instructional Centre was the first building realized north of Ellesmere Road on
the north campus. It is roughly triangular in shape, aligning with Ellesmere Road
and Military Trail, and successfully anchoring the intersection of the two roadways.
The primary volume, clad in silver-gray brick, is set back at the intersection to create
a welcoming forecourt that leads to an interior atrium. A slender L-shaped wing
running southward defines a courtyard and is clad in an attractive, pale-green
and white curtain wall, visually reminiscent of the 1950s but incorporating twenty-
first-century technology that offers rapid installation and long-term high performance. The Instructional Centre includes spaces for research, teaching, and study,
along with a finance lab that resembles a high-tech trading floor, complete with
an LCD stock ticker.

In the lovely four-story atrium, take note of the wall-mounted artwork
Interregnum: Corner Displacement for John Andrews (2011) by Daniel Young and

Instructional Centre, exterior (ABOVE) and atrium (OVERLEAF)

Christian Giroux, winners of the 2011 Sobey Art Award. This piece, achieved through the stacking and cantilevering of quadrilateral forms, is based on an interior fragment of John Andrews's Scarborough College building—a kind of "Andrews quotation" and subtle nod to institutional memory.

148 Environmental Science and Chemistry Building

Diamond Schmitt Architects, 2015

The third building on the evolving north campus—a simple block by the same architects who designed the nearby Instructional Centre—hints at the midrise urban strategy for construction along Military Trail. The east volume of the Environmental Science and Chemistry Building is clad in silver-gray brick like the Instructional Centre next door and sports a jazzlike pattern of yellow fins. At grade, glass-fronted spaces anticipate future retail shops, facing onto a future pedestrian mall. The west volume is clad in wavy vertical fins. Inside, an atrium showers natural light deep into the efficient building, which achieved a LEED Gold rating.

Environmental Science and Chemistry Building

A unique aspect of this structure is its system of six huge, winding underground tubes that precondition air for the building, producing a 40 percent reduction in annual energy consumption. Air intake devices for the underground air-conditioning system are sculpturally expressed in a public outdoor area, aptly named Earth Tube Plaza.

149 Toronto Pan Am Sports Centre

NORR Architects, 2014

Located at the intersection of Morningside Avenue and Military Trail, on the north campus, this c$205 million field house and aquatic center was constructed for the Toronto 2015 Pan Am & Parapan Am Games—specifically for swimming, diving, fencing, sitting volleyball, and parts of the Modern Pentathlon events. In 2009 UTSC students approved a tuition levy that will contribute c$30 million to the project over a period of approximately twenty-five years. The Sports Centre is now co-owned by the University of Toronto and the City of Toronto, serving the UTSC and surrounding Scarborough communities as well as high-performance and national sport organizations. It is also home of the Canadian Sport Institute Ontario, one of seven such centers across Canada.

Architecturally, the sprawling building is somewhat deconstructivist in style, composed of angular wedge-like forms and a roofscape of 1,800 solar panels. Approaching from the parking lot, visitors are greeted by a large yellow canopy and a nearby sculpture titled *Water Velocity* (2014) by the Québec City–based artist consortium BGL. Constructed of aluminum and stainless-steel cables with small, colorful circles and squares laced through it, the sculpture flutters in the breeze and practically sings with a sound like rippling water.

Inside, one finds a beehive of activity in what feels like a friendly community center. The swimming pool and gymnasia are impressive, to say the least, accommodating not only professional athletes but *everyone*, at any age with any level of physical ability. In the modernist sense, it is an exhilarating social condenser, promoting the admirable "be healthy" agenda of the University of Toronto Scarborough's current principal and vice president, Bruce Kidd, himself a former Olympic star.

The facility has been showered with awards, including the LEED Gold certification by the Canadian Green Building Council, the Ontario General Contractor's Association award for Best Project Built in Ontario, the Best of Best Large Project Achievement Award from the Toronto Construction Association, a Facilities of Merit award from Athletic Business, and the PRO Excellence in Design Award by Parks & Recreation Ontario.

As the north campus develops into an urban village over the next fifty years, the Sports Centre and nearby Morningside Athletic Fields will become increasingly significant as community anchors—symbols of the importance of physical well-being.

**Toronto Pan Am Sports Centre, exterior (TOP)
and diving pool (BOTTOM)**

Centennial College Morningside Campus

150 Centennial College Morningside Campus, 755 Morningside Avenue

Kuwabara Payne McKenna Blumberg Architects with Stone McQuire Vogt Architects, 2004

Although not administratively part of the University of Toronto Scarborough, the Centennial College Morningside Campus (formerly the Centennial HP Science and Technology Centre) sits on land owned by the university, southwest of the north campus, and the two institutions share several joint-degree programs, such as paramedicine and journalism. Centennial College was established in 1966 as Ontario's first community college and now has four campuses and seven satellite locations. It is recognized as one of the most culturally diverse postsecondary institutions in Canada.

This V-shaped facility is reminiscent of a magnificent ocean liner that has somehow plowed into and comfortably come to rest in a south-facing hillside. Gleaming white in some places and metallic in others, this is undeniably optimistic architecture embodying a liberating spirit. Inside, it feels like a small, bustling city with students coming and going amid the central atrium commons space, classrooms, laboratories, exercise rooms, and a multifaith prayer room. Wandering through the facility, one is reminded of Canada's aspirations as a microcosm of tolerance and social well-being, of which this humming place can serve as a rewarding everyday example.

Within this great ship of a building, a dramatic four-story commons space steps down the hillside on several levels, flooded on the south by sunlight. A wood-clad lecture theater and classroom volume hovers above. This space has a convincing grandeur and sophistication while, at the same time, feeling relaxed and welcoming.

151 The Ravine

The preservation and thoughtful development of the Highland Creek Valley ravine is integral to the UTSC visionary master plan. The natural beauty and ecology of the ravine will be protected while, simultaneously, areas will continue to be developed for recreation, sports, hiking, foraging, and firsthand immersion in a remarkably diverse landscape.

A sanctuary for wildlife and a favorite destination for hikers and naturalists, the ravine lands link with Rouge Valley, Canada's first national urban park. UTSC continues to strengthen its program of environmental stewardship as Parks Canada's primary research and education partner, and by collaborating with the City of Toronto and Toronto Region Conservation Authority on projects that include ecological restoration, wildlife protection and conservation, water quality monitoring, and recreational opportunities.

In addition to natural habitats, the campus's beautiful ravine zone features two multisport grass fields suitable for soccer, rugby, football, cricket, and more. The Dan Lang Field is a full, high-performance baseball diamond and home to U of T's Varsity Blues baseball team. In 2011 University of Toronto President David Naylor named the field for Dan Lang, the beloved professor and the longest-serving head coach of the Varsity Blues who led the team to two Ontario University Athletics league championships and two silver medals.

UTSC has a strong tennis tradition with facilities supporting community, tournaments, intramural teaching, coaching, and play. A new tennis facility, with eight courts and a stadium court, opened for the 2015 Pan Am & Parapan Am Games.

152 Miller Lash House and Coach House
Attributed to Edward B. Green Sr., 1913

At the southern edge of the Scarborough campus overlooking the ravine is the stately Miller Lash House, which serves as a conference center, guest house, and community events facility. Completed between 1911 and 1913 by Toronto businessman Miller Lash, whose father owned the Brazilian Traction, Light and Power Company, the seventeen-room house was the set piece of his family's 375-acre summer estate in the Highland Creek Valley.

Legend has it that in 1911 the wealthy Lash was out for a Sunday drive along what is now Old Kingston Road, which descends into the valley of Highland Creek. Lash was supposedly so impressed by the land with its grassy fields, forest, and rushing stream that he promptly bought the property and commissioned architect Edward B. Green Sr., of the prominent Buffalo, New York, firm Green & Wicks, to design his new estate.

The design of the Miller Lash House generally follows the style of the arts and crafts movement. The walls of the house are constructed of poured-in-place concrete and integrally faced with river stones collected from the Highland Creek

Miller Lash House, exterior (ABOVE) and living room (OPPOSITE)

bed, which meanders by the house. The heavy beams and trusswork that support the cathedral ceilings are squared pine timbers, while natural clay was used for the roof and floor tiles.

Lash died in 1941, and the house was sold to insurance broker E. L. McLean, who, in 1963, sold the estate to the University of Toronto. The university renovated the house to serve as the UTSC principal's residence, in conjunction with the establishment of Scarborough College in 1964. A. F. Wynne Plumptre, appointed as the college's second principal, was the first principal to reside in the house. Principals continued to live there until 1976.

In 1998 the Miller Lash House was designated under the Ontario Heritage Act, and the university lovingly restored the house, providing a stimulating venue for social events.

University of Toronto Mississauga (UTM)

University of Toronto Mississauga (UTM)

Along winding Mississauga Road, twenty miles (twenty-three kilometers) west of downtown Toronto, a structure of stacked, jutting stone boldly announces the University of Toronto Mississauga (UTM). This sculptural gateway at the main entrance to the campus symbolizes UTM's origins on a quarry site fifty years ago, along with the institution's dynamic thrust into the future. The gateway's fossil-filled limestone, extracted nearby, links us back through thousands of years to nature and to the Iroquois, then the Mississauga peoples, and, later, French trappers who lived along the Credit River, above which UTM's modern campus is now perched.

In 1963 the University of Toronto Plateau Committee recommended the establishment of two off-campus colleges: Scarborough College to the east of Toronto and Erindale College to the west. Erindale College held its first classes

Dr. Carl Williams, vice president for planning for the suburban campuses and principal, Erindale College (left) with William Davis, premier of Ontario, at sod turning, Erindale College, 1966

in 1965 in the T. L. Kennedy Secondary School. The first class of ninety students graduated in 1970. Known since 1998 as the University of Toronto at Mississauga and more recently as simply University of Toronto Mississauga, the institution now has nearly fourteen thousand students, 90 percent of them commuters. Growth is expected to reach an enrollment of 16,000 students by 2023.

The physical shape of the campus retains the traces of numerous master plans. In the thirty-five-year period from 1965 to 2000, UTM generated five different plans, resulting in the campus collage of divergent impulses that now exists. This history of moving in one direction for several years and then shifting to another has left behind superimposed, half-filled visions. Although the university's other suburban campus, at Scarborough, has also seen major shifts in planning in recent decades, it at least has John Andrews's distinctive original buildings as a reminder of what a coherent campus plan might be. (For more on the campus at Scarborough, see Walk Nine, pages 270–72.)

UTM has not had the good fortune of Scarborough's Andrews legacy, but it almost did. In December 1966 the architect drafted an impressive thirty-one-page document titled *Erindale Campus Master Plan*—a bold, comprehensive proposal for consolidated, dense built form at the south end of the 224-acre campus and environmentally conscious conservation of the rest of the site. In terms of land use, it was a progressive proposition. Andrews had just completed his visionary project for the Scarborough campus, and the May 1966 *Report of the User's Committee on the Construction of the Erindale Campus, University of Toronto* stated, "We have been strongly impressed by the excellence of the Scarborough design, and have endeavored to profit from that example." It is thus not surprising that Andrews was called on again.

For Erindale, the architect's innovative team included planner Donovan Pinker, landscape architect Michael Hough, and housing consultant Evan Walker. Their proposal has several similarities with Scarborough: respect for and response to topography, separation of pedestrian and vehicular traffic, a climate-controlled pedestrian street system, integration of resident and commuter students, avoidance of rigid departmental structures, a strong emphasis on meeting and communal spaces, the use of television as a teaching aid, experimentation with modular building systems, and, throughout, an elaborate orchestration of architectural space, as evident in the section drawings drafted by the Andrews team.

The master plan gave special attention to commuting students. Andrews asserted:

> The major innovation at Erindale will be the inclusion of a significant amount of "bunk and carrel" space within the residential complex. This will mean that commuting students will be able to rent a bunk and carrell [*sic*] for overnight use whenever they wish to stay late on campus to work, or for some specific event.…In this way it is hoped that commuters will become 2 or 3 day commuter residents, able to join more easily in the total student life of the university.

Erindale College, perspective view, A. D. Margison and Associates, 1968

Andrews's vision was rigorously knit together in a proposed megastructure that grabbed the upper ridge of a former quarry and stepped down its slope. This building would be surrounded by carefully planned athletic fields, botanical gardens, research fields, and meadowlands (along with 2,500 car spaces in four enclosed parking quays). The rollout of the plan was to happen incrementally, starting with five hundred students and growing to five thousand. Andrews prophetically imagined that eventually Erindale College would become a "town" of ten to twelve thousand students. The model prepared by Andrews's team gives a sense of the project's orthogonal, labyrinthine conception.

For reasons that remain unclear, however, within a year of the planning committee's recommendation, the Andrews team was out of the picture, replaced by A. D. Margison and Associates, with Raymond Moriyama as planning and architectural consultant and J. Austin Floyd as landscape architect. Through late 1967 and early 1968, Moriyama developed a similarly ambitious megastructure, to be sited in exactly the same location that Andrews had selected, along the ridge of the quarry. Megastructural projects were de rigueur through the late 1950s and early 1960s, and both Andrews and Moriyama were undoubtedly influenced by European projects built during this period by architects such as Alison and Peter Smithson, Jacob B. Bakema, and Shadrach Woods. Many aspects of the officially adopted Margison-Moriyama plan were akin to Andrews's 1966 plan, such as the loop road, the separation of pedestrians from vehicles, the internal pedestrian street system, and the residence wings overlooking the river valley. It was a monumental conception that encompassed more than one million square feet (92,903 square meters).

Although the working relationship between Moriyama and the Margison firm from 1967 to 1968 is difficult to discern precisely, documentation from the period clearly reveals that Moriyama was involved in the Erindale project at key junctures. The forms that evolved during Moriyama's involvement were not as rigid as Andrews's and presented a somewhat more relaxed, organic approach. Indeed, the first part of the imagined megastructural colossus constructed at UTM— the Phase One Research and Laboratory Block, designed by Moriyama from 1967 to 1968 and opened in 1971—convincingly cranks and bends across the site. A. D. Margison and Associates designed the second phase—the Library, Lecture, Theatre Complex (1973)—which resembles Moriyama's first phase but lacks that design's material richness and formal finesse. Only these two phases of the Margison-Moriyama megastructure, which came to be known as the South Building (later renamed Davis Building), were realized.

By 1972 the Queen's Park government thought Ontario had excessive college and university capacity and put a halt to expansion. This, along with growing public and institutional skepticism about introverted, grandiose projects, put an end to UTM's imposing vision. By the 1970s and 1980s, funding was scarce and architectural ambition low. During that time, five architecturally undistinguished, entirely suburban town-house complexes for students were built around the campus, far removed both conceptually and physically from the original megastructure vision. By 2000, when Mark Sterling and Mary Jane Finlayson completed their master plan for UTM, collective thinking had shifted to ecological performance and a more incremental approach to building, underscored by the concept of landscape as the connective, community-making tissue. Sterling and Finlayson's campus plan established an intelligent framework for development and expansion at UTM and received a City of Mississauga Urban Design Award in 2005. The Sterling and Finlayson plan was revised by a UTM in-house working group in 2011, providing guidelines for development and growth of the original south campus and the newly defined north campus, through the year 2020.

Remarkable change has unfolded over the past five decades. As its founders imagined from the start, UTM is commuter-intensive, but there are now diverse living options on campus. In addition to the town-house clusters, three residence halls have been realized, bringing the total on-campus accommodations to nearly 1,500 beds. Phased renovation of the town-house clusters will commence soon, along with incremental build-out of additional student residence halls. The completions of new academic buildings, a library/learning center, a student center, a recreation/athletic center, and a health sciences building—along with a surge in construction of housing for students—have dramatically changed the feel of UTM. During the past twenty years the campus has transformed from a loose agglomeration of structures to a bustling village-like place. As Sterling and Finlayson suggested in their 2000 master plan, landscape has become the connective tissue. If not highly integrated in the Andrews and Moriyama modes, incrementally the UTM campus has nevertheless become more coherent, providing a vibrant framework for intellectual and social life in the twenty-first century.

This architectural transformation seems particularly significant and timely in the context of the phenomenal growth of Mississauga as a city. UTM is a sophisticated anchor in this sprawling city of 750,000, Canada's sixth largest. Created in 1974 from a disparate collection of small towns, Mississauga has become a bizarre, highly complex urban-suburban landscape, hosting Pearson International Airport and dotted now with sixty-story, futuristic residential towers. The city struggles to retain remnants of its original geography and social history. Indeed, most of the natural landscape of its indigenous peoples, the Mississaugas, has been radically changed, layered with a vast network of technology-driven infrastructure, of which UTM is a vital part. But, admirably, the campus retains swaths of fields and forests and bedrock, anchoring the institution in place and time.

153 Gateway Entrance
Kearns Mancini Architects, 2013

This powerful, asymmetrical structure of Credit Valley limestone was designed by Kearns Mancini Architects to welcome people to the campus and to recall UTM's beginnings in the 1960s on a former quarry site. As well, it suggests shifting tectonic plates and recalls the important research of UTM's second principal, Dr. John Tuzo

Gateway Entrance

Wilson, an internationally acclaimed geophysicist and geologist who advanced plate tectonics theory. Simultaneously raw and friendly, this gateway is a memorable introduction to the UTM campus.

154   William G. Davis Building (formerly South Building)

Phase One: Research and Laboratory Block (J. Tuzo Wilson Research Wing)

A. D. Margison and Associates with Raymond Moriyama (design consultant), 1971

Phase Two: Library, Lecture, Theatre Complex

A. D. Margison and Associates, 1973

Centre for Applied Biosciences and Biotechnology (CABB)

Stantec Architecture Ltd., 2002

Renovation

Kearns Mancini Architects, 2010

Renovation

Moriyama & Teshima Architects, expected completion 2019

Arriving from Mississauga Road at either the main or middle entrance to campus, one encounters a large pond. Just beyond is the William G. Davis Building, which serves as the front door to the campus. Derived from a vast, megastructural concept by architect Raymond Moriyama, the Brutalist-style Davis Building is constructed of reinforced concrete and presents an aggressive expression of horizontal and vertical circulation elements and, in Phase One, of laboratory ducting systems. The Research and Laboratory Block (1971) is architecturally accomplished, employing sculpted forms and a robust material palette. The softly curved towers that house the stairs; naturally lit corridors; recessed wooden window frames; rugged pine railings; and rust-colored clay tiles covering the walls of the corridors combine to create a visceral interior environment that is rewarding to the senses.

Phase Two (originally the Library, Lecture, Theatre Complex) architecturally mimics Phase One, but, with its painted concrete-block walls, feels like a dowdy cousin. This portion of the Davis Building has served for forty years as the center of campus life and contains classrooms, a bookstore, health services, food services, counseling areas, athletic facilities, and the central meeting place that was and continues to be a gathering point for commuters. UTM's main administrative offices are on the second floor.

In 2002 UTM completed a small addition to the Davis Building, the Centre for Applied Biosciences and Biotechnology (CABB), which provides specialized biotech facilities for faculty, graduate students, and doctoral students. It houses research on combining the precision of DNA chemistry with the speed of fiber optics, leading to rapid testing and screening for life-threatening infections and diseases, such as hepatitis and AIDS. The de Stijl–like composition of the CABB recalls the Rietveld Schröder House (1924) in Utrecht designed by Gerrit Rietveld, but dressed up, rather heavily and mysteriously, in a cloak of charcoal black. This small wing is able to hold its own next to the giant alongside it.

William G. Davis Building

In recent years the university broke up the bulk of the Davis Building—which continues to be a somewhat perplexing maze—with the creation of through routes and linkages to other structures: a connection to the Recreation, Athletics, and Wellness Centre to the southeast; connections to the Communication, Culture & Technology Building at the northwest; and connection to the Health Science Complex to the north are welcome improvements. The 2010 renovation of the former library block into classrooms and offices is particularly noteworthy. While respecting the Brutalist architectural character of the building, Kearns Mancini Architects inserted carefully detailed skylights and a clerestory to introduce swaths of natural light into the deep floorplate. UTM's next phase of renovation for the Davis Building will include a new entry sequence and updating of the food court.

155 Innovation Complex (formerly Kaneff Centre for Management and Social Studies)

Shore Tilbe Henschel Irwin Peters, 1992

Addition and renovation

Moriyama and Teshima Architects 2014

The Kaneff Centre for Management and Social Studies opened in 1992. Rather humdrum, the mildly postmodern building was typical of commercial architecture in the late 1980s and early 1990s and stood alone, with no easily discernable relationship to nearby structures. Two decades after it opened, the Kaneff Centre was completely transformed, reborn as UTM's Innovation Complex.

Innovation Complex, exterior (TOP) and central atrium (BOTTOM)

The building's square footprint was largely retained, and the exterior was reclad in elegant, vertical white fins made of powder-coated aluminum. The central, 120-foot-diameter (36.6-meter-diameter) circular space from 1992 (an outdoor courtyard) was enclosed to make a beautiful, light-filled atrium for year-round use. Wrapped in warm, creamy travertine, the atrium has white oak fins accenting the upper band of windows circling the rotunda. The Innovation Complex is a multiuse building, housing the registrar's office, the Institute for Management & Innovation, cafés, and the Blackwood Gallery. The gallery is named to honor Canadian artist David Blackwood, who was appointed in 1969 as the first artist in residence at UTM (then Erindale College). The Blackwood Gallery has become a major player in the Toronto art scene, hosting exhibitions of leading contemporary artists.

156 Recreation, Athletics, and Wellness Centre (RAWC)
Shore Tilbe Irwin & Partners, 2006

In 2006 the university added the Recreation, Athletics, and Wellness Centre (RAWC) onto the Davis Building, fully integrating the two spaces and generating a new southeast gateway into the campus from the adjacent parking lots. A granite-paved grand stair that rises through three levels signifies this gateway condition and unifies the RAWC with the Davis Building.

The architects employed multiple transparencies to provide visual connections between the building's various gymnasia, Olympic-class swimming pool,

Recreation, Athletics, and Wellness Centre

and running track. On a typical day the facility is abuzz with activity, presenting a scene of bodies moving through and engaging the architectural space. With simple means, the design creates a recreational/athletic machine that recalls the social goals of health and well-being promoted by early-twentieth-century modernist architects such as Le Corbusier.

At the northwest, a series of terraces step up from the RAWC to the Davis Building.

157 Student Centre

Kohn Shnier Architects, 1999

The Student Centre resulted from a 1996–97 national design competition that garnered more than a hundred entries and launched the architectural renaissance that UTM has enjoyed for the past twenty years. Kohn Shnier Architects won the competition with a rigorous design that functions as a gateway for the Five Minute Walk, the route between the central academic buildings and the wooded area to the northeast where most of the student residences are.

The center contains student clubs, the campus radio station CFRE, newspaper and student union offices, lounges, a restaurant/pub, a multifaith prayer room, and generous outdoor areas—all nestled under a butterfly roof. The architects organized the building into four horizontal bands: restaurant/pub, multipurpose rooms, linear lobby/lounge, and student activity offices. Within each of these bands

Student Centre

there is flexibility to adjust programs and activities, and there is also functional flexibility between the bands. The competition brief required an existing two-story retail structure, the Crossroads Building, to be incorporated into the new project, and Kohn Shnier Architects used it as their fourth band, the student activity offices.

A dramatic red fireplace lounge and an elegant white music room face the forest and provide contained counterpoints within the building's otherwise network-like composition. The minimalist restaurant/pub space—with tall walls of glass forming three of its sides—was immediately controversial, seen by some students as too exposed and public. Partly because of this, students altered the space to be more like a cozy recreation room, without seeking much guidance from the architects. Other areas of the building have been modified haphazardly in recent years, including the covered terrace along the south facade. These changes have undermined the Student Centre's minimalist, modernist verve, which brought it international attention at the end of the twentieth century. Nevertheless, the architects' conceptual banding has survived and enables waves of student life to flow robustly in the twenty-first century.

158 Roy Ivor Hall

*Baird Sampson Neuert Architects in joint venture with
Fliess Gates McGowan Easton Architects Inc., 1999*

Roy Ivor Hall, a residence for 190 students, is loosely based on the University of Oxford model. It is organized into four volumetrically distinct house clusters, each with its own stair. The typical living arrangement consists of an apartment with four bedrooms. The site plan preserved mature trees, and the building focuses on a garden of indigenous plants surrounding a small pond. Realized on a modest budget, Roy Ivor Hall is impressive for its imaginative embedding in the landscape (which takes advantage of subtle topographical shifts), gentle humanizing scale, handsome material palette, and tectonic rigor.

The building's concept flows from an approach that balances Bauhaus rationality (note, for example, the large, thoughtfully designed windows in student rooms that provide ample light and pleasant views) with phenomenological preoccupations that owe something to Frank Lloyd Wright and Canadian architect Ron Thom. What results is an intricate architectural composition with a strong sense of context.

Roy Ivor Hall's varied material and color palette—iron-flecked orange-brown brick, blue-gray slate tile, red-brown horizontally corrugated steel panels—is masterfully orchestrated and proportioned. It can be argued that less is not always more, and the visual complexity of the building makes a convincing case for this statement, its textures merging with the surrounding landscape.

In terms of urban design, Roy Ivor Hall is intelligently resolved, presenting a long and regular rhythm along Mississauga Road, while communicating a looser, picturesque quality from Residence Road on the campus side. The complex also kindly engages the Schreiberwood town houses to the north. In 2004 Roy Ivor Hall won both an Ontario Association of Architects Design Excellence Award and a City of Mississauga Urban Design Award.

The residence was touchingly named for the "Bird Man of Mississauga," Roy Ivor, who lived in a mobile home in the woods across from the campus. He took in and cured injured birds and created a sanctuary for them.

Roy Ivor Hall

159 Oscar Peterson Hall

Cannon Design, 2007

This residence hall honors Oscar Peterson, the late Canadian jazz musician and longtime resident of Mississauga. The largest residence on campus, it accommodates over 420 students, who are housed in suites composed of two bedrooms that share a bathroom. Oscar Peterson Hall also houses the Colman Commons, a food court for all UTM residences.

Oscar Peterson Hall

The building is sited in the center of the heavily wooded western sector of the campus, facing Roy Ivor Hall and backing onto Erindale Hall. It is S-shaped, generating a courtyard directly across from Roy Ivor Hall's pond and garden. Given the careful siting strategies and architectural sophistication of the earlier Roy Ivor Hall and Erindale College residences, which are gently tucked into their sites, it is both surprising and regrettable that the university seemed to lose architectural focus and courage in the realization of Oscar Peterson Hall. This five- and six-story brick-clad dorm feels too large for its site, and there is little tectonic finesse.

160 Lislehurst

Herbert Harrie Schreiber, builder, 1885
Renovation
Reginald Watkins, 1928

Lislehurst is the home of the principal of UTM. Nestled deep in the heavily wooded area at the north end of the campus, it was built of Credit Valley stone in 1885 by the Schreiber family, who hailed from England and were descendants of Sir Isaac Brock, the major general responsible for defending Upper Canada (now Ontario) against the United States in the War of 1812. (There were originally three Schreiber houses in the area, but, other than traces of foundations, only Lislehurst remains.) A subsequent owner, Reginald Watkins, a Hamilton businessman, renovated the house in 1928, adding a wing to the west. The property became known as the Watkins Estate and was purchased by the University of Toronto in the mid-1960s to create the new Erindale College campus. Lislehurst is designated under the Ontario Heritage Act, recognized for its architectural and historical importance.

Lislehurst

Inside, the house exudes English country coziness, from the wood beams in the entrance hall to an array of exquisite fireplaces to view of the deer that frequently pass by and peer through the living room windows. Throughout hang lovely etchings and paintings by Charlotte Mount Brock Schreiber, wife of Herbert Harrie Schreiber and an accomplished artist. Do not miss the delightful Lislehurst Bridge, not far from the historic home and a popular spot for wedding photographs.

161 Terrence Donnelly Health Sciences Complex

Kongats Architects, 2010

In 2006, when the Province of Ontario approved the expansion of medical programs, including the University of Toronto Faculty of Medicine's expansion to the Mississauga campus, a UTM medical academy was created in conjunction with local hospitals. This academy occupies two-thirds of the Terrence Donnelly Health Sciences Complex, located to the northeast of the Davis Building and to the southeast of the Communication, Culture, and Technology Building. The structure consists of four stories, each level designed as a sculptural programmatic box that expresses its internal function. (The first floor has lecture halls, the second floor contains seminar rooms, the third floor comprises offices, and the fourth floor has laboratories.) These stacked boxes are offset to create outdoor, landscaped decks and terraces. The box volumes are clad in vertical stainless-steel panels that

OVERLEAF: Terrence Donnelly Health Sciences Complex

also act as louvers (or fins) and generate a rhythmic, varied facade that ranges from opaque to transparent. The building skin captures and manipulates light rather magically.

The interior character is minimalist with white terrazzo floors, white walls, and lovely anigre wood doors. The main stairwell is an exquisite essay in folded stainless steel—perhaps the most beautiful stairway on campus. An equally beautiful bridge links the complex, diagonally, to the Davis Building.

162 Research Greenhouse

Baird Sampson Neuert Architects, 2017

This tiny structure is a lovely addition to the campus. Accommodating plant research, its precisely detailed, delicate high-tech structure sparkles in the sunlight, and the lit interior glows at night. Six bays were completed in 2017 with provision for future expansion.

Research Greenhouse

THE NORTH CAMPUS

With six buildings constructed from 2004 to 2018 and a final infill piece planned, the renaissance of the north campus is nearly complete. Although the area is thought of as the new campus, it is actually the old campus, dating back to 1967. Today's students are generally unaware that the north campus was the location of the first new structure built after the founding of Erindale College, the forerunner of UTM. The building was referred to on early drawings simply as "Olympia York," shorthand reference to Olympia and York, the Toronto-based property development firm founded in the early 1950s by the Reichmann brothers who assisted with the project. Opened in 1967 and expanded in 1969, the old North Building served as a major academic building and as a gateway to the campus at the northern edge. The original North Building was demolished in stages, fully erased by 2016 to make way for Phases One, Two, and Three of the new North Building.

Now the north campus green and its playing fields are circled and defined by a necklace of attractive buildings ranging from four to six stories. These structures have given a strong identity to the bucolic north campus. Take note of the materials and colors of the buildings, which, rather subtly, link one to another. For example, the striped-orange terra-cotta cladding of Deerfield Hall, Phase One of the North Building, picks up on the rusty-orange brick of Erindale Hall; then the Phase Two extension of the North Building continues the use of terra-cotta, but in a metallic hue that in turn links to the moss-green copper of the Instructional Center. Like jewels in the necklace surrounding the north campus green, these low-slung buildings have highly individual characters while transitioning, one to the other, gracefully. Responsive to the environment, the architecture recedes, politely and quietly, into the dense forest setting.

163 Communication, Culture & Technology (CCT) Building

Saucier + Perrotte, 2004

The Communication, Culture & Technology (CCT) Building was the first new building constructed in the emerging north campus precinct, adding a significant edge along the southeast. Architecturally, it set a high standard for the other buildings that would follow around the edge of the north campus green, and its academic ambitions are equally provocative. Simply stated, the central question of the CCT interdisciplinary community is: how can communication, in all its dimensions, build knowledge and create culture? The elegant, minimalist structure that houses the CCT program provides a suitable environment for engaging intellectual questions such as this.

The T-shaped, four-story CCT building comprises nearly 113,000 square feet (10,500 square meters) and contains interactive computer classrooms and laboratories, editing suites, faculty offices, a multimedia studio theater, a five-hundred-seat lecture theater, an "e-gallery" for electronic art exhibitions, and underground parking. It also houses the Human Communication Lab and the Institute of Communication and Culture. The building created two new courtyards and links the South Building and the heart of the campus northeastward to the Hazel McCallion Academic Learning Centre. With its parallel pedestrian "streets"—one outdoors, one indoors—straddling a reflective glass wall, it is experientially reminiscent of the mirrored environments created by artists such as Lucas Samaras. The sculpted northeast facade has hard-edge glass boxes that weave in and out and incorporates strips of mirror. It demonstrates how architecture can both embrace notions of movement and be simultaneously solid and transparent.

Communication, Culture & Technology Building

Communication, Culture & Technology Building, interior

Inside is a monumentally scaled commons area that, in its highly controlled spatial complexity, is reminiscent of the soaring, mysterious spaces of the eighteenth-century Roman architect-theorist Giovanni Battista Piranesi. In the CCT building, though, Montreal-based architects Saucier + Perrotte also offer contrasting intimate spaces, and the whole design is joined together by a cool palette of black, white, and gray.

The greatest success of the CCT Building is its strong integration with adjacent structures and the surrounding landscape. This is particularly apparent at the south and east areas of the building, where the folded planes of an expressive black auditorium mirror a series of folded, grass-covered ground planes. Saucier + Perrotte have developed a sophisticated understanding of landscape, both natural and artificial, that enables them to generate an architecture that is abstract and universal but also deeply embedded in the particulars of a specific place. From this, they seek what they refer to as a building's "soul," which they clearly found in the CCT building.

Indeed, it is not surprising that the building won the Ordre des Architectes du Québec Award for Best Institutional Building and an Ontario Association of Architects Design Excellence Award, both in 2007, and a Governor General's Medal in Architecture award in 2008. It set an appropriately high benchmark for future projects.

164 Erindale Hall

Baird Sampson Neuert Architects, 2005

Erindale Hall was the second building constructed on the newly defined north campus green. The name of this two-hundred-student residence honors the campus's transition from Erindale College to the University of Toronto Mississauga. The curved primary volume—which parallels and reinforces the Five Minute Walk and contributes to the definition of the southwest edge of the north campus green—consists of a long "bar building" supported by nineteen V-shaped piers that form the edge of a colonnade. The meandering back wall of the colonnade is faced in alternating zones of coarse, fissured capstone (removed in the quarrying

Erindale Hall

of Algonquin limestone) and sleek, mullionless glass; overhead hangs a rhythmic soffit with lighting slots cut into it and finished with delicate blue ceramic tiles. At the bend in the slender bar building, a small entrance foyer is glazed on both sides to provide views of the surrounding wooded areas, which are protected ecological zones. The roofs of the building collect rainwater, which is used to recharge adjacent wetland. The east convex side of Erindale Hall has three five-story residence towers that branch out from the main bar building. Between these towers, in the primary volume, run carefully detailed glazed corridors. Many aspects of this handsome, rusty-orange brick building are reminiscent of the work of the modernist architects Le Corbusier and Alvar Aalto, from the spirited piers to the sophisticated material palette.

165 Hazel McCallion Academic Learning Centre

Shore Tilbe Irwin & Partners, 2006

This striking building is named in honor of Hazel McCallion, the mayor of Mississauga from 1978 to 2014. Hazel, as she is affectionately called by her admirers, was an unwavering champion and booster for UTM. So it is fitting that the university's library bears the name of this energetic woman who led the city successfully for thirty-six years.

The architects based the four-story building's design for a technology-driven, information-obsessed society on the concept of an architectural "puzzle box" that users can open to discover an inner cabinet of stored knowledge (in both print and digital formats). Movable sliding units of compact shelving efficiently accommodate the library's entire collection of print material. The facade's interplay of rectilinear volumes, alternating between Prodema wood-veneer panels from Spain and large glazed areas with bluish glass fins, represents the puzzle box notion. Within this box, light wells bring sunlight deep into the library's interior and introduce dynamic diagonal views.

A glazed passageway links the Academic Learning Centre to the CCT building to the southwest. Along this route one can glimpse landscaped courtyards

and a lovely wooded area that is particularly spectacular in the fall, when the red, orange, and yellow leaves complement the library's reddish-brown cladding.

Hazel McCallion Academic Learning Centre

166 Instructional Centre

Shore Tilbe, 2011

This handsome building, which reaches out to but does not physically connect with the Academic Learning Centre, was conceived volumetrically as three "teaching towers" with atrium spaces between. The sequence of spaces includes a two-story glazed social gallery along the south edge of the building, overlooking the north campus green. With its distinctive green-tinged copper cladding and dark glass, the structure exudes an "of the forest" feel. The copper is applied in vertical panels, which, when seen up close, appear like tree bark or moss, furthering the building's

Instructional Centre

organic sensibility. The UTM master plan proposes that the Instructional Centre be linked to the final, forthcoming third phase of the North Building. This has merit, given that it would provide spatial closure of the northeast corner of the north campus green.

167 Deerfield Hall (North Building Phase One)
Perkins + Will Architects, 2014

Orange-striped Deerfield Hall is the first phase of the new North Building and accommodates the mathematical and computational sciences, drama, English, and psychology departments. Between two large volumes, the architects created an

Deerfield Hall, North Building Phase One (TOP) and an architectural rendering of North Building Phase Two (BOTTOM)

atrium that brings natural light deep into the structure, enlivening circulation routes, stairs, the café, and study lounges. Deerfield Hall's distinctive big boxes are clad in vertical-striped terra-cotta in shades of orange, relating the building to the rusty-orange brick of nearby Erindale Hall, constructed a decade earlier. Deerfield Hall is linked to Phase Two of the North Building, stretching to the northeast.

168 North Building Phase Two

Perkins and Will Architects, 2018

Phase Two of the North Building, encompassing 210,000 square feet (1,950 square meters), shares a landscaped courtyard with Deerfield Hall (Phase One). Space is provided for numerous departments: English, drama, philosophy, historical studies, language studies, political science, and sociology. Similar architecturally to adjacent Deerfield Hall, Phase Two features two large rectangular volumes embracing an atrium; but here the primary volumes rise to six stories, the easterly one being somewhat monumental, giving it an appropriate scale in relation to the expanse of the north campus green. Each expressed "box" includes a top-floor covered terrace, one that faces the north campus green, and one that faces Outer Circle Road. Clad in metallic terra-cotta with an iron oxide metallic glaze, Phase Two of the North Building relates visually to the nearby copper-clad Instructional Centre, completed in 2011 and also designed by Andrew Frontini of Shore Tilbe and later of Perkins and Will Architects.

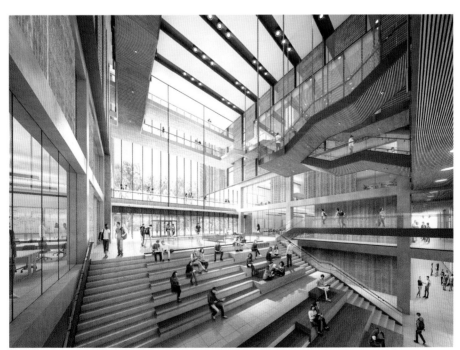

Deerfield Hall, North Building Phase Two, atrium (architectural rendering)

University of Toronto Off Campus and Surroundings

University of Toronto Off Campus and Surroundings

This last walk focuses on four of the University of Toronto's off-campus buildings and fourteen architecturally noteworthy buildings in the immediate area around the downtown (St. George) campus. The immediate area spans from Richard A. Waite's Ontario Legislative Building (1892) to the 7 St. Thomas project by Hariri Pontarini Architects, completed in 2017. They not only present an engaging cross-section of 125 years of Toronto architectural history but also serve as a reminder of how tastes change and styles come and go, and that controversy in the world of architecture is nothing new.

Most importantly, these diverse buildings near the campus reveal the city's long tradition of architectural innovation and excellence, something that

ABOVE: President's House
PREVIOUS: Toronto Athletic Club (Stewart Building)

Torontonians tend to overlook or even deny. These formidable works of architecture constitute an appropriate final footnote. They complement the university buildings and places presented earlier in this guide and underscore the rich cultural relationships and flow of ideas that exist between town and gown.

169   President's House, 93 Highland Avenue
Wickson & Gregg, 1910

This home in Toronto's Rosedale neighborhood is attributed to the firm of Wickson & Gregg, which was formed in 1905 and designed nearly forty large residences in Toronto. The President's House was originally built for David Alexander Dunlap, a gold-mining magnate whose philanthropist wife, Jessie, donated the David Dunlap Observatory to the university in 1935, honoring her husband. (The university sold the observatory in 2008.)

In 1956 the university purchased the Dunlap mansion to serve as the official residence for the president and his or her events. University social occasions are gracefully accommodated in the sophisticated sequence of spaces that the house provides. From a porte cochere, guests enter a vestibule leading to an elegant receiving room, off of which are a formal yet intimate dining room with ornate plaster work, a paneled library, and a large living room with an adjacent, plant-filled solarium. The rear of the house opens onto extensive lawns and gardens. Perched above one of Toronto's twenty-nine ravines, the President's House offers magnificent views to the downtown skyline.

170   Dr. Eric Jackman Institute of Child Study (JICS), 45 Walmer Road
Sproatt & Rolph, 1932
Addition
Gordon Adamson & Associates, 1955
Renovation and addition (Margaret and Wallace McCain Pavilion)
Taylor Smyth Architects, 2018

Named in honor of clinical psychologist and benefactor Dr. Eric Jackman, the JICS is part of the Ontario Institute for Studies in Education and focuses on an integrated approach to the study of human development, family dynamics, and childhood education. Its tripartite mission is carried out through three components: a graduate teacher education program, a research center, and a laboratory school. The school has two hundred students, ranging from those in nursery to those in grade eight. The JICS evolved from the St. George's School of Child Study, established in 1925 by Edward Bott, the first head of psychology at the University of Toronto. During the 1930s, this St. George's School came into national and international prominence for its role in the early education of the Dionne quintuplets. The school also became an important contributor to Canada's war effort, helping to establish war nurseries in England.

The Georgian house that accommodates the JICS was designed by the talented Henry Sproatt and was one of his last works before he died in 1934. The home originally belonged to Leighton Goldie McCarthy, who donated it to the university in 1955. The McCain Pavilion, facing Spadina Road, was added in 2018 and includes a multipurpose auditorium/gymnasium and new classrooms for the laboratory school. The second floor projects dramatically over the new Spadina Road entrance with a deep, inhabitable window for children.

171 Chestnut Residence, 89 Chestnut Street

Armstrong & Molesworth, 1971

Located next door to Toronto City Hall, this former hotel was purchased by the university in 2003 and adapted as a residence accommodating 950 students. It was originally the Civic Square Holiday Inn, touted as "the largest Holiday Inn in the world with 750 luxury rooms and suites." Its twenty-seventh floor deluxe eatery, La Ronde, was the city's only revolving restaurant until the CN Tower opened in 1976.

Chestnut Residence

The concrete-clad building consists of a twenty-four-floor tower rising from a three-story podium that is linked by a bridge (no longer in use) to the podium of city hall. The facades of the tower present a grid of alternating pairs of windows and tiny recessed balconies.

172 University of Toronto Institute for Aerospace Studies (UTIAS), 4925 Dufferin Street

Gordon Adamson & Associates, 1959

Microsatellite Science and Technology Centre

Kearns Mancini Architects, Inc., 2012

The University of Toronto's Institute for Aerospace Studies (UTIAS) is located fourteen miles (twenty-two kilometers) north of downtown Toronto and offers undergraduate studies along with master's of applied science and doctoral degrees. The history of UTIAS goes back to World War One, but its substantial formation unfolded through the pioneering work of Dr. Gordon Patterson, who established the Department of Aeronautical Engineering in 1947, then the Institute of Aerophysics in 1949. UTIAS's sprawling complex includes the Multifunctional Structures Lab,

University of Toronto Institute for Aerospace Studies

the Flight Research Simulator, the Advanced Combustion Energy Research Facility, and the Autonomous Space Robotics Lab.

In 2012 UTIAS opened its impressive Microsatellite Science and Technology Centre (MSTC), which focuses on nanotechnology and microsatellites for use in outer space. The MSTC's elegant industrial architecture is expressed through sophisticated details, such as the curved, louvered sunshades. Kearns Mancini Architects created a building that, in its unity, reflects the nature of satellites: simple forms housing sophisticated and precise instruments. A soaring "in flight" canopy graces the entrance.

173   Koffler Scientific Reserve, 17000 Dufferin Street
Principal residence
Mathers & Haldenby, 1953
Renovation of principal residence
B. Napier Simpson Jr., late 1960s to early 1970s
Gazebo
Raymond Moriyama, 1972
Dining and Operations Centre + Seasonal Bunkies
Montgomery Sisam Architects, Inc., expected completion 2020

It is not generally well known that the university owns a spectacular 860-acre property (formerly a horse farm) an hour north of Toronto. Situated in King Township in the west portion of the Oak Ridges Moraine, Joker's Hill, as the horse farm was called, was generously donated to the university by Murray and Marvelle Koffler in 1995. Recognizing the biological and geological diversity of the area, the university established a scientific research station at Joker's Hill in 2002 and uses this significant environmental landscape for teaching and research.

Koffler Scientific Reserve, Dining and Operations Centre (rendering)

The original building at Joker's Hill was designed by Mathers & Haldenby and completed around 1953. It was a rambling, wood-clad ranch-style house, built for General C. Churchill Mann and his wife, Billie Mann, the second owners of the property. Billie Mann was the daughter of the original owner, Colonel R. S. McLaughlin, founder of the automobile industry in Canada and breeder of champion thoroughbred racehorses.

When the Kofflers bought the farm in 1969, they commissioned the noted Canadian architect B. Napier Simpson Jr. to renovate and add to the house. He completely transformed it, adding grand extensions that created a U-shaped courtyard accommodating a swimming pool. The house is a good example of Simpson's signature use of locally sourced material, such as wood, stone, iron, slate, and barn board, which, through his rhythmic and imaginative manipulation, generates a unified architectural vocabulary.

The couple also engaged landscape architect J. Austin Floyd, one of Canada's first modern landscape architects, to redesign the grounds and reshape the ponds on the property; and the Kofflers commissioned noted Canadian architect Raymond Moriyama to design a chalet-like recreational structure on the edge of one of the ponds. Known to researchers and students as "the gazebo," the rugged yet playful wood structure focuses on a 360-degree stone fire hearth and surrounding table with a copper-clad hood. Rising from this is a chimney, which penetrates the peak of the roof and the center of a double-glazed skylight. Joker's Hill, now protected by the Oak Ridges Moraine Conservation Act, has become a significant oasis of green and calm amid the alarming urban sprawl creeping northward from Toronto. In 2017 the university launched a master planning initiative for Joker's Hill that includes housing for researchers, along with related facilities. The proposed structure by Montgomery Sisam Architects strives to fit organically into the Ontario agrarian landscape. Joker's Hill will be transformed once again, hopefully with the same imagination and care displayed in the twentieth century by the Manns and then the Kofflers.

174 Toronto Athletic Club (Stewart Building), 149 College Street

Edward James Lennox, 1894

Constructed on what had been cricket grounds in the nineteenth century, the Toronto Athletic Club, also known as the Stewart Building, was originally equipped with a gymnasium, dining rooms, a room dedicated to the card game whist, and the city's first indoor swimming pool. Although its original front steps were crudely replaced, and the building today sits in a sea of asphalt-paved parking lots, this Richardsonian Romanesque, palazzo-like structure retains much of its original grandeur. (See photo on page 323.)

Its architect, Edward James Lennox, better known as E. J. Lennox, was responsible for many important Ontario buildings, including the Toronto City Hall (opened in 1899 and now called Old City Hall), the King Edward Hotel of 1903, the flamboyant Casa Loma residence of 1911, and the monumental Toronto Power Generating Station at Niagara Falls, finished in 1913.

The Stewart Building has housed numerous institutions and organizations over the years, including the Central Technical School, the fifty-second division of the Toronto Police, Collège des Grands-Lacs, and the Ontario College of Art and Design University, which owned the building from 1979 to 1997, using it as a second campus. The University of Toronto currently leases space in the Stewart Building to accommodate overflow from the Faculty of Arts and Science, the Faculty of Medicine, and the Rotman School of Management.

PROVINCE OF ONTARIO QUEEN'S PARK CAMPUS

The large complex of nine Ontario government buildings at the southeast corner of the University of Toronto's St. George campus includes styles ranging from Romanesque Revival to International Style modernism. An entire book could be written about this collection of fine buildings.

175 The Ontario Legislative Building (Queen's Park)

Richard A. Waite, 1892

Rebuilding of west wing

E. J. Lennox, 1912

North library addition

George W. Gouinlock, 1910

In Toronto the term "Queen's Park" applies to many things: a large urban park, a street, a subway station, the numerous buildings housing the offices of the Province of Ontario, or the Ontario Legislative Building at the head of University Avenue. Even the provincial government is casually called "Queen's Park." The park itself, named in honor of Queen Victoria, was planned by Edwin Taylor, an English landscape gardener who had trained with Sir Joseph Paxton. It was completed in 1860. Before

The Ontario Legislative Building (Queen's Park)

the crude traffic overpass was constructed at the southwest corner in the 1950s, the urban space of Queen's Park flowed unencumbered into the University of Toronto campus, past Hart House, to King's College Circle.

The other Queen's Park, the imposing, pink-stone Ontario Legislative Building, was completed in 1892 on the site of the former King's College (demolished in 1886). It took from 1852, when Cumberland & Storm won a competition for a building on the King's College site, to 1892—forty years of angst, wrangling, and aborted attempts—before a new legislative building was finally built. Even though the provincial government proceeded to dismantle King's College, they refused to commit money for Cumberland & Storm's building. Designs by government architect Kivas Tully were advanced in 1877 and 1880, but, again, nothing happened. Finally, an international competition was held in 1880, and the jury favored two entries: one by Darling & Curry and the other by Smith & Gemmell. However, the jury was soon to discover that both greatly exceeded the declared budget. The government revived the building project in 1885, raising the budget to c$750,000 and calling on one of the jury members, Buffalo, New York–based architect Richard A. Waite, to decide between the two designs. Waite declared both defective. Then, incredibly, the government appointed Waite himself to design the new legislative building. Construction commenced in 1886, and the building was completed in 1892, costing nearly c$1.4 million.

Waite's Romanesque Revival design is organized in a U shape, with the legislative chamber at the center, on the second floor. Four domed turrets flank a steep slate roof, and side wings with galleried halls extend to the east and west, each terminated by round-arched porte cocheres. The interiors, detailed with carved wood, wrought iron, and cast iron, are sumptuous. Following a 1909 fire, the west wing was rebuilt by E. J. Lennox, and George W. Gouinlock designed the north library wing completed in 1910. The north entrance to the library is through a beautiful Romanesque portal, which incorporates an Ontario coat of arms and realistically sculpted animals (a moose, deer, and a bear).

A throned Queen Victoria, sculpted in 1903 by Mario Raggi, is positioned at the southeast corner of the building. She seems content with the architecture behind her, unprovoked by the bickering and lavish budget overruns that surrounded Waite's appointment and the construction of this place more than a century ago. Maybe she is simply happy that everything around her is, rather strangely, "Queen's Park."

176 Whitney Block, 99 Wellesley Street West
Francis Riley Heaks, 1926
Tower addition
Francis Riley Heaks, 1932

Located across the street from the Ontario Legislative Building, this lovely neo-Gothic ensemble faced with Queenston limestone houses several provincial ministries. The sixteen-story, south-facing tower of the Whitney Block, added in 1932, is magnificent. It has art deco touches, and the facade is ornamented with sequences of quatrefoils and figures designed by Charles Adamson, which represent abstract ideals, like justice, along with physical pursuits such as mining and farming. The

Whitney Block, looking northeast, late 1920s

tower is no longer in use because it does not meet today's building code standards. However, it still has an operational hand-cranked elevator, one of the few remaining in Toronto. Between 2018 and 2020, the main Whitney Block will undergo renovation, including window replacement and updating of the heating and cooling systems.

177 Ontario Government Buildings

The Associated Architects for Queen's Park Project: Gordon S. Adamson & Associates, Allward and Gouinlock, Mathers and Haldenby, Shore and Moffat (later, Shore Tilbe Henschel Irwin Architects); landscape architects: Sasaki Strong and Richard Strong Associates

Phase One: Macdonald, Ferguson, and Hepburn Blocks

1964–66

Phase Two: Mowat and Hearst Blocks

1966–71

Queen's Park Reconstruction Project

2016–24

The concept for this group of five government office buildings, bounded by Bay Street, Wellesley Street West, and Grosvenor Street, is attributed to Douglas Glenn Creba, chief architect of the Ontario Public Works Department, starting in 1958. A consortium of Toronto architects formed a temporary company, the Associated Architects for Queen's Park Project, to design the large project, which houses most of the ministries of the Province of Ontario.

Completed in 1971, the complex was designed in the International Style. It is composed of four precast-concrete-clad towers in a pinwheel arrangement,

Ontario government buildings: the Whitney Block (left) and (clockwise from top left) the Ferguson, Hearst, Mowat, and Hepburn Blocks, with the two-story Macdonald Block connecting the four, aerial view, December 19, 2009

linked by a long, two-story, black-granite-clad podium. Sculpture, paintings, and design work were commissioned from twenty-nine artists and are integrated into the buildings, courtyards, and outdoor public spaces. These include pieces by Jack Bush, A. J. Casson, Alan C. Collier, Louis Archambault, Gerald Gladstone, Harold Town, Walter Yarwood, and Paulosie Kanayook.

Starting in 2018, the aging complex is being vacated to enable the Queen's Park Reconstruction Project, entailing replacement of electrical, plumbing, cooling, and heating systems, along with the rationalization of space allocation. The multiyear project of installing new green infrastructure will preserve aspects of the buildings that are architecturally and historically important while creating new efficiencies, accessibility, and an environmentally responsible workplace for the twenty-first century.

178 Frost Building, 95 Wellesley Street West
North Block
George N. Williams (chief architect, Ontario Public Works Department), 1955
South Block
Mathers & Haldenby, 1966

The Frost Building consists of two blocks linked by a five-story glass-enclosed bridge. The older North Block, completed in 1954 for the Treasury Department, is an unremarkable background building, while the South Block, opened in 1966, is one of Toronto's most interesting International Style structures. Together, they are named to honor Leslie M. Frost, premier of Ontario from 1949 to 1961.

The six-story South Block curves gently to embrace and define the urban space of Queen's Park Crescent. Resting on a raised terrace, the ground-floor facade is clad in white marble and dark brown granite, while the upper five floors, with deep-set windows, are clad in limestone.

179 One St. Thomas Residences, One St. Thomas Street
Robert A. M. Stern Architects, 2008

During the early twenty-first century, Toronto spawned hundreds of condominium towers, and the city now ranks second to New York in the number of people living in high-rise buildings in North America. Architecturally, the dramatic verticalization of Toronto has been a mixed blessing, with a few truly beautiful residential towers added to the urban fabric. A notable exception to the proliferation of architectural mediocrity is the creamy-white, twenty-nine-story luxury tower on St. Thomas Street by Robert A. M. Stern.

Stern is a native New Yorker, author of *New York 1960: Architecture and Urbanism Between the Second World War and the Bicentennial* (1995) and former dean of the Yale School of Architecture, so it comes as no surprise that the urbane architect has taken cues from the 1920s and 1930s, the grand era of New York

apartment buildings, and translated them into an eye-catching, stepped high-rise building for Toronto, anchored at the base by a porte cochere, formal garden, and wing of elegant town houses running eastward. A sculpted marble wall by artist Carl Tacon graces the driveway along the north.

The stepped silhouette of Stern's design is interesting to observe from a few blocks south, in relation to the 1933 Whitney Block tower at Queen's Park, which is similarly stepped and exquisitely detailed. (See photo on page 332.)

180   The Colonnade, 131 Bloor Street West

Gerald Robinson Architect with Tampold & Wells, 1964

Among many factors contributing to Toronto's success as a dynamic, contemporary city is its array of mixed-use buildings—structures that have more than one use and that, typically, mix these uses for economic and social advantage. The Colonnade, which encompasses luxury apartments, retail shops, restaurants, offices, and a parking garage, was completed in 1964 on land owned by Victoria University and was one of Toronto's first ambitiously mixed-use buildings. It recalls many of the intentions of Le Corbusier's Unité d'Habitation in Marseilles, completed just twelve years earlier.

ABOVE: The Colonnade
OPPOSITE: One St. Thomas Residences

The upper apartment volume, which includes over 160 apartments, presents a screenlike facade of concrete, made of dominant horizontals punctuated with a rapid rhythm of short verticals. This volume rests on a podium that houses publicly accessible offices, shops, and restaurants. Along Bloor Street, this podium is convincingly inflected to form a semicircular plaza and welcoming entry. The second-floor shopping area has ample height and a sectional development that brings in generous amounts of natural light. At the rear south face of the podium, the curved second floor has a row of fifteen elliptical windows that are worth seeing.

181 The Royal Conservatory of Music and the TELUS Centre for Performance and Learning, 273 Bloor Street West

Baptist Theological College
Langley, Langley & Burke, 1882
Castle Memorial Hall
Burke & Horwood, 1901
Science Hall
Burke & Horwood, 1907 (demolished 2002)
Renovation and additions
Kuwabara Payne McKenna Blumberg Architects, 1997, 2009

Founded in 1886 as the Toronto Conservatory of Music, this venerable institution (which counts Glenn Gould among its graduates) has been located at 273 Bloor Street West since 1962 and gained independence from the University of Toronto in 1991. Tightly bounded by the Royal Ontario Museum and Philosopher's Walk on the east and the university's Varsity Centre at the south and west, the conservatory engaged in a ten-year program of expansion and renovation that bound together its magnificent Victorian fabric with sympathetic contemporary additions. Due to the small site, Kuwabara Payne McKenna Blumberg Architects also had to make sacrifices, including the demolition of the fine south wing and stair tower of the original 1882 building by Langley, Langley & Burke.

The revitalized complex centers around the historic McMaster Hall (originally the Baptist Theological College, then McMaster University) and features three concert spaces: the intimate Mazzoleni Hall, a rehearsal hall, and a classic shoebox concert hall. The latter is positioned east–west, floating over the west edge of Philosopher's Walk and grafted onto McMaster Hall with a dramatic skylit court.

One of the most successful aspects of the reborn conservatory is the forecourt along Bloor Street West, framed on the west by Mazzoleni Hall, at the south by McMaster Hall, and on the west by an entrance pavilion. The wing containing the west entrance pavilion is boldly scaled and colored, smoothly fitting in with the heritage structure while refusing to kowtow to history. Together, these elements create a pleasing, public urban space.

182 The York Club, 135 St. George Street

David Roberts Jr., 1892

What is now the prestigious York Club was once a private mansion built for George Gooderham, president of the Gooderham and Worts distillery, a complex of buildings at the east edge of downtown that has been recently restored and christened the Distillery District. After Gooderham's death in 1905, the York Club purchased the mansion in 1908, and the university's board of governors often held meetings there. It remains one of the best examples of Romanesque Revival architecture in Toronto.

The geometrically complex, luxuriant structure is anchored by a muscular tower on the southwest corner and presents strong facades on both Saint George and Bloor Streets. To the right of the front door, the carved ornament includes a portrait of Henry Sproatt, who worked on the design with David Roberts Jr. and who later was one of the architects of the university's Hart House.

Constructed of red stone, brick, and terra-cotta, the York Club is a landmark in the city's Annex district. With the construction of numerous new condominium towers nearby, along Bloor Street West, and given the increasing densification of Toronto, the York Club and its gardens are a reminder of the key importance of both human scale and robust color and texture in urban environments.

The York Club

Lord Lansdowne Public School

183 Lord Lansdowne Public School, 33 Robert Street

Frederick C. Etherington, 1961

The Lord Lansdowne Public School presents a striking image on the corners of Robert Street and Spadina Crescent. What is this spiky eruption? A former world's fair pavilion? A lost fragment of Sputnik? Whatever one's reading of the building, it is fortunate that this exuberant work of modern architecture from 1961 not only still exists but also continues to provide a stimulating environment for students.

The school is knit together by steel, concrete, brick, and metal. However, it is the very slender steel pylons supporting a circular, folded roof that grab so much attention and make the building memorable. The sculpted pylons also define a kind of dramatic porch that flows around the central classroom pavilion.

Frederick C. Etherington, who graduated from the Ontario College of Art and Design University and apprenticed with the Toronto firm of Sproatt & Rolph, was the imaginative architect of the project. He was appointed chief architect of the Toronto Board of Education in 1951 and continued in that position until his retirement in 1965.

At a time when Toronto is losing many fine mid-twentieth-century works of architecture, one can only hope that the Lord Lansdowne Public School will continue to be appreciated and preserved.

184 Orde Street Junior School, 18 Orde Street

Charles Hartnoll Bishop, 1915

Located at the southeast corner of the university's St. George campus, just north of Chinatown, this century-old, Prairie Style public school is an important part of Toronto's architectural heritage. The building is attributed to Charles Hartnoll Bishop, who served as an architect's apprentice in England before becoming super-intendent of buildings for the Toronto Board of Education. The school opened in 1915 to serve an influx of immigrants to Toronto—to this day it continues to serve students from more than thirty countries.

Associated with the Midwestern United States, particularly Chicago, the Prairie Style was developed by a like-minded group of architects known as the Prairie School, a movement that evolved from the English arts and crafts movement in the late nineteenth and early-twentieth centuries. Emphasizing solid construction, craftsmanship, and disciplined ornament, the term "Prairie School" was coined by H. Allen Brooks, an architectural historian and longtime professor at the University of Toronto. Frank Lloyd Wright was a leading proponent of the movement.

Orde Street Junior School

Seen in comparison with Wright's Midway Gardens (1914) in Chicago, the Orde Street Junior School (1915) is a somewhat timid example of the Prairie Style. Nevertheless, Toronto has few examples of the style remaining, making it increasingly important to preserve this school.

185 Lillian H. Smith Branch Library, 239 College Street
Phillip H. Carter, 1995

This branch of the Toronto Public Library has special collections devoted to children's books and can be traced to the 1922 founding of the Toronto's Boys and Girls House, the first library in the British Empire devoted exclusively to children. One of the branch's key collections is the Osborne Collection of Early Children's Books, which includes gems such as Florence Nightingale's childhood library. The building itself is one of Toronto's strongest examples of the postmodern style.

There is little agreement about the date range of postmodernism, but it is generally thought of as emerging in the 1970s, reaching its zenith in the 1980s, and losing steam in the 1990s. This library, completed in 1995, is a late example of the style. Although postmodernism has endured a lot of contempt in recent years, the library, with its simple cubic volumes, substantial materials, and integral ornament, is curiously satisfying.

Embedded in the classical tradition, the four-story building is massive, monolithic, and bilaterally symmetrical with a carefully articulated copper roof.

Lillian H. Smith Branch Library

Its facades, clad in pale-cream brick, are well scaled, with two-story windows rising to a band of smaller windows on the third floor. A fourth-floor attic features diamond-brick patterning and tiny square windows. An elaborate, arched entry graces the College Street facade, accentuated by a pair of giant bronze griffins (guarding the library's treasures) and further marked above by a deep three-story cleft. Other pleasant aspects include a hefty, wood-clad service door on the east facade and a community garden at the rear.

186 Seven St. Thomas

Hariri Pontarini Architects, Inc. with ERA Architects Inc., 2017

The real estate boom that exploded in downtown and around the university over the past decade—sometimes referred to as the Manhattanization of Toronto—has resulted in a denser, more vibrant city. However, Toronto has struggled to balance heritage preservation with profit-driven enterprise, often resulting in formulaic development, facadism, and architectural mediocrity. Seven St. Thomas, at the southeast corner of Sultan and St. Thomas Streets, on the eastern edge of Victoria University, is a notable exception to this kind of generic, same-thing-everywhere approach, and it demonstrates how the old and the new can be elegantly harmonized.

Seven St. Thomas consists of three interlocking parts: six three-story red-brick Romanesque Revival town houses from the 1880s; a three-story podium wrapping around the town houses; and a six-story curvilinear glass-clad volume hovering above. The luxury project, which offers the purchase of commercial units rather than the typical lease arrangement, houses retail at ground level and office space above. The sensuous, fritted-white glass curtain wall reduces thermal transmission for this sustainable project. A miniplaza at the corner of St. Thomas and Sultan Streets offers a public amenity in the densely built area.

Here we find a model of intelligent, imaginative adaptive reuse and the kind of distinctive place-making that Toronto, at its best, can do brilliantly.

Seven St. Thomas

Bibliography

BOOKS

Arthur, Eric. *From Front Street to Queen's Park*. Toronto: McClelland & Stewart, 1979.
———. *Toronto, No Mean City*. Toronto: University of Toronto Press, 1964.
Baraness, Marc, and Larry Richards, eds. *Toronto Places: A Context for Urban Design*. Toronto: City of Toronto and University of Toronto Press, 1992.
Blackburn, Robert H. *Evolution of the Heart: A History of the University of Toronto Library Up To 1981*. Toronto: University of Toronto Press, 1987.
Blake, Samuel H. *Wycliffe College, An Historical Sketch*. Toronto: Wycliffe College, 1911.
Browne, Kelvin. *Bold Visions: The Architecture of the Royal Ontario Museum*. Toronto: Royal Ontario Museum, 2008.
Bureau of Architecture & Urbanism. *Toronto Modern: Architecture 1945–1965*. Toronto: Coach House Books and Association for Preservation Technology International, 2002.
Burwash, Nathaniel. *The History of Victoria College*. Toronto: The Victoria College Press, 1927.
Byrtus, Nancy, Mark Fram, and Michael McLelland, eds. *East/West: A Guide to Where People Live in Downtown Toronto*. Toronto: Coach House Press, 2000.
Carr, Angela. *Toronto Architect Edmund Burke: Redefining Canadian Architecture*. Montreal and Kingston: McGill-Queen's University Press, 1995.
Carter, Brian, ed. *Works: The Architecture of A. J. Diamond, Donald Schmitt and Company, 1968–1995*. Halifax: TUNS Press, 1996.
Dendy, William. *Lost Toronto*. Toronto: Oxford University Press, 1978.
Dendy, William, and William Kilbourn. *Toronto Observed: Its Architecture, Patrons, and History*. Toronto: Oxford University Press, 1986.
Diamond, Jack, Don Gillmor, and Donald Schmitt. *Insight and On Site: The Architecture of Diamond and Schmitt*. Vancouver: Douglas & McIntyre, 2008.
Dobney, Stephen, ed. *Barton Myers: Selected and Current Works*. Victoria: Images Publishing Group, 1994.
Ede, Carol Moore. *Canadian Architecture 1960/70*. Toronto: Burns and MacEachern, 1971.
Freedman, Adele. *Sight Lines: Looking at Architecture and Design in Canada*. Toronto: Oxford University Press, 1990.
Friedland, Martin L. *The University of Toronto: A History*. 2nd ed. Toronto: University of Toronto Press, 2013.
Gournay, Isabelle. *Ernest Cormier and the Université de Montréal*. Montreal: Canadian Centre for Architecture, 1990.
Hart House: University of Toronto. Toronto: The Board of Governors, University of Toronto, 1921.
Ibelings, Hans, and PARTISANS. *Rise and Sprawl: The Condominiumization of Toronto*. Montreal/Amsterdam: Architecture Observer, 2016.
Kalman, Harold. *A History of Canadian Architecture*. 2 vols. Toronto: Oxford University Press, 1994.
Kilgour, David, ed. *A Strange Elation: Hart House, the First Eighty Years*. Toronto: University of Toronto, 1999.
Kuwabara Payne McKenna Blumberg. *Kuwabara Payne McKenna Blumberg*. Gloucester, MA: Rockport Publishers, 1998.
Lambert, Phyllis, Deflet Mertins, Bruce Mau, and Rodolphe El-Khoury. *The Architecture of Kuwabara Payne McKenna Blumberg*. Basel: Birkhauser Ltd., 2004.
Litvak, Marilyn M. *Edward James Lennox: "Builder of Toronto."* Toronto: Dundurn Press, 1995.
Mays, John Bentley. *Emerald City: Toronto Visited*. Toronto: Viking, 1994.
Martyn, Lucy B. *The Face of Early Toronto: An Archival Record, 1797–1936*. Ontario: Sutton West/Paget Press, 1982.
McClelland, Michael, and Graeme Stewart, eds. *Concrete Toronto: A Guidebook to Concrete Architecture from the Fifties to the Seventies*. Toronto: Coach House Press and ERA Architects, 2007.
McHugh, Patricia and Alex Bozikovic. *Toronto Architecture: A City Guide*. Toronto: McClelland & Stewart, 2017.
Reed, T. A. *The History of Trinity College, 1852–1952*. Toronto: University of Toronto Press, 1952.
Reid, Dennis, ed. *Frank Gehry: Toronto*. Toronto: Art Gallery of Ontario, 2006.
Richardson, Douglas. *A Not Unsightly Building: University College and Its History*. Oakville, Ontario: Mosaic Press, 1990.

Rickets, Shannon, Leslie Maitland, and Jacqueline Hucker. *A Guide to Canadian Architectural Styles*. Peterborough, Ontario: Broadview Press, 2004.

Rochon, Lisa. *Up North: Where Canada's Architecture Meets the Land*. Toronto: Key Porter Books, 2005.

Simmins, Geoffrey. *Fred Cumberland: Building the Victorian Dream*. Toronto: University of Toronto Press, 1997.

——. *Ontario Association of Architects: A Centennial History, 1889-1989*. Toronto: Ontario Association of Architects, 1989.

Sisam, David. *Place and Occasion: Montgomery Sisam Architects*. Artifice Books in Architecture, London (UK), 2013.

Stackhouse, Reginald. *The Way Forward: A History of Wycliffe College, Toronto, 1877-2002*. Toronto: University of Toronto Press, 2002.

Stanwick, Sean, and J. Flores. *Design City Toronto*. Chicester, England: John Wiley & Sons, 2007.

Westfall, William. *The Founding Moment: Church, Society, and the Construction of Trinity College*. Montreal and Kingston: McGill-Queen's University Press, 2002.

White, Richard. *The Skule Story: The University of Toronto Faculty of Applied Science and Engineering, 1873-2000*. Toronto: Faculty of Applied Science and Engineering, University of Toronto, 2000.

Zeidler, Eberhard. *Buildings Cities Life: An Autobiography in Architecture*. 2 vols. Toronto: Dundurn Press, 2013.

BOOKLETS, GUIDES, REPORTS, AND SELECTED ARTICLES

Averill, Harold. *The University of Toronto: Snapshots of Its History*. University of Toronto Library, 2002.

A. D. Margison and Associates. "University of Toronto: Interim Report for the Complete Design and Supervision of Construction of Buildings and Site Development for the Erindale Campus." April 5, 1967.

——. "University of Toronto: Master Plan Report on Phasing and Planning for the Erindale Campus" 3, vol. 1 (December 1972) and 3, vol 2. (May 1972).

A. D. Margison and Associates with Raymond Moriyama, Planning and Architectural Consultant. "University of Toronto: Master Plan: Report on Phasing and Planning for the Erindale Campus." no. 1 and no. 2, Summer 1967.

Andrews, John, Michael Hough, Donovan Pinker, and Evan Walker. "Erindale Campus Master Plan, University of Toronto." December 1966.

Bissell, Claude. "University of Toronto Expansion Program—A Reflection of Academic Policy and Ideals." *Royal Architectural Institute of Canada Journal* 37 (January 1960): 6-10.

Black, J. Bernard. "Familiar Landmarks: Four Walks Through the Historic Campus of the University of St. Michael's College." Toronto: University of St. Michael's College, 1984.

"Brief Guide to Massey College, A." Toronto: Massey College, June 1994.

Centre for Engineering Innovation & Entrepreneurship. Office of the Dean, Faculty of Applied Science & Engineering, University of Toronto, 2018.

Chapman, Howard. "The Campus Development Plan." *Royal Architectural Institute of Canada Journal* 37 (January 1960): 24-26.

Fleming, Bryant, "A Report Accompanying A Preliminary Plan for the Landscape Improvement and General Expansion for the University of Toronto, Toronto, Ont." November 1917.

Greer, William. "Trinity College Quadrangle." Report for the Trinity College Provost's Quadrangle Committee, January 2006.

Hill, Robert, ed. *Biographical Dictionary of Architects in Canada, 1800-1950*. http://dictionaryofarchitectsincanada.org.

McGeer, Eric. "Redeveloping U of T's Back Campus a break with history," *The Globe and Mail*, Toronto, June 6, 2013.

New Woodsworth College, The. Woodsworth College, 1994.

Office of the Assistant Vice-President (Planning). "University of Toronto Plan (Discussion Draft)." University of Toronto, 1991.

Office of Convocation. "Trinity College: A Walking Guide. University of Trinity College," University of Toronto, 2001.

Percy, John, and Sabeen Abbas, eds. *Celebrating 40 Years of History at the University of Toronto Mississauga*. Toronto: U of T Mississauga, 2007.

Richards, Larry W., and Craig Handy. "A Report on the Education Centre Architecture and Art," April 2004.

Robarts Common, Diamond Schmitt Architects, 2015.

Seymour, Kathryn. *An Architectural-Historical Report on The Koffler Scientific Reserve at Joker's Hill.* Commissioned by the University of Toronto, June 2004.

Students' Administrative Council. *The Campus as the Campus Centre: A Manual.* Toronto: Students' Administrative Council, University of Toronto, 1971.

University of Toronto Scarborough / Campus Master Plan. University of Toronto Scarborough, April 2011.

University of Toronto Scarborough Environmental Science and Chemistry Building. EllisDon / Diamond Schmitt Architects, undated.

Urban Strategies. "Investing in the Landscape (Open Space Master Plan)." 1999.

VG Architects. "University of Toronto—School of Graduate Studies: Heritage Impact Assessment." February 2016.

Wright, C. H. C. "University of Toronto." *The Journal of The Royal Architectural Institute of Canada.* ii, January–March 1925, 2–23.

COLLECTIONS AND FILES

Archives of Ontario
Campus and Facilities Planning, University of Toronto
City of Toronto Archives
City of Toronto Heritage Properties Inventory
Department of Facilities Management, University of Toronto Scarborough
Facilities and Services Department, University of Toronto
National Gallery of Canada
Ontario Heritage Trust
Public Archives of Canada
Real Estate Department and Capital Projects Department, University of Toronto
University of Toronto Archives, Fisher Rare Book Library
Utilities and Grounds Department, University of Toronto Mississauga

Image Credits

All photographs are by Eugen Sakhnenko unless otherwise noted.

401 Richmond and Zeidler family: 267 (bottom)

Archives of Ontario: 82 (top)

Arsié, Laura: 40

Art Gallery of Ontario and Mary Handford: 260

Art Gallery of Ontario and the Henry Moore Foundation: 261

Bata Shoe Museum: 256 (middle and bottom)

Bell, Ken / University Advancement and University of Toronto Press: 34, 36

Campus and Facilities Planning, University of Toronto (architectural renderings provided by): 10, 52–53 (top), 53 (bottom), 105, 170 (top), 185 (bottom), 220 (top), 221, 277, 320 (bottom), 321, 328

City of Toronto Archives: 8–9, 73, 86, 246, 270, 331

City of Toronto Archives and Panda: 33

Farrugia, Kevin: 332

Gardiner Museum: 257 (middle)

Hafkenscheid, Toni: 24–25, 252, 253

Hall, Dennis / University Advancement and University of Toronto Press: 32

Horwood Collection, Archives of Ontario: 12

Library and Archives of Canada: 14

Li, Norm: 178

Robert Lonsdale Photography / University of Toronto Archives: 35

Royal Canadian Academy of Arts diploma work, deposited by the architect, Toronto, 1880 (photo © National Gallery of Canada, Ottawa): 16–17

Royal Ontario Museum: 254 (bottom), 255

Ryerson Image Centre: 265 (bottom), 266

Textile Museum of Canada: 264

Toronto Reference Library / Toronto Public Library: 11, 15, 18, 19, 243

University of Toronto Archives: 23, 26, 27, 28, 29 (top), 29 (bottom), 32, 39, 51, 68–69, 71, 73, 88, 89, 92, 95, 96, 99 (top), 103, 145, 184, 250, 298, 300

Acknowledgments

My interest in the architecture of the University of Toronto goes back to 1980, when I had just arrived as a young professor and been invited by the dean of the architecture school at the time, Blanche van Ginkel, to develop an introductory course on architecture for University College undergraduates. Teaching at the historic University College thirty-eight years ago triggered a desire to explore other buildings on the university's three campuses—something that I did casually from time to time over the next two decades. However, a structured opportunity to fully study the university's buildings did not present itself until the spring of 2005, when Princeton Architectural Press approached the university to discuss creating a comprehensive campus guide (the publisher's first one about a campus outside the United States). The resulting first edition in 2009 was well received by the university community and by its neighbors and visitors. I was delighted to be invited by the university, including President Meric S. Gertler, and by Kevin Lippert, publisher at Princeton Architectural Press, and Jan Cigliano Hartman, the Campus Guide series editor, to complete this updated second edition. It was enormously rewarding to once again engage my passion for architecture.

For the first edition, which was researched and written between 2005 to 2009, I remain indebted to the Campus Guide series editor emerita, Nancy Eklund Later, and to key people at the university who enthusiastically supported the book idea: Vivek Goel, vice president and provost at the time; Ron Venter, who was vice provost of space and facilities planning; Rivi Frankle, chief operating officer and assistant vice president of alumni relations; and Professor David Rayside at University College. Elizabeth Sisam, assistant vice president of campus and facilities planning, and George Baird, dean of the John H. Daniels Faculty of Architecture, Landscape, and Design, provided encouragement, criticism, and support throughout the process of producing the first edition. Professor Emeritus Martin Friedland, whose comprehensive knowledge of the history of the University of Toronto is without equal, has been invaluable for both the first and second editions.

Conceptualizing, researching, writing, and illustrating a guide of this sort requires a team of dedicated, talented people. I was fortunate to bring Eugen Sakhnenko on board as the photographer, and the pictures he produced are striking, to say the least. His careful documentation will serve as an important visual record of the university's buildings for decades to come. Michal Kuzniar produced detailed, digital base maps of the three campuses, later enlivened by the extraordinary artistic talent of John Wang. The book might never have gotten to the finish line without the assistance that I received from University of Toronto colleagues like Scott Mabury, vice president, University Operations; Christine Burke, director of campus and facilities planning; and Lisa Neidrauer, senior planner, who generously shared their knowledge on architecture and planning at the university. Also, I am most grateful for the professionalism, patience, and precision of Linda Lee, project editor, and Nolan Boomer, copy editor at Princeton Architectural Press. It is also important to note the skill and sophistication of the book designer, Ben English.

For the first and second editions, scores of people have, directly and indirectly, helped move the books along, and I wish I could list and thank every one of them. Trusting that I might be forgiven for imperfect recall, in addition to all those mentioned earlier, I express my appreciation to Jennifer Adams, Tom Arban, Harold Averill, Nicola Bednarek, Alex Bozikovic, Shirley Blumberg, John Buckley, Robert Burley, Ultan Byrne, Bradley Chi, Brent Cordner, Charles Cox, David Curtin, Bob Davies, Ray deSouza, Lisa Doherty, Barbara Fischer, Adele Freedman, Susan Ford, Marne Gamble, Matthew Gourlay, William Greer, Mary Handford, Beth Hannah, Alan Hayes, Robert Hill, Joel Legault, Mary Louise Lobsinger, Mary Markou, Judy Matthews, John Bentley Mays, Janice Oliver, Ian Orchard, Stephen Otto, Mariangela Piccione, Heather Pigat, Stephen Phillips, Irene Puchalski, Edward Relph, Michelangelo Sabatino, Joseph Schner, Paolo Scrivano, Brigitte Shim, Geoffrey Simmins, Scott Sorli, Luke Stern, Mary Alice Thring, Nancy-Ann Wilson, and Fan Zhang. I am also grateful to Nene Brode, Ralph Burgess, Evelyn Collins, John Court, Anne Dale, Gilbert Delgado, Jim Derenzis, Don Dewees, Dale Duncan, Mike Filey, Mark Fram, Yvonne Hilder, Spencer Higgins, John Howarth, Evonne Levy, Yuri Lomakin, Elaine Marerolle, Michael Marrus, Dale Martin, Doug McBean, Anastasia Meletopoulos, Teresa Miniaci, Steve Miziak, Eha Naylor, Mandy O'Brien, George Phelphs, Sabina Pampor, Daniel Payne, Pina Petricone, Komala Prabhakar, Jacqueline Raaflaub, Dennis Reid, Douglas Richardson, Kathryn Seymour, John Smegal, Richard Sommer, Graeme Stewart, Paul Stoooer, Kim Storey, Rudy Tyono, Alex Waugh, Linda Wicks, Tom Wilson, and Margie Zeidler.

Throughout this exploration of some 186 buildings, I have been supported by my partner of fifty-one years, Frederic Urban, whose insights into history, architecture, and culture continue to propel me forward.

Larry Wayne Richards
Toronto, Canada

Index

Page references for illustrations appear in *italics*.